MEDITERRANEAN SEA
THE NORTH AND THE CENTRE
SLIEMA AND ST JULIAN'S
VALLETTA
THREE CITIES
THE SOUTH
MALTA
Ras il-Qawra
Salina Bay
Ras il-Qrejten
Bahar ic-Caghaq
Ras I-Irqieqa
Il Ponta tad-Dragunara
Il-Ponta Ta'Dragut
Burmarrad
Madliena
Gharghur
Ta' Giorni
Birkirkara
Balzan
Lija
Tal-Mirakli
Ta'Qali
Attard
Gwardamanga
Santa Venera
Wied is Sewda
Hamrun
Qormi
Hal Muxi
Zebbug
Hal Mula
Hal Dwin
Ghammieri
Paola
Tarxien
Luqa
Kalkara
Xghajra
San Leonardo
Zabbar
Zonqor
Buleben Iz-Zghir
Marsaskala
Marsaskala Bay
Il-Gzira
Tas-Sienja
Ponta tal-Mignuma
St Thomas Bay
Zejtun
Bir id-Deheb
Misrah Strejnu
Siggiewi
Mqabba
Ghaxaq
Marsaxlokk
Il-Ballut
Il-Hofra z-Zghira
Tal-Providenza
Ta' Haxxluq
Kirkop
Borg in-Nadur
Qrendi
Safi
Zurrieq
Tal-Bajjada
Birzebbugia
Marsaxlokk Bay
Delimara
Ghar Lapsi
Ras il-Hamrija
Bubaqra
Wied iz-Zurrieq
Ta' Ghammer
Kalafrana
Ponta ta'Delimara
Hal-Far
Benghisa
Ponta ta'Benghisa
L-Artal

INSIGHT GUIDES

MALTA

www.insightguides.com/Malta

Walking Eye App

YOUR FREE DESTINATION CONTENT AND EBOOK AVAILABLE THROUGH THE WALKING EYE APP

Your guide now includes a free eBook and destination content for your chosen destination, all for the same great price as before. Simply download the Walking Eye App from the App Store or Google Play to access your free eBook and destination content.

HOW THE WALKING EYE APP WORKS

Through the Walking Eye App, you can purchase a range of eBooks and destination content. However, when you buy this book, you can download the corresponding eBook and destination content for free. Just see below in the grey panels where to find your free content and then scan the QR code at the bottom of this page.

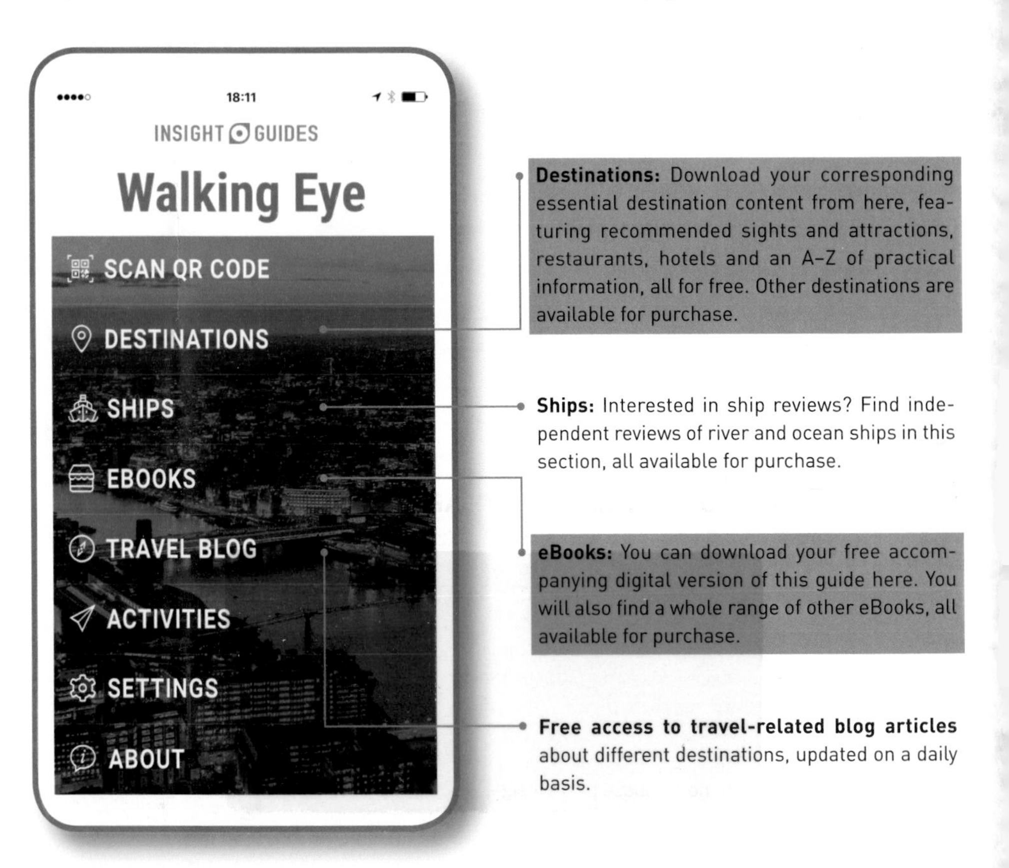

HOW THE DESTINATION CONTENT WORKS

Each destination includes a short introduction, an A–Z of practical information and recommended points of interest, split into 4 different categories:

- Highlights
- Accommodation
- Eating out
- What to do

You can view the location of every point of interest and save it by adding it to your Favourites. In the 'Around Me' section you can view all the points of interest within 5km.

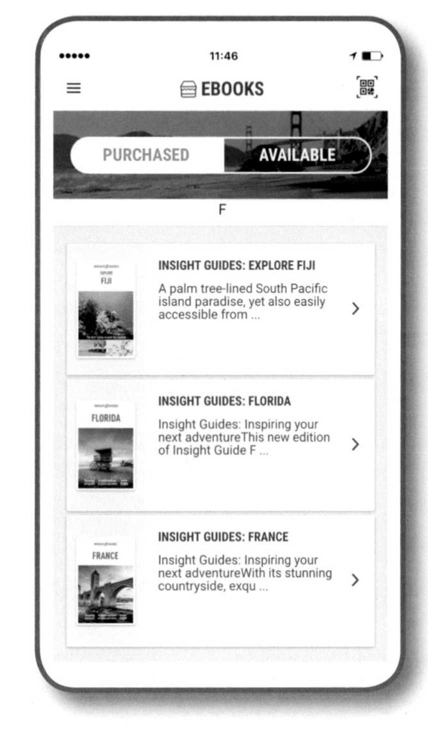

HOW THE EBOOKS WORK

The eBooks are provided in EPUB file format. Please note that you will need an eBook reader installed on your device to open the file. Many devices come with this as standard, but you may still need to install one manually from Google Play.

The eBook content is identical to the content in the printed guide.

HOW TO DOWNLOAD THE WALKING EYE APP

1. Download the Walking Eye App from the App Store or Google Play.
2. Open the app and select the scanning function from the main menu.
3. Scan the QR code on this page – you will then be asked a security question to verify ownership of the book.
4. Once this has been verified, you will see your eBook and destination content in the purchased ebook and destination sections, where you will be able to download them.

Other destination apps and eBooks are available for purchase separately or are free with the purchase of the Insight Guide book.

Contents

Travel Tips

TRANSPORT

A – Z

LANGUAGE

FURTHER READING

Maps

THE BEST OF MALTA: TOP ATTRACTIONS

There really is so much to see and do across Malta, Gozo and Comino, but this is our pick of what simply can't be missed.

△ **Valletta**. This Unesco World Heritage Site is going through some changes, but is still one of the most beautiful parts of the island. Don't miss St John's Co-Cathedral, St George's Square and the Manoel Theatre. See page 117.

▽ **Upper Barrakka Gardens**. Recently restored, these lovely gardens enjoy some of the most stunning views anywhere in Malta. The perfect place to snap pictures of Grand Harbour. See page 134.

△ **Ggantija Temples**. The oldest of Malta's temples, as well as one of the oldest free-standing stone structures in the world, Ggantija dates back to 3,600 BC. See page 207.

▽ **Ta Pinu, Gozo**. This simple church houses a shrine to Our Lady, with touching stories and artefacts that are truly inspiring. See page 210.

△ **The Blue Lagoon, Comino**. The best beach on uninhabited Comino, take a boat trip here to bathe in the turquoise waters. See page 215.

△ **The Azure Window, Gozo**. Adjacent to the striking Dwejra inland sea, this landmark is truly extraordinary. Best seen from the sea. See page 211.

◁ **The Palace of the Grand Masters**. One of the proudest buildings in Valletta, go inside to explore the Armoury and see incredible tapestries. See page 126.

▷ **Mellieha Bay**. With its crystal-clear waters and great facilities for all the family, it's no wonder this is one of the most popular sandy beaches. See page 175.

◁ **The Cittadella, Gozo**. Take the steep climb up to the old, walled capital and explore the bastions. It has great 360-degree views of the island below. See page 201.

▷ **Mdina**. Known as the Silent City, this is Malta's medieval jewel. Explore the winding backstreets surrounded by imposing walls, or take a romantic, lamp-lit stroll at night. See page 149.

THE BEST OF MALTA: EDITOR'S CHOICE

From family fun to historic gems, Malta promises a little something for everyone, and these are our top recommendations.

BEST FOR FAMILIES

Popeye Village. Since the 1970s, this one-time movie set has been a popular place for children to let their imagination run riot with the characters from the *Popeye* film. There is also a beach, a restaurant and boat rides out to sea. See page 177.

The Melita Trackless Train. Leaving from just beside Rabat's Domus Romana, the whole family will love a trip on this trackless train. See page 156.

Ta' Qali Family Adventure Park. This adventure park has become a new favourite with local families, with climbing frames and open spaces the whole family can enjoy together. See page 161.

Splash & Fun. This water park makes for a great day out, with slides, "a lazy river" and a wave pool. See page 173.

Qui-Si-Sana Gardens. With a lovely lawn and plenty of space to play, this Sliema park – which overlooks the sea – is ideal for all ages. See page 166.

Splash & Fun water park.

The Malta Experience.

BEST MUSEUMS

National Museum of Archaeology. Originally built in 1574 by the Knights of St John, this beautiful building now houses the islands' most prized archaeological treasures. See page 120.

The Malta Experience. This audiovisual experience is the perfect introduction to the islands, and takes spectators on a journey from their early history to the present day. See page 133.

Casa Rocca Piccola. This beautiful Valletta home has been opened to the public and is still run by the noble family that has owned it for centuries. See page 131.

St James Cavalier Centre for Creativity. Also in Valletta, this fort was transformed into a centre for the creative arts. Culture vultures will love it. See page 135.

Carmelite Priory Museum. Set on Mdina's main street, this friary threw open its doors to the general public for the first time a few years ago and is a historical gem well worth exploring. See page 155.

Exhibit in the Archaeology Museum.

BEST FESTIVALS AND EVENTS

Malta Arts Festival.

The Malta Arts Festival. Fast becoming one of the biggest arts festivals in the Mediterranean, this three-week event takes place every July and showcases artists from the worlds of music, theatre, dance, street performance, art and more. See page 75.

The Jazz Festival. Also held in July, the Grand Harbour has become the well-loved backdrop for this incredible international music event that annually attracts some of the world's biggest names in jazz. See page 76.

The Farsons Great Beer Festival. An event for beer lovers and foodies, August has become synonymous with a trip to Ta' Qali for the great atmosphere and brilliant live music performances (www.farsonsbeerfestival.com).

Isle of MTV. The largest open-air concert in Europe now takes place in Malta every June. Past acts have included Lady Gaga, the Black Eyed Peas and Snoop Dogg (www.isleofmtv.com).

BEST BEACHES

Mellieha Bay, Malta. Below the town of Mellieha, this is the island's longest sandy beach. With full facilities, it is a favourite for family outings. See page 175.

Ghajn Tuffieha, Malta. A delightfully attractive beach; quieter than it might be because of its hillside access and limited facilities. See page 178.

Gnejna, Malta. An unsophisticated beach for undemanding people, in a charming location outside Mgarr. See page 179.

Ramla Bay, Gozo. This is the smaller island's great sandy stretch, with stunning red sand. Ideal for picnics. See page 209.

San Blas, Gozo. Tiny cove with difficult access, signposted on road from Nadur. No facilities, so take all your needs. See page 209.

Blue Lagoon, Comino. The turquoise bay draws boats of every shape and size to gather in its idyllic but stark surroundings. See page 215.

Hikers in Gozo.

BEST WALKS

Buskett Gardens. As Malta's largest woodland area, this expanse beneath beautiful Verdala Castle is well worth exploring. Look out for indigenous plants and stop to mingle with the cat colony as you return back to base. See page 190.

Delimara. This picturesque part of southern Malta is a little hard to get to but well worth the trek. Look out over Marsaxlokk Bay and the historic Delimara Lighthouse (though more industrial sights are sadly common, too). See page 186.

Dingli. Head past Rabat to get to one of the most beautiful countryside areas of Malta. The cliffs promise striking views, and you can look across to the uninhabited island of Filfla. See page 190.

Golden Bay. The countryside above this stunning stretch of golden sand is positively bursting with local fauna and flora, as well as a number of historical sites. See page 178.

Gordan Lighthouse, Gozo. Located close to the pretty village of Ghasri, this is a great place to take in the island's picturesque natural surroundings and people watch. See page 210.

Golden Bay.

Boats at Marsaxlokk Harbour.

MFC 502
DIEGU

Interior of St John's Co-Cathedral, Valletta.

NO
FLASH

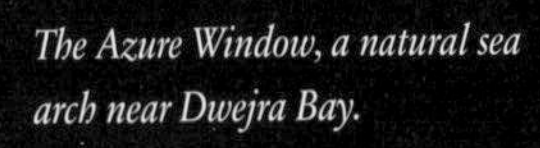

The Azure Window, a natural sea arch near Dwejra Bay.

A view of Valletta from Manoel Island.

SUN, SEA AND HISTORY

Eclectic Malta, the heart of the Mediterranean, offers a great deal to curious visitors, in spite of its small size.

A fishing boat in the azure waters.

In the middle of a remarkably clear and unpolluted expanse of blue Mediterranean Sea, some 90km (60 miles) due south of Sicily, the Maltese archipelago consists of three inhabited islands – Malta, Gozo and Comino – and a number of minuscule uninhabited rocks. Malta is the largest of the inhabited islands (yet not much bigger than England's Isle of Wight), Gozo is half its size and Comino is smaller still. The population is around 420,000, most of whom speak English as well as the native Malti.

Malta is shaped like a wedge, sloping from the northwest to the east, with most of the resort developments on the eastern shore, which is indented with harbours and bays, rock beaches and beautiful sheltered coves.

Maltese bandsmen.

Like all islands subject to the vagaries of modern tourism, Malta throws up sharp contrasts, which are made all the more striking because of the island's tiny size. Ancient temples – some of the oldest structures on earth – and the massive fortifications and *palazzi* of the Knights of St John rub shoulders with the increasing sprawl of modern Malta and its tourist infrastructure. Considerable wealth mingles with a simple, hard-working rural lifestyle.

The biggest changes have come since the island's accession to the European Union in 2004. More and more multistoreys shape the skyline, huge infrastructural developments have taken place, and a truly cosmopolitan atmosphere prevails. Visitors to the islands now want for nothing – whether that's a lively nightlife scene, designer fashion, international cuisine or luxury resorts.

Just across the water, however, Gozo retains much of its unspoilt charm – although developments have occurred here, too. If you're hoping to get away from it all, consider a tranquil long weekend at a traditional farmhouse on the sister island – then head back to Malta for a holiday offering the best of both worlds.

Traders at Marsaxlokk Market.

THE MALTESE PEOPLE

Warm, passionate and friendly, the Maltese are one of the islands' greatest assets, but they are fast forgoing traditionalism in favour of a more cosmopolitan approach.

The Maltese can easily be regarded as one of the most resilient peoples in the world – they have remained steadfast, proud and patriotic in the face of an ever-changing array of rulers and strong outside influences.

In spite of being conquered, subjugated and led over the centuries by the powerful nations of the times – and bearing faces that even now reflect some of that past, with features recalling the Romans, Arabs and Phoenicians – the Maltese have doggedly clung to insular individuality. With roots planted firmly in a group of tiny islands, whose total area adds up to no more than 316 sq km (122 sq miles), there is a strong sense of identity born out of a mixture of self-preservation and stubbornness, qualities the Maltese have in abundance. And the same applies to Maltese emigrants settled abroad.

Family

Family remains the most important part of life in Malta and, for the majority of the population, getting married and having children remains a priority. Most young men and women will find a spouse from within their village or extended community, and big, lavish wedding ceremonies are the order of the day, flamboyantly celebrating the start of a new couple's life together.

Regular family events are also the norm. Most Maltese are never happier than when sitting around a large table and enjoying a sumptuous meal with their relatives. The old, young and very young muddle together, relishing each other's company and sharing stories. There remains a genuine respect for the family's elders and their wisdom, and it is still common for the *nanna* or *nannu* to reside with the younger generations into their retirement.

Bus driver.

House-proud

The Maltese are proud of their homes. These are spotlessly clean inside, with gleaming, patterned marble-tiled floors, and everything in its prescribed place. Almost everyone, whatever their social level, maintains a formal sitting room, to be used only when guests are invited to the house. It is here that wealth and social achievement can be demonstrated. Even in the most unsophisticated villages, these rooms will have furniture made to order, sofas and armchairs and wall units to hold whimsical china figurines and framed pictures.

However, most locals still take a disproportionate amount of pride in their homes when compared with their localities. Women can often be seen sweeping dust and dirt out of their homes and into the street, and national campaigns are now in place to encourage locals to take as much pride in their country as they do in their belongings.

Politics

Up to the mid-1990s, politics played an important part in daily life. All Maltese were politically aware and were "born" into the party supported by their parents, an allegiance that normally lasted a lifetime, for better or worse. Businesspeople expected to do better when their side was in power. As the governments changed, so did the people in key positions in the civil service and in government-run organisations. As bureaucratic power changed, so were new ropes oiled. The "floating voter" status hardly existed.

However, the pattern began to change dramatically from 1995 onwards when it became evident that increasing numbers of youths were more independent from the political influence of their parents and were definitely much less interested in politics and political issues. The zenith of cross-voting was reached in the 2003 general election when thousands of Malta Labour Party (MLP) supporters cast their votes in favour of the pro-EU Nationalist Party, to defy the MLP's anti full-EU-membership policy, thus assuring Malta of full membership of the European Union.

A Catholic festa procession in Sliema.

HOME AND AWAY

There is a population of about 420,000 on the Maltese Islands, with an equal number in Australia, Canada, the United Kingdom and the United States of America. These are the emigrants and families of Maltese who set sail for the lands of golden promise in the days of expansive migration at the end of World War II, when hope was offered to poorer communities.

Many, homesick after making their fortunes in a modest manner, return to build modern villas that are named in fond memory of chances given: Villa Wallaby, Melbourne Court, Brentford House, Casa Orlando or, simply, Bondi.

Religion

For many years, the Church played a key role in life, both secular and political, making its views known on all key issues as well as running many of the better schools. In election years, parish priests often exhorted congregations to vote for the Nationalist Party. But, as has happened elsewhere in Europe, the sway of the Church has diminished. The annual parish *festa* is still the most important event in the calendar, but church attendance, although still proportionately among the highest in Europe, is declining.

Brain drain

A welcome benefit of the islands' accession to the EU was the fact that the Maltese can now work across Europe at will, as well as study more easily at foreign institutions. This exciting development opened doors for many young people, and a good number will now choose to spread their wings overseas. While a great opportunity for Malta's youth, it has created

Off to the market.

something of a brain drain for the islands, with many of the most accomplished or promising young people leaving for Britain, Belgium (the seat of the EU, where Maltese is recognised as an official language) or beyond. The government has recently launched a variety of initiatives to encourage career development for young people choosing to stay local, especially in the booming IT industry.

The tourist influence and internationalisation

Although the Church still has a very strong influence on a good portion of the population, parish priests have ceased to function as moral policemen, with the ability to prescribe and enforce standards of conduct within their territory. And the fact that foreign visitors now easily outnumber local people (in 2014 a record 1.7 million tourists visited the islands) has undoubtedly had a greater influence than most Maltese would care to admit on their attitude towards both unorthodox behaviour and established authority.

Yet to every cloud there is a silver lining, and perhaps now there is more opportunity for directly confronting modern-day issues. The islands have come a long way since the days when girls were whisked away by police for wearing bikinis.

Young Maltese women at festa time.

POLITICAL CHOICES

Surprisingly, despite the traditional Maltese passion for politics, there are only two major parties from which to choose – Nationalist or Labour. However, a newer Green party (known as Alternativa) is slowly beginning to make its mark and establish itself as a serious contender. In the past it was automatic for young people simply to vote the way their family did, as most were either staunchly loyal to one party or another following the political upheaval of the 1980s. Today, everyone feels freer to make decisions based on manifestos and politicians' promises rather than automatically sticking to party colour or family tradition.

Contraception and sex before marriage are now reasonably accepted subjects for discussion and, while the clergy may insist on decorum in dress whilst walking through the streets and in the churches, topless bathing is tolerated on some beaches, despite it being illegal. Nude bathing is also against the law and those who bare all may well find themselves facing prosecution.

The divorce debate

May 2011 saw a big milestone for Malta, when 53 percent of the voting population opted to legalise divorce in a national referendum (the last time divorce was legal here was during Napoleon's brief rule, and the law was soon overturned). Previously, Malta was one of only two countries in the world where divorce was illegal (the other being the Philippines) and locals had to travel overseas to get one. Alternatively, they could seek a legal separation, or a church annulment, but the latter was a complex procedure that could take up to nine years and cost thousands of euros.

Throughout the debate, both the campaigning "yes" and "no" camps (the latter heavily endorsed by the church) fought to get their views across and the margin was slim until the end. MPs finally passed the law through Parliament with 52 votes to 11 and it took effect in October 2011.

Another procession in Sliema.

Joie de vivre

The Maltese, although industrious, are determined to enjoy life to the full. They delight in any opportunity to throw a party and there is a ribald sense of humour devoted, for the most part, to *double entendre*. Malti may be a relatively unsophisticated language but it gives ample opportunity for double meanings. As a result, political and social farce is probably the most popular form of entertainment, both on TV and at Maltese-speaking theatre venues. The Maltese love nothing more than to poke fun at those in the limelight, and blogging is now popular, with many taking to cyberspace to express themselves anonymously. These, usually written in Maltese or Minglish (a witty blend of Maltese and English), tend to be hilarious, and poke fun at the government, the opposition and the Church.

On the minus side, the Maltese, in true Latin tradition, can be hard on each other, prone to jealousy and quick to take advantage or pick a quarrel. A crossed Maltese stays cross.

Tradition vs Modernism

Beautiful old buildings standing beside modern high-rises, and centuries-old traditions jostling with modern-day approaches. How do the Maltese Islands blend the two?

The Maltese Islands have always been heavily influenced by the outside world, whether that was by cultural differences introduced by their many and varied rulers throughout the years or, more recently, by tourists who brought their more cosmopolitan ideas into the country's traditionally conservative ways of life. It hasn't always been easy to blend the two.

Today, that conflict of old vs new still reigns and there is a feeling of change in the air. As a result, holiday-makers who might have been here a decade or so ago will probably not recognise many of the more built-up areas.

Nevertheless, village life, within the core of each town, remains traditional. Life tends to revolve around the local church and its calendar, with feast days taking pride of place among the picturesque hamlets made up of little houses of character. If this is the Malta that you want to experience, head to traditional villages such as Rabat and Siggiewi in Malta, or Nadur in Gozo. Here the pace of life feels authentically Mediterranean and very far removed from that of the cities. You may even spot a key hanging in a front-door lock – a level of trust that demonstrates that some Maltese still feel as though they can invite the whole world in – although, admittedly, this is changing fast. In areas such as these, religion and its practices are still followed to the letter, and many modern-day topics of discussion, such as abortion and gay marriage, are considered extremely distasteful.

Contrarily, in the more cosmopolitan areas of the islands, such as Sliema and St Julian's, very little is taboo today – whether that's gay bars, cohabiting couples or "gentlemen's clubs", all of which would have raised more than a few eyebrows less than a decade ago. The EU has certainly played its part, with more and more foreigners choosing to base themselves here and to integrate within local life.

The IT and iGaming industries have also boomed, bringing with them thousands of young, hip professionals, keen to take full advantage of the benefits that such growing industries can offer to employees. As a result, the expat community has exploded, creating an interesting social crowd. This has led to more and more openings of upmarket restaurants, bars and clubs, and has pushed prices up in many parts. In fact, Malta recently registered the highest cost-of-living increase in the eurozone area.

That said, the impact of such rapid change has been considerable and the islanders now want for nothing; vast ranges of international products line supermarket shelves, the health-care system is one of the best in the Mediterranean, and low-cost airlines have made it easy to travel to many parts of the world at the drop of a hat from Malta. In fact, it has become customary for Maltese people to holiday abroad at least once or twice a year.

Cooling off, Maltese style.

So, in many ways, the islands feel as if they are on the cusp of something great – teetering between old and new, tradition and modernity, with older generations clinging to the past while youngsters strive to propel themselves into the future and achieve the same goals as their mainland European peers. Now it just remains to be seen to what extent modern Malta will continue to develop and balance all angles in the next phase of its multi-faceted existence.

Prehistoric temples at Ggantija, on Gozo.

DECISIVE DATES

Prehistory

Before 5,000 BC
First settlers arrive in Malta. The earliest temples are built from 4,800 BC.

Sculptures in the Gozo Archaeological Museum.

3,200 BC
The megalithic temples of Hagar Qim, Ggantija and Mnajdra are built. They survive today as the oldest free-standing edifices in the world.

c.2,000 BC
The Bronze Age.

c.700 BC
Hellenic influence begins.

c.800–480 BC
The Phoenicians settle on the islands and use their safe harbours as a trading post.

c.480–218 BC
Carthage conquers Malta.

The Roman Period

218 BC
A Roman expedition captures Malta and incorporates the islands into the Republic of Rome.

AD 60
St Paul is shipwrecked in the area now known as St Paul's Bay. He converts the islanders to Christianity.

AD 117–138
During Hadrian's reign, Malta, is declared a Roman municipality.

Dark Ages to Arab Arrival

AD 395–535
Division of the Roman Empire and collapse of the western half (including Malta).

AD 535
Justinian, head of the eastern Roman Empire conquers Malta and Sicily in the name of Byzantium.

AD 870
The Aghlabite Arabs arrive. The Islamic religion is also adopted by the islanders.

Europeans Take Power

1090
The Normans invade under Count Roger. Arabic remains the national language but the islanders revert to Christianity.

1194–1266
After the Norman kings die out the island passes to the Swabian (German) kings.

1266–1283
The French House of Anjou drives out the Germans.

1283–1530
The Aragonese rule Malta and Sicily.

1479–1516
Affiliation of the houses of Castile and Aragon means that Malta becomes part of the new Spanish Empire.

The Knights of St John

1530
The 4,000-strong army of the Order of St John arrives to take formal possession of the islands.

1551
Corsairs from the Barbary Coast attack Gozo and enslave almost the entire population.

1561
The Inquisition is established in Malta.

1565
The Great Siege of Malta. For three months, Suleiman the Magnificent's fleet lays siege to the Knights. Eventually help arrives from Sicily and the Ottoman forces are defeated.

1566
Urgent construction begins on Valletta. It becomes the finest fortified city in Europe.

1683
A century-long phase of consolidation and construction begins. However, with no enemies to fight, the Order of the Knights declines into decadence.

1789
The French Revolution weakens the already faltering Order.

Napoleonic Period

1798
Napoleon takes Malta without a fight.

1800
The Maltese rise against French domination and seek outside help. Britain and Naples intercede. French force capitulates.

The British Influence

1802
Peace of Amiens decides that Malta should be returned to the Order of St John, but the Maltese vote to come under the protection of the British. At the 1814 Treaty of Paris, Malta formally becomes a British Crown Colony.

1850 onwards
Malta experiences an economic upswing as a trading harbour and an important British naval base.

1914–18
World War I. Malta becomes known as the "Nurse of the Mediterranean".

1919
The *Sette Giugno* riots. An angry crowd riots in Valletta, causing troops to be called in. Four Maltese in the crowd are shot.

1921
Self-government is granted. The first Malta Parliament is opened.

World War II 1940–43
Malta receives most severe aerial bombardment in its history while undergoing its second Great Siege. In 1942, in recognition of their inhabitants' heroism, Britain awards the islands the George Cross.

Post-War Period

1947
Self-government restored.

1964
Malta becomes an independent state within the Commonwealth of Nations.

1972
An agreement is signed with Britain and Nato to use the islands as a military base.

1974
Malta officially becomes a republic but remains within the Commonwealth.

1979
The last British forces leave the island.

1989
The Malta Summit. US President George Bush Snr and Soviet leader Mikhail Gorbachev use the island as a meeting place to mark the end of the Cold War.

2003
Malta signs the full EU Accession Treaty in Athens for full EU membership in 2004.

2007
Pope Benedict proclaims Dun Gorg Preca the first-ever Maltese saint.

2008
The euro replaces Maltese currency. Nationalist Party narrowly re-elected.

2010
Works start on the milestone City Gate project, which will see the capital restored to its former glory for the first time since World War II.

2011
The parliament passes a bill allowing divorces following a national referendum on the issue.

2013
Labour Party wins snap elections and returns to power after 15 years.

2014
Hundreds of African migrants drown as their ship sinks off Malta coast.

2015
EU leaders meet in Valletta for a two-day summit to tackle the immigration crisis as waves of immigrants pour into the EU.

2016
The so-called Panama Papers reveal Malta was used to filter millions by shell companies set up by the notorious Mossak Fonseca law firm.

2018
Valletta is set to be the official European Capital of Culture.

Commemoration of the George Cross awarded to Malta.

BUCKINGHAM PALACE

The Governor,
Malta

To honour her brave people
I award the George Cross
to the Island Fortress of Malta
to bear witness to a heroism and
devotion that will long be famous
in history.

George R.I.

April 15th 1942.

Stone statue of a fertility goddess, dating back to 3,000 BC.

IN THE BEGINNING

The first inhabitants of the Maltese Islands built giant temples to pagan gods, long before the pyramids were constructed in Egypt.

It is widely believed that the Maltese Islands once formed part of a causeway that joined Europe to Africa, and so became a thoroughfare for animals escaping from the encroaching ice of Northern Europe. Many died en route or were trapped by the rising sea, which turned the causeway into a necklace of island stepping stones. Today, evidence of this can be seen at Ghar Dalam, near Birzebbugia, a museum and cave that contain the bones of several prehistoric and extinct animals, including dwarf elephants and hippos, from around 100,000 BC.

Little is known of the people who inhabited the islands. Among the animal bones found at Ghar Dalam were a couple of Neanderthal human teeth from about 40,000 BC, and it seems that there was a fairly sizeable human population that lived in caves along the coastal cliffs. Eventually, they emerged from their troglodytic dwellings to live in settlements of huts.

Ruins at Ggantija, Gozo.

Temple builders

In about the 4th millennium BC, the Maltese were engaged in the construction of great megalithic temples. The Ggantija temples on Gozo were probably the first, but they were soon joined by the temples of Mnajdra and Hagar Qim on the main island of Malta.

The temples were an assembly of massive slabs of rock, similar to Stonehenge in Britain, with alcoves for altars and statues associated with ancient religious rituals. The temple at Hagar Qim incorporates a stone that is 6 metres (20ft) long – a testament to the considerable engineering skills of those who manoeuvred it into position. These great temples were mostly erected outdoors, yet Malta's most remarkable Neolithic remains were revealed only last century by a builder who was digging to lay the foundations of a house.

The Hypogeum of Hal Saflieni (the last part of the name refers not to some ancient deity but to the area where the builder was proposing to construct the house) is a vast, three-storeyed underground chamber carved by human hands out of solid rock. It is supposed that the chamber once housed an oracle and was used for "initiation into the mysteries of priestcraft". Later it became a burial chamber, and the Hypogeum is so huge that it is estimated to have held up to 7,000 bodies. Yet, apart from the fact that they lived about 5,000 years ago, practically nothing is known about the people who built this temple.

Shortly after the Hypogeum discovery, close by in Tarxien three more temples were found, embellished with carvings that are remarkably sophisticated for their time.

A Mediterranean staging post

Malta edges into recorded history on the fringes of the momentous three-cornered power struggle for the then-known world between Phoenicians, Greeks and Persians. The Phoenicians set the ball rolling by sailing the breadth of the Mediterranean, from the cities of Tyre and Sidon (in what is now Lebanon) to semi-secret copper and tin deposits in Spain.

Evidence of ancient cart tracks at Misrah Ghar il-Kbir.

Phoenicians and Carthaginians

The most famous of the new Phoenician colonies was Carthage, founded in modern-day Tunisia. Soon this was almost as prosperous and powerful as the Phoenician homeland, but the connection between the two was severed after a bungled attempt by Phoenicians and Persians acting in concert to crush the Greeks. The Greeks beat both enemies in surprise victories that are reputed to have taken place on the same day in 470 BC, and the Mediterranean was effectively cut in half: with Greeks supreme in the east and Phoenicians (now more properly called "Carthaginians") in the west. In the middle of the dividing line was little Malta.

The Carthaginians used Malta as a training base for their galley crews. They also began to cultivate olives and carobs and used the excellent-quality local clay for pottery. These innovations must have improved the islands' economy, but the terrible price paid by the local inhabitants was to see many of their number carried off as slaves to Carthage.

Today, aside from some cave tombs, there is little to tell us that the Carthaginians were ever here, but there is one priceless exception. In 1697, a pair of marble *cippi* (columns) were discovered, inscribed with a dedication by two brothers to the god Melqarth. Normally, this would have been of no great interest, but astoundingly, next to the cursive Phoenician script (the progenitor of the Roman alphabet) was a Greek translation. These *cippi* – one in Malta's Museum of Archaeology, the other in the Louvre in Paris – thus became the key to deciphering Phoenician in exactly the same way as the Rosetta Stone unlocked the secrets of ancient Egypt's hieroglyphics.

The Malti language

By modern analysis, Malti, the language of the Maltese, appears to be a living legacy of spoken Phoenician (subject, of course, to 2,000 years of natural evolution and later additions), which helps to explain its often outlandish appearance to other European eyes.

In its earliest form, the language was only spoken, never written. It was the language of a simple people and, possibly because of this, had a basic vocabulary, short of the flowery pretensions that mark the language of a more sophisticated society.

When the Arabs arrived in the 9th century they brought their own language and, because of similar Semitic language roots, many of their words were incorporated by the Maltese. Similarly, in later centuries, the European nations began imposing their influence on Malta, and borrowed words from the Romance languages were also assimilated into Malti.

The Punic Wars and Roman rule

The three Punic (Phoenician) Wars raged between Rome and Carthage between 264 and

146 BC and culminated in the destruction of the Carthaginian empire.

Malta was tossed about in this struggle-to-the-death between the two superpowers, although there are few specific references to its fate in Roman accounts of the war.

After the first Punic War, records tell us that Malta was ceded to Rome as part of Carthage's indemnity. According to sources, Hamilcar (Hannibal's father) was in Malta when he surrendered with 2,000 men. But the Carthaginians must somehow have regained the island because it was ceded again after the second war. In any event, the islands were firmly in Rome's orbit for a good millennium after the Punic Wars.

Although Malta had a certain degree of autonomy under Roman rule, it was generally lumped together with Sicily for administrative purposes and prospered under unobtrusive Roman rule.

Diodorus of Sicily, one of the very few Latin historians who so much as mention Malta, describes the inhabitants as "Phoenicians". In fact, the Maltese coins of the period bore Phoenician symbols with Latin or Greek

The remains of Mnajdra Temple, dating back to 4,000 BC.

MYSTERY OF THE CART TRACKS

Strange formations found on the ground in both Malta and Gozo pose one of the islands' most taxing enigmas. Known as cart tracks (or cart ruts), these are parallel furrows – V-shaped and generally 15–50cm (6–20ins) wide – that run through the hard rock. Were they first cut with tools or were they simply worn this size and shape by constant use? What is surely beyond coincidence is that they are uniformly around 135cm (54ins) apart – which corresponds exactly to the width of the axle still used on the modern Maltese country cart.

The obvious question is: to what use were these tracks put? What were the carts carrying and where were they going with this cargo? Some lead apparently pointlessly up hills or plunge over the edge of cliffs. Maltese archaeologist Sir Themistocles Zammit surmises that "the material handled must have been abundant, cheap, and of the greatest value to those who carted it". In Malta, that could well have meant soil, as everywhere on the islands the bare rock is topped by only the thinnest layer of earth. "When the increasing population required as much land as possible under cultivation on which to grow foodstuffs, they could only do this by carrying earth from the valleys up on the sides and tops of hills." Later experts believe that the tracks are evidence of an elaborate transport and communication system on the islands.

inscriptions, and the tradition of cremation and burial in pit tombs was maintained. In general, therefore, it would seem that the Roman presence was confined to a garrison which had no impact either on the local culture or on the language.

St Paul

The greatest single upheaval in Maltese culture occurred AD 60, when a ship bound for Rome with 275 passengers, including a famous prisoner, was caught in a dreadful storm off the northeastern coast. "They knew not the land but they discovered a certain creek with a shore, into which they were minded, if it were possible, to thrust in the ship ... The forepart stuck fast, and remained unmoveable, but the hinder part was broken with the violence of the waves ... And when they were escaped, then they knew that the island was called Melita. And the barbarous people shewed us no little kindness: for they kindled a fire, and received us every one, because of the present rain, and because of the cold".

The catacombs of St Paul in Rabat – evidence of early Christianity on the islands.

The author of the quotation was St Luke (Acts of the Apostles: XXVIII) and the prisoner was his fellow passenger, St Paul. The shipwreck victims clambered ashore at what is known today as St Paul's Bay and remained on the island for three months. During this period, St Paul is said to have lived for most of the time in a grotto at Rabat, but also, for three days, as the guest of Publius, "the chief man of the island", whose father he also cured "of a fever and of a bloody flux".

According to tradition, St Paul not only converted Publius to Christianity, but also made him bishop, with his house being nominated as Malta's first church. The present-day Mdina Cathedral is reputed to stand on that very site.

If, as is surmised, the Maltese were still speaking a fairly pristine form of Phoenician with Canaanite origins, St Paul's preaching would have been greatly facilitated by the fact that he, as a native of Tarsus, also spoke a Canaanite dialect. In any case, Malta was one of the first Roman colonies to become Christian, which is reflected in the existence of catacombs from the 2nd century onwards.

After the Romans

Malta seems to have escaped the attentions of the Vandals and the Goths, who between them first destroyed the Roman provinces in North Africa and then Rome itself, and life continued in what must have been blessed obscurity. However, history records that in 535, Belisarius, the Byzantine conqueror of the northern scourges, won Malta on behalf of Justinian, the emperor of the eastern empire.

The islands seem to have been relatively unaffected by the Islamic tide that swept westwards across North Africa in the 7th century. Malta was not, in fact, occupied by Arabs until the year 870, and even then probably only as an adjunct to their wider ambitions in Sicily and on the European mainland. The Arabs took over the old Roman fortifications, including what was later to become Fort St Angelo, and the city, which they renamed Mdina. The latter became their island capital and stronghold, and parts of the walls they added are still in evidence today. A number of Arab graves have been found, but the greatest legacy of their 200-year rule undoubtedly lies in the Arabic words and phrases added to Malti, a language that they would have readily understood.

The return of Christianity

The Muslim hold on Malta was ended in 1090 by the Norman count Roger I of Sicily, who fooled the Arab garrison with a mock attack on St Paul's Bay, while other troops scaled the perilous western cliffs.

Roger was probably less interested in taking over the island than in making sure that the Arabs living there were not in a position to trouble him in Sicily. This was no religion-inspired invasion. In fact, Arabic remained the island's national language for some time and Islam was only gradually replaced as the principal religion by Christianity.

It was the Romans who first called the islands Melita, meaning honey, after the rich, sweet variety produced by local bees. Today, honey remains an important resource for the islanders, with numerous varieties available.

A mosaic at the Domus Romana.

The islands passed from hand to hand, by marriage, inheritance or war, the Maltese themselves having little say in the matter – although a rebellion in 1428 managed to exact certain rights under a royal charter. Eventually, the islands reached the hands of Spain's redoubtable Catholic monarchs, Ferdinand of Aragon and Isabella of Castile.

Seeds of conflict

Ferdinand and Isabella's determination to rid Europe, particularly Spain, of the "Moors" (a catch-all term for the Arabs and North African Berbers who had crossed the Mediterranean under the protection of Islam) was to have unforeseen consequences for Malta. The implications would be fully realised when, in 1530, their grandson, Emperor Charles V, made a gift of the islands to the homeless Knights of the Order of St John of Jerusalem.

THE DOMUS ROMANA

The islands of the Maltese archipelago prospered immensely under Roman rule, yet, somewhat oddly, few tangible remnants of this era have ever been unearthed. That said, a major breakthrough did occur in 1881, when workers happened upon the remains of a Roman house on the outskirts of Rabat. The site was later explored in great detail and transformed into a museum that proudly showcases a variety of interesting and priceless Roman items that have been discovered in the area, including tombstones, marble statues, terracotta ornaments, glassware, lamps, mosaics and theatrical masks.

Armour sentinel in the Palace of the Grand Masters.

THE KNIGHTS OF ST JOHN AND BEYOND

Malta may not have been their first choice, but the Knights of St John came here and embraced it, changing the island's face forever.

Once upon a time, the Knights of the Order of St John of Jerusalem were the most fabulous figures in Christendom. They were, quite literally, gallant white knights on chargers, heroes who, at heart, deplored violence, but, as a last resort in the face of unspeakable evil, were more than capable of climbing into suits of armour and proving their worth on the battlefield.

Humble beginnings

The Order was originally formed in about 1085 as the Knights Hospitallers, a community of monks set up to nurse Christians who fell ill while on pilgrimage in the Holy Land. As pilgrims came increasingly under attack from the Infidel, however, they needed physical protection rather than cures for minor ailments, and young Knights were recruited specifically to provide that protection.

These fighting Knights, led by their leader the Grand Master, were drawn from aristocratic families in France, Italy, Spain, Portugal and England. This was not considered to be ordinary mercenary work. "To volunteer in a Crusade against the Infidels in possession of the Holy Land", relates E.W. Schermerhorn in her masterful history of the Order, *Malta of the Knights*, "aside from the great service rendered to Christianity, and the safe and sure place it promised in the world to come, was the sport *par excellence* of the Middle Ages."

The Knights of Rhodes

As powerful as the Knights had become, the rising tide of Islam eventually drove them out of the Holy Land. They regrouped on the island of Rhodes. However, as leadership of the Islamic world had now passed to the Ottoman Turks, Rhodes was an intolerable provocation. Ottoman forces seized Constantinople in 1453 and Belgrade in 1520. The whole of Europe knew Rhodes would be next, but when the assault came, it was claimed "no Christian King lifted a finger; all were too busy killing each other".

Phillipe de Villiers de L'Isle-Adam seizing control of the island in 1530.

The opposing commanders in the battle for Rhodes were Suleiman the Magnificent, greatest of all the sultans, and, for the Knights, Grand Master Philippe de Villiers de L'Isle-Adam, now in his seventies but still "the embodiment of the soldier and gentleman". But Rhodes fell.

In contrast to their stereotyped brutal image, the Turks were gracious in victory and allowed the Knights to make a dignified departure with all their possessions, not least the cherished relic of the hand of St John the Baptist. The Greek inhabitants had misgivings about remaining on Rhodes under Turkish rule, so 100 families were given places in the Christian galleys. As Suleiman the Magnificent suspected, however, the Knights had no idea where they were going.

Between a rock and a hard place

The prospect of these illustrious veterans adrift in the Mediterranean was more than could be countenanced by the King of Spain, Charles V, who was also Holy Roman Emperor and therefore the symbol of almost everything the Knights stood for. A new home had to be found for them. He had, as it were, a couple of surplus properties in his inheritance, one of which was Malta.

Needing more information about the comparatively unknown Malta, the Knights sent commissioners to look into what was on offer.

Malta, they reported disdainfully, was "merely a rock of a soft sandstone ... scarcely covered with more than three or four feet of earth ... no running water, nor even wells ... wood was so scarce as to be sold by the pound ... about 12,000 inhabitants, of both sexes; the greatest part of whom were poor and miserable". In short, "a residence in Malta appeared extremely disagreeable – indeed, almost insupportable – particularly in summer".

But Malta it would be, as Tripoli, the only other option, seemed worse.

Portrait of Charles V from 1548.

In 1530, the Maltese Islands were gifted to the Knights of St John by the Holy Roman Emperor. The one condition was that they, in return, give one Maltese falcon each year.

IN THE SERVICE OF CHRIST

Ambitious parents put their son's name forward for the Order as soon as he was born and paid a hefty registration fee while he was still an infant.

Rules of membership were stringent, yet even popes tried to bend them. A particular problem was that an applicant's pedigree on both sides of the family should not have been blemished by illegitimacy for several generations. Vows of poverty, obedience and celibacy were also required, but openly flouted, and many Knights begged for a release from the last. As Edward Gibbons observed, they "neglected to live, but were prepared to die, in the service of Christ".

An island of "mongrels"

The arrival of the Knights and hapless Greeks seven years later put Malta under the spotlight of Europe for the first time. The 12,000 poor inhabitants of the islands were regarded as human detritus and diverse vagabonds.

One of the results, according to the Knights' commissioners, was that the inhabitants had been left speaking "a sort of Moorish". However, the barefooted fishermen and peasants of Malta welcomed the influx of Knights as the prospective employers, customers, and protectors against Barbary-coast Corsairs who routinely raided the islands for slave labour.

An island transformed

Although the Maltese peasants welcomed the protection of the Knights, the local nobility were not at all keen on being displaced by a superior force enjoying a special relationship with the Pope and Holy Roman Emperor. But in spite of the sullen reservations of the indigenous ruling class, the face of Malta was soon transformed. Accommodation had to be found or built immediately and great urgency was given to the construction of defences, which had to be capable of withstanding the attack by Ottoman troops that was only a matter of time in coming.

The Barbarossa band

Well before the arrival of the Knights, the Barbary Corsairs, as the pirates of North Africa were generally known, had been frequent raiders in this part of the Mediterranean. The profits from piracy enabled the Ottoman *deys* and *beys* (leaders) in control of the Barbary ports to employ the finest fighting commanders and crews available. The best (or worst, if you were a Christian) at the beginning of the 16th century were the brothers Barbarossa from the Greek island of Lesbos. Their protégé Dragut was equally infamous.

Born on the Caramanian coast opposite Rhodes, Dragut joined the Turkish navy as a boy and was recognised as "a good pilot and a most excellent gunner". He joined the Barbarossa band based at Algiers and quickly rose to the rank of lieutenant with the command of 12 galleys.

After years of roving, Dragut decided to join the Ottoman navy, and in 1551 he sailed out of the Dardanelles as second-in-command of a fleet of nearly 150 galleys and 10,000 soldiers.

The sack of Gozo

The Ottoman fleet was heading straight for Malta. By then, the Knights had been on the island for 20 years, steadily improving the defences. When the Turks landed they were intimidated by the mighty sight of Fort St Angelo, even though it was not yet complete. Instead of attacking Malta, they redirected their assault and plundered the relatively defenceless island of Gozo.

Five years earlier, the Gozitans had captured a Corsair, and the people, who were infuriated by years of terror and plunder, had burnt his body

Hayreddin Barbarossa defeats the Holy League of Charles V.

A CHANCE MEETING

There is a legend that, some 25 years before the Great Siege, two of the protagonists met face to face. In 1540, Dragut was captured and put to work as a galley slave in a Christian ship. One of the ship's officers had once been captured by the Turks and spotted him straining at the oars and cried: *"Señor Dragut, usanza de guerra!"* ("'tis the custom of war!"). To which the prisoner, recognising the officer, replied *"Y mudanza de fortuna!"* ("and a change of luck!"). The Christian officer was Jean Parisot de la Valette, the future Grand Master. Dragut was ransomed soon afterwards by the Barbarossas for 3,000 crowns.

on the bastions of their citadel. The Corsair was in fact the brother of Dragut and now he had come for revenge. The Turks devastated the island and carried off almost the entire population of 5,000 into slavery.

Preparing for the worst

Grand Master La Valette, approaching 70 years of age, did not expect to wait long before his old adversary Dragut came looking for him. To face the impending invasion, the fortification of Malta was augmented. The entrances to the harbour and the sheltered creeks of the

The fresco scenes from the Palace of the Grand Masters in Valletta are the most accurate known depiction of the Great Siege of 1565.

Borgo were guarded by a ferocious chain of stakes and metal. La Valette ordered the granaries filled and the cisterns kept topped up with water. A chain of warning beacons was erected around the coast. He asked the Viceroy of Sicily to be ready to help and appealed to all absent Knights to return to Malta at once. In the meantime, 700 Knights and 3,000 Maltese troops, supplemented by about 5,000 mercenaries, waited.

The siege begins

On 18 May 1565, the huge Ottoman fleet hove into view. It consisted of 180 ships carrying more than 30,000 of the best troops the Sultan could muster, but Dragut himself was delayed and word was received that it would be two weeks before he could assume overall command of the operation. Mustafa Pasha, the senior army officer, and the fleet admiral, Piali, had little choice but to begin without him.

The beacons along the coast flared warnings. Peasants rushed into the fortresses with the last of the food and their livestock. Mdina closed its gates and poison was dropped into the wells at Marsa, where the enemy were expected to make their camp.

The Turks took their time, building earthworks ready for an attack on the relatively small garrison of St Elmo before moving on to the main targets, Birgu and St Michael. Arriving at last, Dragut disagreed with these tactics but the preparations were too far advanced to be abandoned. Mustafa professed himself confident that St Elmo would fall within five days.

The sheer weight of the attack when it was launched put the Turks in possession of the ravine in front of the gate within just three hours. The defenders, no more than 60 Knights and a few hundred men, doubted that they could withstand a second assault and sent a message to the Grand Master. La Valette replied that, if necessary, he would personally come to take over St Elmo's defence. Dragut threw a bridge across the ravine and ordered his men to take the fort.

The battle raged on the bridge for five hours, in the course of which the Turkish losses were heavy. The many stories of the Battle of St Elmo are the stuff of legend but one incontrovertible fact is that, during the action, Dragut himself was mortally wounded – according to the Maltese, by the shrapnel of a shot fired from Mount Scebberas. Mustafa is said to have thrown his cloak over the prostrate Dragut until he could be carried to the safety of his tent.

The fall of St Elmo

The battle continued. La Valette gave up asking for the promised help from Sicily and the St Elmo defenders in turn asked no more for reinforcements. On 22 June, the St Elmo Knights set to their final hand-to-hand combat with the Turks and, by the next day, a Turkish flag was run up over the fort.

It is said that word reached the dying Dragut in his tent that St Elmo had at last fallen without a single survivor, whereupon he lay back dead. In fact, there may have been a handful of Christian survivors – some say there were nine Knights, who were never heard of again, and five Maltese, who swam to safety across Grand Harbour. The Turks had lost 8,000 men. Mustafa proposed terms of capitulation to La Valette. His reply was to point at the depth of the ditch around the two as-yet-untouched forts with the remark: "Let your Janissaries come and take that".

The final assault

Turkish guns were manoeuvred into position to bombard the forts, but the rock-hard ground provided little cover for crews who were exposed to brisk counterfire.

Mustafa would have liked to have brought the Turkish ships to lend fire support to his infantry and gunners; La Valette's spiked barrier, however, blocked the entrance.

The Turks threw 10 assaults at St Michael, supported by fire from ships dragged across the lower slopes of Mount Scebberas to circumvent the defences laid at the harbour entrance. Janissaries swarmed up scaling ladders but were hurled back, "a huddled mass of mangled flesh". Knights defended by dropping huge blocks of masonry on to the heads of their assailants.

Still no help came from Don García de Toledo, the Viceroy in Sicily, although it seems that messages passed freely backwards and forwards during the long weeks. Then, on 7 August, Mustafa threw 20,000 men at the two bastions. A mine brought down a long line of battlements, and with a gigantic roar, the Turks, sensing victory, poured through the breach into the town of Birgu itself. "At that supreme moment even the aged Grand Master ... came down to the front of battle and used his sword and pike like a common soldier."

Reinforcements at last

The Turks seem to have been distracted at the very moment of their victory by the sight and sound of cavalry riding down from the Old Town, Mdina. Assuming that they were the long-anticipated reinforcements from Sicily, the soldiers turned tail, retreating over the 2,000 dead who lay there after eight hours of fighting and ignoring their commander's entreaties that this cavalry was merely the 200 members of the Old Town garrison.

Mustafa managed to regroup, but his men had lost the stomach for a fight. The Turkish offensive thereafter was left to the gunners, amid growing concern about the prospect of being stranded in Malta during the approaching winter. Mustafa's concern was increased on 7 September by reports of the arrival of 28 enemy ships and some 8,000 men. This time the rumours of reinforcements were true; the exhausted Turks marched to engage them at Naxxar. Realising that he must withdraw,

Further scenes from the fresco depicting the Great Siege of 1565.

Mustafa formed a rearguard with Dragut's son, Hassan, to protect a retreat that nevertheless left St Paul's Bay choked with Turkish bodies.

Victory

At nightfall on 8 September, the battered gates of Senglea and Birgu were opened and the Knights' Cross again flew over St Elmo. The survivors emerged on to the ruined battlefields outside their fortifications. An account stated: "The Grand Master and his few surviving Knights (the entire force was reduced to some 600 men) looked like phantoms, so pale and grisly were they, faint from their wounds, their hair and beard unkempt, their armour stained and neglected ... men who had hardly slept without their weapons for more than three memorable months."

The anniversary of the ending of the siege on 8 September has, ever since, been the most important holiday on the Maltese calendar. It was thought that no moment of pain or glory could equal it – until Malta's second Great Siege in 1940.

After the siege

Grand Master Jean Parisot de la Valette was the hero of Europe, and monarchs lavished honours and money on him and the Order. But rebuilding was the main task on his mind. Malta needed to be fortified against any future attack. With the Order's coffers overflowing, expense was no object. The site chosen was Mount Scebberas, the high ground from which the Christian forces had taken so much Turkish fire.

The Knights in their role as hospitallers, tending the sick in the Great Ward.

The Grand Master, after whom "The Most Humble City of Valletta" was named, did not see the city completed. He suffered a stroke, after a day's hawking, and earned the distinction of being the first person to be buried in Valletta.

Nevertheless, work began. Levelling the site on Mount Scebberas proved more difficult than expected and was abandoned prematurely; this accounts for the number of streets that end in a steep dive down a flight of stairs to the sea. In general, though, Valletta was laid out as an example of pure Renaissance symmetry, a homogeneous blend of large and small, public and private buildings.

The forts of St Angelo and St Michael were rebuilt and enlarged, as were the fortifications around Birgu – renamed Vittoriosa to commemorate the victory – and Senglea, which sensibly resisted attempts to impose on it the pompous name Invitta (Invincible).

La Sacra Infermeria

In 1574, the Order built La Sacra Infermeria, a great hospital immediately outside Fort St Elmo. Technically, it was the most advanced in Europe, with surgeons boiling their instruments in water before use. It could accommodate 746 patients, and lunatics and galley slaves were "treated" on a lower floor. Patients were well fed – 200 chickens went daily into broth alone.

Langues and auberges

The Knights were divided into *langues* (literally "tongues") and each lived in their particular *auberge* (or inn). The *langues* represented eight major divisions on the political map of Christian Europe as it then existed: Auvergne, Provence, France, Aragon, Castile, Italy, Germany and England, although the last was withdrawn following Henry VIII's mutiple and fierce conjugal disagreements with the papacy. The links with religion were very strong; indeed, the Order as a whole was frequently referred to as the "Religion" and its base as the "Convent".

Religious interference

The Grand Master was officially on a par with the monarchs of Christendom but, as Sir Harry Luke wrote, "he had to endure two rival authorities, the Bishop and the Inquisitor, who in their several ways sought to make his life a burden and often succeeded in their purpose".

In granting Malta to the Order, the Emperor had reserved the right to nominate the local bishop who, moreover, had to be Spanish and be given a say, if not a vote, in the Order's affairs. The bishop therefore came to be regarded as a semi-secret agent reporting to the King of Spain. The Inquisitor, originally invited to Malta by the bishop to look into "pestilential heresies", stayed on to emerge as the papal agent. They thereupon schemed to maximise their influence within the Order.

The simple expedient employed by the bishop to obtain information was to "confer the tonsure" (shave the crown of the head), which, apart from the unusual hairstyle, signified that the persons concerned (many of whom had absolutely no intention of abandoning the lay life) were "clerks" in his service and therefore technically beyond the jurisdiction of the Grand Master.

A depiction of Valletta and the Three Cities.

The Inquisitor dispensed with such subtleties, offering potential informers the unattractive alternative of being thrown into the dungeon of his palace in Vittoriosa on suspicion of heresy. When Bishop Cagliares decided to build a new palace for himself, the Pope refused to allow him to include a dungeon.

Protocols

The three-cornered struggle for power between an independent-minded Grand Master and the two church agents, bishop and Inquisitor, was most likely to show itself in petty occasional issues, such as the right to shoot rabbits, or in daily rules of precedence and protocol. Unforeseen encounters in the street between any two or, heaven forbid, all three of these worthies were very tricky.

If, for example, Grand Master and Inquisitor both happened to be in their coaches, the Inquisitor was expected to stop to allow the former to pass. If the Grand Master happened to be on foot, the Inquisitor was required to descend from his coach and compliment the Grand Master, who was equally obliged to

AN EYE FOR AN EYE

The Great Siege was a brutal and bloody fight to the finish. During the battle for St Elmo, the ravine beneath Dragut's bridge overflowed with putrefying corpses, while the flowing white robes of the Christian defenders on the wall were set alight by fire hoops and plunged into the ravine like comets. After the battle was over, the Turks – trying to demoralise the Knights further – sent five wooden crosses floating across the harbour towards St Angelo, each bearing the headless body of a Knight who had died bravely. La Valette's riposte was to execute all his Turkish prisoners and to fire their heads back at the Turkish lines as cannonballs.

stop to receive the compliment. If the Grand Master was in his coach and the Inquisitor on foot, the latter was supposed to salute but not to advance towards the coach.

Decline into decadence

With no enemy to fight and in this kind of climate, the Order began to lose its sense of purpose. Knights drank, brawled and duelled over honour, as well as for the favours of local women. Petitions and counter-petitions, edicts and counter-edicts flew furiously between Valletta and Rome.

The City Gate entrance to Valletta, with its original drawbridge and narrow bridge over a dry moat.

As if to compensate for a decline in their real power and importance, the Grand Masters adopted ever more ostentatious uniforms, not to mention redundant suits of armour. Some pursued eccentric interests, such as Grand Master Emanuel Pinto, who employed a notorious scoundrel known as Cagliostro (who had been involved in a scandal with Marie Antoinette in France) to carry out experiments "to concoct an elixir of life designed to keep a man sound in health". Whether or not Cagliostro deserves any credit, Pinto lasted until he was 92.

The once-dreaded fleet of the Knights similarly sacrificed efficiency for flamboyant show. The Knights were soon to be looked down upon, according to a local account, as "a corrupt, fanatical and hypocritical lot, as cruel as the Turks and as morally loose as the Popes and Cardinals they catered to".

The French Revolution

The Order was usually dominated by the French contingent, and it was to be expected that when the French Revolution came along, they were firmly on the side of the monarchy, even to the extent of sending money to Louis XVI. The victorious revolutionaries exacted revenge. A large part of the Order's income was derived from property and investments in France. These were sequestered and the French *langue* was stripped of its nationality.

The Little Emperor

Napoleon was convinced that he needed Malta to pursue his designs on British influence in the Mediterranean in general and Egypt in particular. The Grand Master of the time, the German Ferdinand von Hompesch, could see trouble coming and opened negotiations to bring the Order under the protection of Tsar Paul of Russia. These negotiations were in progress when 300 French warships appeared off the Maltese coast demanding a supply of water. Von Hompesch insisted on not more than four ships entering at a time; Napoleon demurred. Within two days, the islands were in French hands.

The feeble surrender to the French cost the Knights the last vestiges of Maltese respect.

The island looted

On Napoleon's orders, French troops looted the various *auberges* and palaces of paintings and tapestries. Napoleon personally helped himself to the jewelled sword presented to La Valette by Philip II of Spain. French became the official language of Malta overnight.

Napoleon stayed on Malta only a week before launching himself on Egypt. He left behind a garrison of 1,000 men under General Claude Vaubois. The Royal Navy under Nelson, however, caught up with him at Alexandria and, at the ensuing Battle of the Nile, the French fleet was annihilated. One of the notable casualties was the *Orient*, which took to the bottom much of the treasure so recently looted from Malta.

The French garrison left behind was not deterred by these setbacks from further plundering Maltese churches; the crowning insult was a public auction held in Mdina of the contents of the Carmelite Church.

The local backlash

This was the final straw for the furious Maltese, who slaughtered the small garrison in Mdina and set off in pursuit of Vaubois, who speedily locked himself in the safety of Valletta. A siege was laid by a local force, under the command of the canon of Mdina Cathedral, aided and abetted by the British ship *Orion* which supplied 1,000 muskets, and the King of Naples and Admiral Lord Nelson, who provided ships to blockade Valletta.

Vaubois was not to be intimidated, however, and he led his men out of the city against the 10,000 rebellious islanders who had now declared themselves to be subjects of the King of Naples.

The French are ousted

Although Vaubois proved remarkably resilient, initially the British commanding officer, Captain Alexander Ball, was not inclined to do more than patrol the coastline to prevent French reinforcements from slipping in. It was left to the Maltese to sustain the pressure on the ground with the help of supporters within the walls. The French unmasked some of these and, on one occasion, executed 43 men.

However, as the 19th century dawned, Britain decided to turn the screw by sending additional forces, who raised a local regiment. The mass of volunteers who came forward thereby became the Maltese Light Infantry – part of the British Army, a new departure in Maltese military history.

The French hung on in Valletta for two months, eventually conceding defeat and giving themselves up when their stock of bread was reduced to just three days' supply. The British flag was run up over Malta on 5 September 1800. The departing French troops took with them the ghost, if not the corpse, of the Knights.

The Auberge de Provence.

PIRATE KNIGHTS

The Knights could only support their extravagant lifestyles by indulging in the brutal piracy that they were supposed to contain. The oars of their galleys were manned by whomever came to hand: usually prisoners-of-war, or convicts, who were stripped naked, chained six to a bench, and flogged with whips – "ten, twelve, even twenty hours at a stretch, without the slightest relapse or rests, and on these occasions the officer will go round putting into the mouths of the wretched rowers pieces of bread soaked in wine to prevent them from fainting". If someone did faint, "he is flogged until he appears to be dead and is then flung overboard".

THE KNIGHTS OF MALTA TODAY

The warrior Knights began as Hospitallers, caring for pilgrims to the Holy Land, and have never forgotten their healing tradition.

The Sovereign Military Hospitaller Order of St John of Jerusalem, of Rhodes, and of Malta, to give it its full name, is still a powerful force. It has 11,000 Roman Catholic members spread around the globe and co-operates with many other Christian orders. Its modern mission is purely humanitarian, from the running of refugee camps, to caring for children in South American slums. It has leprosy hospitals in Africa and Asia and, quite appropriately, a maternity clinic in Bethlehem. It also runs blood banks and dispatches field hospitals to disaster areas.

The Order's headquarters in Rome's elegant shopping street, Via Condotti, is, like the Vatican (with which it is closely linked), a sovereign state. It issues is own stamps, has its own diplomatic corps, and has a sovereign head with the title Prince and Grand Master. But these days, only the top echelons of the Order take vows of chastity and poverty, and they require an impeccable pedigree of more than two centuries of nobility.

Depite its chic Rome address, there is a real desire for the Order to return to the site of its most famous victory, Fort St Angelo, Malta's last bastion of defence during the Great Siege. The Order has a lease on part of the fort and would like to turn it into a mini state.

Dressed for the occasion – a participant in a re-enactment wearing the old clothing of the Knights' officers and men-in-arms.

Regular In Guardia parades re-enact the pomp of the Knights. Shows are held at Fort St Elmo most Sundays (except in August).

The rotation of the Maltese Cross is said to symbolise the spiritual regeneration brought about by Christ's crucifixion.

The Beheading of John the Baptist by Michelangelo Caravaggio.

THE LEGACY LIVES ON

If you keep your eyes peeled, Malta is literally an open-air museum for striking remnants of the Knights' many years here. Across the islands you can spot everything from architecture to paintings that hail from this incredible era and prove that the legacy of the Knights lives on today. For instance, architecturally, the Grand Master Pinto Stores along the Valletta Waterfront now provide the beautiful backdrop for this busy commercial spot. Meanwhile, if you choose to wander through the countryside, you'll be likely to spot one of the 13 watchtowers that were built to defend the coast. The oldest is Wignacourt Tower in St Paul's Bay, which dates back to 1609. Other gems include the public clocks of St John's Co-Cathedral, and Pinto's Clock at the Magistral Palace in Valletta, which has been marking time since 22 June 1745. Finally, don't miss one of Malta's true treasures – the painting of *The Beheading of St John* (above) by Michelangelo Merisi da Caravaggio. Now housed within St John's Co-Cathedral, it was commissioned under Grand Master Alof de Wignacourt.

Many of the Order are buried at St John's Co-Cathedral including Grand Master Jean Parisot de la Vallette, who built Valletta.

An engraving of the Great Siege of Malta in 1565, when the Knights successfully protected Malta from the invading Turkish armies. It is one of the most celebrated events in Malta's history.

The Order of St John is still active today. It no longer governs any territory, but is recognised as a soveverign nation by the Vatican.

Statue of Queen Victoria in Republic Square.

ENTER THE BRITISH

With the Knights and Napoleon both expelled, the arrival of the British signalled a new and completely different era for the Maltese Islands.

The negotiation of the Peace of Amiens between France and Britain in 1802 took an alarming twist in the Maltese's eyes: there was talk of Britain handing back all previously French-owned territories after two years of occupation. The island's bitter taste of French rule made the prospect of this as unsavoury as the resurrection of the discredited Knights. Malta stated its case unequivocally in a Declaration of Rights: Malta must come "under the protection and sovereignty of the King of the free people, His Majesty the King of the United Kingdom of Great Britain and Ireland."

Ancient experience of the islands being passed around different rulers necessitated the proviso that "his said Majesty has no right to cede these Islands to any power … if he chooses to withdraw his protection, and abandon his sovereignty, the right of electing another sovereign, or of governing these Islands, belongs to us, the inhabitants and aborigines alone, and without control".

Anglicisation

Malta's political institutions and law were gradually anglicised, but it was probably in the matter of language that the nuances showed through most clearly. While spoken by all sections of the Maltese people, Malti had never acquired any status – it remained, as far as most foreigners were concerned, "a kind of Moorish". As the language of its nearest neighbour in Europe, Italian was the language of the Church and the law, and was generally used by society in Maltese drawing rooms.

The commercial community in Valletta had picked up some English because of contact

Print of a British ship in Grand Harbour.

DON'T CALL US…

The Civil Commissioner who guided Malta into British ways was Sir Alexander Ball. His first task had been to let the Order of the Knights know that it would definitely not be returning to Malta. However, oblivious to Maltese local feeling, Grand Master Tommasi was waiting in Sicily fully expecting the call to return. When it didn't come, he sent his diplomat, the Bailiff Buzi, to investigate the delay. Buzi assumed he could move into the Palace in Valletta; instead, he was politely advised that Sir Alexander was in residence and found it "absolutely necessary" to remain so. Buzi was told to wait – in vain, as it transpired.

with English men-of-war and merchants who had been regular callers at the Grand Harbour from the 17th century, but the language was no more widely known than that. Instructions to Sir Thomas Maitland on his appointment as the first British governor in 1813 contained the note, significant in the light of later events: "You will be pleased to issue all Proclamations in English as well as Italian, and in a few years the latter may be gradually disused." It was added that, as yet, "no permanent or definite system had been laid down for their Government".

of modern Maltese politics, education, the liberation of the Maltese church from Sicilian domination, and the regulation of the rights of the Maltese nobility.

In various government proclamations, the switch from the earlier routine could not have been more simple: the words "Grand Master" were crossed out and "The King" substituted.

The history of the British period includes, in one of the smaller footnotes, the implications of having a Queen on the throne. During Victoria's reign, a Maltese marchioness became entitled to kiss her cheek (like an English peeress) instead of kissing only her hand. A similar footnote shows Queen Victoria doing her bit for the Maltese lacemaking industry with an order for "eight dozen pairs long and eight dozen pairs short mits, besides a scarf".

Monument to Sir Alexander Ball in Lower Barrakka Gardens, Valletta.

Subjects of the Crown

The final shadow of the Knights that hung over the island was removed when Russia let it be known that, having broken with Napoleon, it no longer wished to pursue the restoration of the Order of St John to Malta. Now the people of Malta and Gozo could formally be made "subjects of the British Crown and entitled to its fullest protection".

As Sir Harry Luke, a British Lieutenant-Governor of Malta (1930–8), observed, the history of Malta under British rule, at least until World War II, may have lacked "the glamour, the international ramifications, the world-wide appeal of the Knights". But what it did bring to the islanders were the beginnings and development

Literary visitors

One of the first of Malta's illustrious British visitors was the poet Samuel Taylor Coleridge, who arrived in Malta in 1804 for health reasons. The governor, Sir Alexander Ball, appointed him Private Secretary and, after having found other accommodation for himself, Ball left Coleridge to live alone in a vast palace. Coleridge recorded that he felt like "a mouse in a Cathedral on a fair market day".

Grand Tourists arrived close in the wake of the British takeover, including another already famous poet. Lord Byron, just turned 21, was offended by the paucity of the reception laid on by Ball for his arrival in 1809. He was pleased, though, with the accommodation in Old Bakery Street, Valletta, and he began to take Arabic lessons. However, he was distracted by what was to become a notorious weakness: an attractive woman. The woman concerned was appropriately special. Still in her mid-twenties, she was the Austrian-born daughter of the Austrian Internuncio in Constantinople and married to Charles Spencer Smith, the British representative at the same court.

Daily business in the Palace of the Grand Masters.

Their affair lasted a furious three weeks, during which Byron had to be restrained from fighting a duel on her behalf with an aide-de-camp. She appears in his poetry as "Florence" and they talked about running away together to Friuli in northern Italy.

Almost inevitably, Byron let her down badly and knew it. But he was probably not so diffident about the collapse of the affair because he was moved to write a lamenting and, it has to be said, a fairly lamentable farewell to Malta (it is regarded as among his very worst work).

Adieu, ye joys of La Valette!
Adieu, sirocco, sun, and sweat!
Adieu, thou Palace rarely entered!
Adieu, ye mansions where
I've ventured!
Adieu, ye cursed streets of stairs!
(How surely he who mounts you swears!)
Adieu…

More men of letters

Sir Walter Scott, paralysed and apoplectic by strokes brought on by his literary efforts to buy off creditors, spent three weeks of the last year of his life in Malta. He attended a ball given in his honour, and noted privately

DRESSING AND DINING

In 1810, Dr Charles Meryon wrote: "The upper classes of the inhabitants dress like the French; but the common people wear a dress resembling Figaro in the opera, with this difference, that they have trousers instead of tight breeches. The women are small and have beautiful hands and feet. They are fond to excess of gold ornaments which they estimate by value more than taste; their ears, necks and arms are stiff with rings, chains and bracelets. They wear shoe-buckles of gold or silver. Although very brown, they are often handsome. The repasts are plentiful; it is common to have three courses, and from five to ten different sorts of wine."

afterwards that it was "an odd kind of honour to bestow on a man of letters suffering from paralytic illness".

William Makepeace Thackeray's visit started fatefully in quarantine on Manoel Island. On being released, he was enchanted by the scenes that surrounded him: "beggars, boatmen, barrels of pickled herrings and maccaroni; the shovel-hatted priests and bearded Capuchins; the tobacco, grapes, onions and sunshine; the signboards, bottled-porter stores, the statues of saints and little chapels which jostle the stranger's eyes..."

Dizzy's debates

Of all these visitors, the one whose impressions had the most profound influence on Britain's political and diplomatic stance towards the islands in the latter half of the 19th century was the future prime minister, young Benjamin ("Dizzy") Disraeli.

"Highly unpopular and unwanted at the regimental messes and parties," Disraeli was too clever by half for the taste of the British officer corps. It was said that, "what rendered matters worse was his great knowledge and memory, which enabled him to make short work of any bold soldier who encountered his argument". And even if Disraeli knew what people thought of him, it is likely that he didn't care. "You should see me in the costume of a Greek pirate," he wrote home to his father.

Disraeli did not forget his enjoyable experience of Malta when it was relevant to the diplomatic tangles that ultimately ground towards the outbreak of World War I. Britain and France had of course patched up their differences by this stage and Winston Churchill, then First Lord of the Admiralty, openly invited his French counterpart "to use Malta as if it were Toulon". It was then that Malta gained her reputation as "the Nurse of the Mediterranean", providing more than 25,000 beds for the care of the wounded during World War I.

Print of Valletta, seen from Grand Harbour, 1840.

A DIFFERENT LANGUAGE

In order to refute Mussolini's claim that the Maltese spoke a form of Italian (and therefore Malta should be handed over to him), the British governor Sir Harry Luke pointed to a translation of the first part of Longfellow's *Psalm of Life*, ("Tell me not, in mournful numbers...")

Tghidulix li id-dinja hi holma,
Mhiex hlief frugha, u niket, u hemm;
Dak li jidher fil-wicc hu qarrieqi,
U jekk torqod ir-ruh taghna tintemm.

As Sir Harry remarked in typical British style, "It doesn't really look much like a dialect of Italian, does it?".

Self-government

Malta's first self-governing constitution came into being in 1921. The constitution separated the responsibilities pertaining to the island's role as an imperial fortress – such as defence and foreign relations – which remained with Britain, from the responsibilities for the island's domestic affairs, which were put into the hands of a Senate and Legislative Assembly. Political activity was fused into the Nationalist Party until, in 1927, it was defeated by the Constitutional Party under the leadership of Sir Gerald (later Lord) Strickland, who had

Benjamin Disraeli.

previously been Chief Secretary of Malta and was Maltese through his mother, the Contessa della Catena.

Ecclesiastical interference

Lord Strickland and the Church did not get along, and he was not pleased when the bishop circulated a pre-election letter to his flock that stated: "You may not, without committing a grave sin, vote for Lord Strickland and his candidates." Moreover, a postscript to priests reminded them that they were "strictly forbidden to administer the Sacraments to the obstinate who refuse to obey these our instructions".

The British government sent a protest note to the Pope over this ecclesiastical intrusion into the freedom of voters in a British colony, only to be told that Lord Strickland and his party's attitude was "undoubtedly and consistently injurious to religion, since it discredits Bishops and clergy, upsets ecclesiastical discipline and tends to destroy the religious traditions of a people so deeply attached to the Church". The British government promptly suspended the general election in 1930.

The elections in 1933 resulted in the return to office of the Nationalists, who immediately undertook the curious course (for Nationalists) of reversing the previous encouragement given

Bust of Winston Churchill in the Valletta War Museum.

to the use of the Maltese language by imposing Italian. The Secretary of State for the Colonies investigated and, having discovered that only about 15 percent of the population spoke Italian and that English was far more widely used and understood, suspected that Italian Fascists were at work.

Mussolini's ambitions

Mussolini's propaganda was determined to persuade Italians that the Maltese were part of the Italian race, their speech was an Italian dialect, and that the Italians ought to back his plan to seize Malta – plus other choice bits of the former Roman Empire – when he gave the word.

HMS Eagle at war.

AIRCRAFT UP

July 1942, after the "raiders passed" signal.

WORLD WAR II

Isolated on the edge of Axis-held Europe, Malta looked doomed. But history was about to repeat itself in the island's second Great Siege.

On 10 June 1940, Italy's dictator Benito Mussolini cast his lot with Adolf Hitler. Italy was at war with Britain and France. That night, Malta heard Il Duce broadcast to jubilant crowds from his balcony overlooking Piazza Venezia in Rome. His "million bayonets", he shouted, would be on the march as from midnight. What they did not know, nor did Hitler for that matter, was that Mussolini's first action would be against Malta, the following day, 11 June.

The battle begins

At 7am the next morning, air-raid sirens wailed for the first time and, minutes later, the whistle of falling bombs could be heard around Valletta and the Grand Harbour as 10 high-flying bombers escorted by fighters droned overhead. A barrage of rapid fire came from the anti-aircraft guns of Malta's artillery batteries, accompanied by the staccato of the 4-inch guns of HMS *Terror*, a survivor from World War I berthed in Pieta creek. It was the first of what were to be eight raids that day.

Faith, Hope and Charity

To face the enemy aircraft, Malta had but three aged Gladiator biplanes, apparently left behind accidentally at the RAF base in Kalafrana when the carrier *Glorious*, to which they belonged, set sail for the North Sea at the time of the German invasion of Norway. They had become known as *Faith*, *Hope* and *Charity*, and on that first raid, one was lost. Folklore has it that it was *Charity* because "Malta never lost Hope or Faith in the final victory".

To fight or to flee?

Even though the War Cabinet had voted against ceding any claims on Malta to Italy,

Heading for the safety of a shelter.

SECRET TALKS

What the Maltese did not know was that the islands' destiny had already been secretly discussed. In a bid to keep Italy from joining Germany, Britain's War Cabinet had, some days earlier, received a proposal from the French suggesting that the Allies offer Italy "belligerent status", and therefore the right to a seat at an eventual peace conference. There, her territorial claims to Malta could be discussed.

It was a close call. The two War Cabinet doves, Neville Chamberlain and Lord Halifax, voted for the proposal; the three hawks, Churchill, Clement Attlee and Arthur Greenwood voted against, and so rejected it.

whether the islands were physically defensible was quite another matter. Both the Army and the Royal Air Force had considered Malta too vulnerable to attack from enemy planes based on neighbouring Sicily and favoured evacuation. The Royal Navy had thought otherwise and its voice carried. It was to be proved right – though at high cost.

The islands were soon fully embroiled in the rigours of 20th-century war. Wartime restrictions were put into force, blackouts introduced and already-deep shelters were dug deeper into the limestone rock. The sirens sounded their warnings and their all-clears. The 30,000 troops divided into equal numbers of British and Maltese. The civilian population stood at about 255,500.

Wartime poster reinforcing the allegiance between Britain and her colonies.

Malta strikes back

As new Allied planes arrived, the island also took on an offensive role. On 11 November an airborne torpedo attack by planes from the carrier *Illustrious* hit the Italian fleet sheltering in Taranto harbour, accounting for the loss of three battleships and two cruisers.

By December, in excess of 200 Italian air raids had been recorded, but Malta held fast; Operation Hercules – Italy's code name for the planned invasion and occupation of the islands – was indeed proving to be a herculean task.

The key to the Mediterranean

Churchill was utterly convinced of the islands' strategic importance. Malta, he insisted, must be held, whatever the cost. And the strength of Malta's strategic position was not lost on the German forces, either.

As the Allies made advances in North Africa, and Italy suffered setbacks with her disastrous venture into Greece, so Hitler turned his attention to the Mediterranean arena. He planned to cut the supply lifeline, and starve the islands into submission.

The battle for HMS Illustrious

Malta suffered a major blow in January 1941 when the vital aircraft-carrier *Illustrious* was attacked while escorting a convoy coming from Alexandria. The flight deck was put out of commission, putting the carrier's own airborne planes in the predicament of needing somewhere else to land. They decided to head for Malta, their mother ship limping towards the Grand Harbour with the remnants of the convoy that evening.

On reaching Malta, as the first two merchantmen passed safely through the defensive nets at the breakwater entrance into the comparative calm of the Grand Harbour, so waves of Stuka dive-bombers and Junker 88s filled the sky. In spite of a relentless onslaught (a 500kg bomb penetrated the flight-deck armour), the *Illustrious* sailed on with fires raging and her steering gear out of order.

On the night of 10 January, she finally made the harbour and berthed in Dockyard Creek. Here she was sheltered by the heights of Kordin on one side, but was otherwise exposed to full view. Every hand in the area was called out. Casualties were evacuated and men from the dockyard swarmed over the carrier. Working around the clock, they carried out repairs.

It was six days before the enemy returned to their attack, time enough for them to rearm themselves for the final kill. But it was six days not wasted in Malta; the Allies had carefully planned their defence against the bombardment.

On the afternoon of 16 January, the attack came. Buildings shook as bombs exploded and the barrage of anti-aircraft fire opened up. Malta had never known noise like it before. People ran to nearby air-raid shelters only to see dive-bombers flying at rooftop level, screaming down to where the carrier was berthed. Shrapnel rained down from the bursting barrage above.

It was a massive raid. Ten enemy planes were destroyed; five by the few fighters Malta could deploy, five by the ground artillery. And the damage to buildings on both sides of the Grand Harbour was the heaviest recorded in any one raid. Casualties were so high, it was decided to evacuate the so-called Three Cities of Senglea, Cospicua and Vittoriosa bordering the dockyard area. Yet only one bomb hit the *Illustrious*, and even that did little damage.

Undaunted, the enemy returned on the 18th. This time their objective was to put the land-based planes out of action by making the runways unusable. They succeeded, but only briefly. As they always did, teams of willing hands soon filled in the craters again.

The stakes increase

The battle for Malta, which had begun almost as a personal crusade on Mussolini's part, took on a different complexion with growing German involvement.

Rommel's Afrika Korps had joined battle in North Africa, and Malta was now pivotal in the North African theatre because its aircraft, ships and submarines were a constant threat to the Germans' exposed supply line between Naples and Tripoli.

German convoys were careful to pass by only at night and never closer than about 240km (150 miles). If Malta-based aircraft missed the supplies as they crossed the sea, they were given a second chance as the supplies trundled east along the North African coast. There was no practical port in the

Fires rage deep in Grand Harbour after another raid by German bombers.

UNDER SIEGE

In spite of the many hardships and grave danger that the Maltese people faced during this time, morale was generally high throughout the siege. However, by February 1941 there were shortages of everything. Stocks of staple foods had run worryingly low, so food rationing was introduced as a countermeasure. Kerosene, the fuel then used in many kitchens, was also rationed.

The black market thrived in these conditions. Ammunition was also becoming scarce, so anti-aircraft gunners were designated with hours when they were to hold their fire, no matter how tempting the target.

hundreds of miles that separated Tripoli and Tobruk, hence the determination by both Allies and Axis to win and hold the latter. Field Marshal Albert Kesselring repeatedly reminded Rommel of this vulnerability, and on one occasion was overheard to say: "You risk everything if you try to reach the Nile while the British still hold Malta."

The islands got off more lightly in the first half of 1941 than would have been the case if Rommel had not gone against Kesselring's advice with a decision to secure Tobruk first and worry about Malta afterwards. However, fewer Allied convoys were getting through the blockade. Many ships were sunk before they reached sight of harbour, others met their fate as soon as they anchored.

But while few convoys were getting through, Malta's submarines and bombers armed with torpedoes could, and did, still inflict heavy damage and losses on ships carrying supplies destined for the Afrika Korps. The good news for Malta was that, with the German invasion of Russia, planes that would have been deployed in Sicily were now serving at the Russian front. The odds

German Messerschmitt Bf110s in the sky over Malta.

SECRET WEAPONS

In July 1941, the Italians revealed a secret weapon that they had not yet called upon, a special unit of fast-motor torpedo boats known by the Allies as E-boats (and by the Germans as *S-boots*) and manned torpedoes.

According to the unit commander, these small, compact and deadly craft had been designed as long ago as 1935, specifically with a Malta campaign in mind, when the claims of territorial rights by Italy had first surfaced.

The job of the pilot was to drive his craft at the target, wait until the last moment, throw a lever that activated the charge, and abandon the torpedo, which would explode on impact. If the shockwaves did not incapacitate the pilot and he was lucky, he would be picked up by an attendant E-boat. Such manned torpedoes had already been used with some success in attacks on both Gibraltar and Crete.

In reality, however, the bravery of the Italian pilots was to count for nothing. They had not anticipated the island's superb radar coastal defence systems, and were spotted leaving Sicily. They were tracked and allowed to enter Maltese waters, then within minutes were shot to pieces by concentrated firepower. Only three pilots survived, and they were taken prisoner.

The defeat of the secret weapon lifted the spirits of the bombarded Maltese and provided another much-needed boost to the morale of the island's defenders.

on getting a convoy through were steadily improving.

The Blitz of Malta

The Germans, becoming increasingly frustrated by this depleting thorn in their side, felt that they could not allow the strategic outpost of Malta to remain in Allied hands any longer. The German objective now was to neutralise Malta, and the islands were about to enter the second Great Siege of their history.

The first waves of bombing came in the middle of January 1942, and then continued with such brutal force that air superiority seemed to be firmly in the hands of the Axis powers. In March and April, twice as many tons of bombs rained down on Malta as in a whole year at the height of London's Blitz.

To crush the population's will to fight on, there were 154 days of continuous day and night raids (London had 57), and 6,700 tons of bombs were dropped on the Grand Harbour area (by comparison, the worst night of destruction in Coventry was achieved with 260 tons). Buildings were flattened, 40,000 homes were destroyed, and casualties were high. "Victory Kitchens" were set up to feed the population who were suffering acute malnutrition. Ammunition was rationed.

The blockade was complete; nothing could reach the islands. Churchill signalled: "The eyes of Britain are watching Malta in her struggle day by day. We are sure success as well as glory will reward your efforts."

He also signalled President Roosevelt: "Air attack on Malta is very heavy." With the *Ark Royal* recently sunk, could Roosevelt allow the United States aircraft-carrier *Wasp* to airlift essential Spitfires to Malta? "*Wasp* at your disposal", came the reply. On 14 April she set course from Britain for Gibraltar. On her decks were 47 vital fighters. Perhaps Malta's luck was changing.

The next day, King George VI awarded the islands the George Cross. The citation read: "To honour her brave people I award the George Cross to the island fortress of Malta to bear witness to a heroism and devotion that will long be famous in history."

Taking cover

It was a traumatic time. Remote villages of no conceivable military significance suffered like everywhere else. Although houses built of stone did not burn, the confined blast of a bomb landing in a narrow alley was lethal. A low-flying plane could drop a bomb and be gone before an unsuspecting pedestrian knew what was happening, so during the worst of the bombing offensives, the villagers took shelter underground. Many passed the danger periods reciting their rosaries, a bucket of water always at hand to wet a handkerchief that went over the nose as a filter against choking dust mixed with the smell of cordite. And if a meal in the government-funded "Victory Kitchen" included a morsel of meat, then it was goat.

The destructive aftermath of a German aerial bombardment on the Maltese Islands.

Flags and bells

As an emergency reaction to each and every air-raid warning would have prevented any work from being done, the degree of probable danger was denoted by a system of signals, a red flag when bombers were expected, a red-and-white one for fighters or mere reconnaissance flights.

The flags were run up on the Governor's Palace and on the Auberge de Castille, but as these were invisible from certain places, boy scouts took it upon themselves to relay the appropriate signal with miniature flags on hand-held poles. Nearly 1,000 scouts were awarded the Bronze Cross for their efforts.

Church bells, whose peal was the concomitant of normal life in Malta, were silent, now for use only to warn of imminent invasion.

Reinforcements

For nearly two years there had been raids at the rate of about three a day, but a chink of hope interrupted this desperate situation. The American carrier *Wasp* was on its way with 47 more Spitfires. They took off unarmed (to save weight) but with extra disposable fuel tanks that enabled them to reach Malta with barely 90 litres (20 gallons) to spare. The Germans had previously been aware of the arrival of new aircraft and had timed raids to catch them en masse on the ground during the day or so that it took to make them fully serviceable. Now, however, two soldiers and two airmen were waiting for each Spitfire, which was led to a pen as soon as it landed, refuelled, armed and loaded – all within the space of six minutes.

Captain Mason, commander of the SS Ohio, with bandaged hand, after his ship's mission to Malta.

The new arrivals were already in the air and waiting when the Luftwaffe made its customary call. The German pilots were evidently caught completely off guard, their radio channels suddenly clogged with cries of *Achtung Spitfeuer!*, and they lost 30 aircraft that day.

At one time, the rubber dinghies of so many downed Stuka bombers were bobbing in the sea between Malta and Sicily that one of the Spitfire pilots likened it to "Henley on Regatta Day".

Aerial superiority

Between August 1940 and October 1942, 718 fighters were flown to Malta, 367 of them Spitfires. On 10 May 1942, the month that logged the 2,000th air raid, it appeared as if the tide of fortune had turned. The Spitfires that day seemed to be clawing the enemy out of the sky in spectacular dogfights that were watched excitedly by Maltese leaving their shelters.

By contrast, the larger picture was bleak. Malta was only two months away from the date the authorities had decided would have to be the day of surrender if supplies did not get through. Conditions had now become so dire that they would have no other choice.

But relief was on its way. Heading towards Malta was a convoy of 14 supply ships with an enormous escort of three aircraft-carriers, two battleships, seven cruisers and 24 destroyers. This one had to get through.

Malta expects

Day and night a moving target, the convoy was attacked by sea and air, taking heavy losses as it sailed through a corridor of fire. Of the carriers, the *Eagle* was ripped open and sunk by torpedoes, and the *Indomitable* put out of action. Nearing Sicily, the heavier warships turned back to the task force in Gibraltar; the convoy's protection was reduced to four cruisers and 12 destroyers. Now the enemy concentrated the attack, but somehow the remnants continued to progress. Two cruisers were put out of action, five merchantmen sunk.

On 13 August, word spread in Malta as the first ships were sighted. Crowds gathered. First to reach harbour were the supply ships *Port Chalmers*, *Melbourne Star* and *Rochester Castle*. Two days later, on 15 August – which was an important day in the Catholic calendar, the feast day of Santa Marija (the Assumption of the Virgin Mary) – in came the *Brisbane Star* and the battered, charred hulk of the tanker *Ohio*, which was barely above water and was being towed by two minesweepers and a destroyer.

Lining the battlements, crowds cheered and waved and wept for joy.

In the nick of time

But for the arrival of the Santa Marija convoy, the islanders would have had to surrender in two weeks. The courageous *Ohio* symbolised the islands' determination to hold out.

Commenting on this event, which was so crucial to the island's survival, Churchill recorded: "Thus in the end five gallant merchant ships out of 14 got through with their precious cargoes. The loss of 350 officers and men and of so many of the finest ships in the Merchant Navy and in the escorting fleet of the Royal Navy was grievous. The reward justified the price exacted. Revictualed and replenished with ammunition and essential stores, the strength of Malta revived."

Thereafter, the Afrika Korps was primarily concerned with defending its retreat to Tobruk and from there to Benghazi, Tripoli and, ultimately, to Tunisia. The changing tide manifested itself to the Maltese when four merchant ships bobbed into Grand Harbour having made the run from Alexandria unscathed. At Christmas it was even possible to announce that there was a special treat in the rations: about half a pound per head of beans and sugar and a quarter of currants.

Glad tidings

There was even better news to come on 23 January 1943 with the announcement that the Allies had taken Tripoli – or, as the Maltese preferred to think of it, the Italians had lost it.

On 12 May the Afrika Korps capitulated, Malta having barred the way to the evacuation of 291,000 Germans and Italians who might otherwise have fought another day. The following month it was possible for King George VI to visit the island, while Montgomery and Eisenhower planned the invasion of Sicily.

Shipping reinforcements to Malta.

The Allied springboard

The Maltese Islands thus became the Allied springboard for the invasion of Sicily (and for the subsequent push into mainland Europe), with military operations planned from within the depths of the subterranean Lascaris War Rooms, situated adjacent to Grand Harbour in Valletta.

On 8 September the Italian fleet surrendered, as the commander-in-chief Admiral Cunningham notified the Admiralty in London, "under the guns of the fortress of Malta". By coincidence, that momentous day was a feast day of the Virgin Mary and also the anniversary of the victory over the Turks in the Great Siege of 1565.

The new City Gate and Parliament at Valletta, designed by Renzo Piano.

LOOKING TO THE FUTURE

Confident and independent, modern Malta continues to build on its individuality while strengthening its ties to the rest of the world.

While World War II raged on, the British government announced that Malta's "outstanding gallantry" called for "special recognition" in the grant, there and then, of £10 million for restoration after war damage, with a further £20 million in the pipeline. The government also pledged to restore "Responsible Government" as soon as possible after the end of the conflict.

Elections in 1947 gave Malta its first Labour government under Dr (later Sir) Paul Boffa. The party proposed a referendum on whether the Maltese people, in post-war circumstances, wished to "submit Malta's case to the United States of America with a view to Malta receiving economic aid and, as a quid pro quo, the USA use of Malta as a base". It later transpired that the original draft, by Dominic (Dom) Mintoff, a future premier, had left the door open for the USA or "any major power", an implicit invitation to the Soviet Union. The draft alternative was attributed to "human error" and quickly deleted.

Demands for independence.

The call for independence

Mintoff came to power in 1955 and suggested that Malta should be "integrated" into the United Kingdom and therefore be represented in the House of Commons. A referendum showed 67,607 out of 90,343 votes in favour of integration, but the British government, while generally sympathetic to the idea, was not confident that the result reflected the feelings of the non-voters.

The matter was still under discussion with Mintoff when it was announced, in 1957, that Britain would be cutting back its defence expenditure, with unavoidable consequences for the Malta dockyard, the islands' greatest

MINTOFF'S BARGAINING CARD

In 1957, Dom Mintoff, desiring the Church's support for independence, resorted to one of the more bizarre manoeuvres in Malta's political history.

Malta's two great paintings, Caravaggio's *The Beheading of St John the Baptist* and *St Jerome*, both part of St John's Co-Cathedral, had recently been sent to an exhibition in Rome. When they were returned to Malta, they were forcibly impounded on Mintoff's orders. Then, as abruptly as they had been seized, they were released. The following day, a declaration of solidarity was issued by the Archbishop demanding independence from Britain.

single employer, providing work for 13,000 people. Mintoff subsequently lost his enthusiasm for integration and raised the cry for full independence.

Farewell to the British

Following Mintoff's appeals, a constitutional deadlock ensued, leading to Britain taking over full responsibility for the islands' government.

By 1959, Malta's dockyard had outlived its usefulness (at least, to Britain), and the Colonial Administration published a five-year development plan that concluded that "put briefly … Malta must get out into the world and earn its own living in other ways than it has done in the past". The means to do so clearly demanded full independence, and this was duly granted on 21 September 1964, albeit subject to a 10-year Mutual Defence Agreement with Britain.

Former Maltese Premier Dom Mintoff in 1972.

The British naval base was finally closed on 31 March 1979 amid politically orchestrated celebrations that were joyous for some and sad for others. Shortly afterwards came independent Malta's first experience of a hostile foreign act when a gunboat threatened an Italian company drilling for oil on Malta's behalf. It seems rather appropriate to the history of the islands that its home port was on the Barbary coast.

Post-war worries

The main problems after the war concerned the economy, with growing worries that the hardships that followed World War I might be repeated. There was, in addition, the need for an extended settlement from Britain that would not only repair the heavy damage caused by the severe bombing but also help the construction of improved housing and infrastructure. For years, Malta and Gozo had been poor colonial relations.

Employment prospects were looking bleak. British dockyards had employed over one in six of all Maltese workers, and British service establishments had injected considerable cash into the economy.

The most dramatic result of this was two decades of mass emigration to Australia and

DOM MINTOFF: HERO AND OGRE

There was a time when the name Dom Mintoff was synonymous with that of Malta. Over a period of 17 years Mintoff was prime minister four times. Although he stepped down in 1984, many assumed that up to 1987, his great influence (including an apparent friendship with Libya's Colonel Gaddafi) still held sway over a variety of political matters.

Born in 1916, he became determined to prove that the Maltese were as good as anyone else. He worked in Britain between 1941 and 1943 before returning home to help reorganise the Malta Labour Party, ready for the first post-war elections. The elections took place in 1947 and Labour won. By 1955, Mintoff was prime minister, calling for the British to leave the island.

At home, Mintoff's actions polarised the nation. People either loved him or hated him. Violence flared in divided communities. In the days when everyone was a practising Catholic, he was not.

But he did improve the standard of living for many. Wages rose, social services improved and he introduced free tertiary-level education.

Mintoff's political career ended on a sad note in 1998 when, at odds with his Labour Party, he crossed the floor of the house in a vote of confidence, condemning them to a single-vote defeat. They lost the ensuing general election and Mintoff declined to stand.

The bogus claims of Mussolini to the islands' Italian language heritage were buried, alongside Il Duce, after the war. English would be the second language, used for administration and education.

Canada, which eased the problems and softened the blow of the inevitable rundown of jobs. The legacy is that, even today, there are as many Maltese and Gozitans living abroad as on the Maltese Islands.

turned down out of hand. It left a festering wound and barbed his tongue. Later, when he asked for US courtesy, no president would receive him.

With no foreign income to bolster the economy, Mintoff was forced to cast around. Potential friends were wary of such a volatile man. President François Mitterrand, although a socialist, took much wooing before he issued an invitation to visit France, and the former USSR set up dialogue only through satellite states. Yet Mintoff was the first leader to be given a stupendous welcome in China, preceding all other Western leaders, including the USA's Richard Nixon.

HMS Striker being refitted in Malta dockyard in 1959.

Courting trouble

In the years leading up to the long-planned British withdrawal, the demands of Malta's controversial prime minister Dom Mintoff were always emphatically made, most concerning money. Malta approached other countries for aid in establishing itself in the commercial world – but only those accepting Mintoff's socialist leanings would be welcomed. The result was suitors unacceptable to the West.

In the US, where the press was equally cool, Mintoff's leftish leanings spelled communism, and although during World War II both Roosevelt and Eisenhower lauded the islanders' bravery, Mintoff's request for Marshall Aid to help rebuild the shattered islands was

Mintoff the mediator

It was one of Mintoff's dreams in those heady days to become a world mediator, to reconcile Jew and Arab. Because of his unconcealed support for the Palestinian cause, however, his position was hardly unbiased. But his relationship with Colonel Gaddafi, although ambiguous, paid dividends. Libya provided Malta with oil at cost price as world oil prices rocketed.

Looking towards Europe

Yet, even before the British departure, Malta had already taken a serious step into the future by signing an Association Agreement with the European Economic Community. The first approach was made on 4 September 1967, when the Nationalist prime minister, George Borg Olivier, asked the Community to commence negotiations to establish "some form of relationship".

Three years later, an agreement was signed. In 15 years, it was concluded, the Maltese Islands would be well on the way to economic viability if they could be assured of an export market that was free of tariff barriers and quota restrictions. The objectives of the Association were clear. The government emphasised that Malta and Gozo were part of Europe geographically as well as through similarities to the continent in culture, religion, sentiment and way of life.

Joseph Muscat, the Prime Minister of Malta, with his wife, Michelle Muscat.

Borg Olivier spoke of a growing awareness among the Maltese that they were living "in an age of economic groupings and trade areas which will make it difficult for those countries which do not join the group to achieve economic progress and this applies particularly to small countries".

Planning to forestall future criticism from the socialist party about following in the steps of the former Mother Country, the prime minister pointed out that Malta's approach to Europe was made before Britain's. The fact that Britain planned to become a member of the European Community made it more evident that Malta's commercial future lay in such a relationship.

In July 1990, convinced that the Association had produced economic benefits, Malta applied for full membership. All seemed set for a future that would allow Malta to develop trade between Europe and the countries around the Mediterranean, even if this would also mean competition from larger European neighbours.

Political divisions

The transition to full European integration in 2004 has been far from smooth. The two main political parties, the Nationalist Party (PN) and the Malta Labour Party (MLP), were always at odds on Malta's stance within the European Union. The PN were always in favour of full EU membership; the MLP wanted close relations with the EU but not full membership. When Labour returned to office in 1996, after 10 years in opposition, it froze Malta's application for membership. Two years later, however, the returning Nationalists asked for the islands' application to be reinstated. It was, and a national referendum held in 2003 confirmed the majority desire for full EU membership, into which Malta evolved in 2004. The country then joined the eurozone in 2008, with the euro replacing the Maltese lira as currency.

Seeking unity

Neutrality doesn't mean going it alone, however. As well as being a member of the Commonwealth, Malta joined the United Nations in 1964 and has played its part in the Council of Europe since 1965. Malta also endorses the principles of democracy and the rule of law as embodied in the Single European Act.

To quote the official view: "Malta seeks to continue the development of its bilateral and multilateral relations with Europe as a full member of the European Community. Its European credentials are not in doubt; its Western democratic values have deep roots that have withstood the test of provocation; and its neutral status and unpretentious but sober efforts for peaceful dialogue are a positive contribution to a new, larger and closer, but outward-looking Europe."

When the Nationalist Party took the reins of government in 1987, areas of foreign policy previously clouded in uncertainty and ambiguity dissipated. Malta's profile improved all round and although the islands held a decisive pro-Western stance, relations with neighbouring Arab countries remained friendly and strong. Malta has healthy relations with both Israel and the Palestinians and supports their rights to nationhood; it is also active in confirming the rights of all Mediterranean countries to secure their borders.

Maltese economy today

Lacking in some natural mineral resources – vast volumes of commercially viable oil still a pipe dream – Malta relies on tourism as one of its main sources of foreign currency. There has been considerable investment in five-star hotel accommodation, as well as in accommodation for foreign students, who continue to flock to the islands to learn English as a foreign language.

Malta Freeport from Pretty Bay at Birzebbuga.

A UNIQUE NEUTRALITY

Malta became neutral and non-aligned in 1987. However, the governement quickly called together diplomats to explain that Malta's neutrality was *sui generis*, a unique arrangement, with Italy (a Nato member) undertaking to come to Malta's defence if so requested, after consultation with other Nato members. Despite being part of the EU, Malta fought to retain its neutral status during the 2010–11 Libya conflict. However, during the Syrian Civil War, the Maltese government, along with many EU states, agreed to lift their arms embargo and supply weapons to the Syrian rebels fighting forces loyal to President Bashar al-Assad.

Several ambitious tourist projects are currently under development. These include the Fort Cambridge and Manoel Island high-rise building projects, consisting of a controversial 5-star, 40-floor urban hotel designed for business visitors and high-end tourists that stands where fortresses once stood. Localities that will vie to match the sophistication of the exclusive Portomaso yacht marina and apartments, as well as the more recent Tigne Point and mall.

Now well established as a local hotspot is the Valletta Pinto Wharf development, known as the Valletta Waterfront, that opened a few years ago. Originally built by the Knights, it now provides the beautiful backdrop for top restaurants, bars and boutiques, with the Grand Harbour and Three Cities directly opposite. This area has also been established as the local base for the many cruise liners that chug into port, bringing an ever-increasing number of people to the capital. Transport between lower Valletta and the centre has been a problem, but a scenic lift between the two has been operational since 2012.

Schoolchildren, Valletta.

In parallel with EU requirements and its own policies, the government has embarked on privatisation campaigns to liberalise several key sectors of the Maltese economy. A leading bank, the public state lotteries and Malta International Airport have already been privatised and more will follow. The recent public-transport overhaul and privatisation has also raised expectations that customer service will improve, putting to bed the bus drivers' long reign over the Maltese roads and their commuters.

Modernising Malta

Education remains a high priority. Schooling is compulsory up to the age of 16. The system includes both technical and trade schools, and every town and village has a state primary school and kindergarten. Both Church-run and private schools flourish. The University of Malta is the oldest in the Commonwealth outside Britain. The presence of sophisticated technological industries on Malta is reflected in the high profile given to technology in education, with specialised apprenticeship schemes and a strong engineering faculty at the university.

As ever, Malta and Gozo are islands of contrast and change. Use of internet and mobile-phone facilities rate among the highest per capita in Europe; cable and satellite companies transmit scores of international channels into homes across the islands. This new way of life co-exists alongside deeply entrenched Roman Catholic traditions and village *festas*, as do all-night discos, house and salsa, bars and casinos.

In line with this, the 2011 divorce debate and referendum really highlighted just how modern Malta is making its voice heard in a sea of more conservative viewpoints. As the polls opened, the islands' elderly were encouraged to make their mark by saying "no" to the legalisation of divorce, while the younger generation were largely keen to shed the shackles of the past and move forward in line with the ideals of the rest of Europe. But the vote went through – much to the horror of many, including several high-level politicians – and parliament passed a bill that made divorce legal on the islands. Now other sticking points, such as the legalisation of abortion and the introduction of gay marriage, could well be on the agenda for the future.

The effect of immigration

Meanwhile, immigration has made its mark. Aside from the many people choosing to move here for business or pleasure, the islands have experienced an influx of illegal immigrants fleeing Africa. For the past few years, refugees from Somalia, Eritrea and other parts of the continent have escaped their countries and found themselves in Malta. Often told by traffickers that they were en route to a new life in Italy or mainland Europe, they were instead dumped at sea within Maltese waters, and quickly became the island's responsibility – a tall order for such a small nation, but one that it took on as best it could.

Today, the effects of this immigration have become evident, with parts of the island cornered off to house refugees until they can be released and integrated into the community. This is especially evident in areas such as Marsa and Hal-Far. The situation has created something of a dilemma for the Maltese as they struggle between hoping to help and also wanting to protect their nation. Xenophobia is rife, and many are worried that cultural clashes could stem from the current situation if nothing is done to resolve it.

The 2010–11 Libyan conflict also brought challenges to the islands. Malta became a humanitarian base and was integral to the safe eviction of thousands of foreign nationals based in Libya. Boatloads of people poured into the calm, welcoming waters of the historic Grand Harbour, as they continued their journey home. Early on in the conflict, many locals feared for the security of the islands in light of Gaddafi's wrath. The problem intensified once more in 2011 with the start of the Syrian Civil War, which produced an influx of immigration. In 2015, more than 800 hundred migrants – mostly women and children – drowned as their boats sunk off the coast of Malta. Following an extraordinary summit on immigration held in Valletta at the end of 2015, EU leaders agreed to implement radical measures to stem the flow of immigrants and overhaul the existing EU asylum system.

The island's soft limestone quarries yield valuable building material.

THE FINAL FAREWELL

Malta bid farewell to beloved politician Guide de Marco in 2010. His death shocked the nation and prompted three days of national mourning.

He served as the sixth President of the islands, but was also a noted statesman and lawyer, as well as Deputy Prime Minister, Minister of the Interior, Minister for Justice, and Minister for Foreign Affairs. Despite his allegiance to the Nationalist Party, he was respected by all; he is regarded as being instrumental in Malta's accession to the EU. Other highlights of his career included presidency of the United Nations General Assembly in 1990 and chairmanship of the Commonwealth Foundation in 2004.

A religious celebration.

Lanterns in Vittoriosa, the Three Cities.

CULTIVATING CULTURE

Delve into Malta's cultural calendar to discover one of its most buzzing attributes – a non-stop array of colour, innovation and Mediterranean passion.

It's really not long ago that Malta's cultural identity was something of an unknown. Of course, the islands had culture, as well as a cultural calendar, but it had been bumbling along for so long that no one really knew how it was going to develop, or where it would end up.

It was around the turn of the new millennium that a shift began to take place. One of the island's biggest projects at that time was the opening of the St James Cavalier Centre for Creativity, a flexible and multi-purpose space (set within one of the beautiful old fortifications built by the Knights) that incorporates a studio theatre, music room, arthouse cinema and several galleries. Its opening served to usher in a new century, as well as a new era for the Maltese arts scene, with many sectors subsequently experiencing a boost in funding and interest.

Today, the government has put culture firmly on the agenda for the future. Led by the Malta Council for Culture and the Arts, the 2010 Cultural Policy aims to incorporate it as one of the pillars of Malta's 2015 vision. It also sets the scene for Malta's turn as European Capital of Culture in 2018.

Theatre

Malta does have a long history of theatre, dating back to the primitive rituals performed here in honour of the fertility goddess during prehistoric times. Throughout the 17th and early 18th centuries, operas, pageants and dramatic productions stopped being exclusive to the nobility and demand boomed. Shows put on by amateurs and theatre professionals were then presented at the Knights' *auberges* around the capital.

Inside the Manoel Theatre, Valletta.

PEN TO PAPER

One of the most celebrated local authors and playwrights is Trevor Zahra, a teacher who has penned more than 120 works throughout his career. He has won the National Book Award 10 times, and in 2004 was decorated with the Medal for Services to the Republic in recognition for his contribution to children's literature. His adult literature has also proved very popular. Not known for his shy-and-retiring work (it has raised a few eyebrows over the decades), his recent plays have included *Minn Wara iz-Zipp* (Zipped Down), a frank comedy about what goes on beneath men's briefs, which packed local theatres for performances on end.

The Manoel Theatre, in Valletta, also carved its niche long ago. Commissioned by Grand Master Manoel de Vilhena in 1731, it is a 623-seat venue spread over three tiers, with boxes constructed entirely of wood and decorated with 22-carat gold leaf. Today it remains one of the most popular venues, attracting throngs of crowds throughout its busy calendar of theatre, dance and musical performances. Most theatre shows will be in English, so it is well worth trying to secure tickets while you are here, if only to soak up the atmosphere at this incredible venue.

Meanwhile the local theatre scene has established itself, too. Ever more edgy, local practitioners keep abreast of international trends and in-your-face, physical and pioneering performances are now presented alongside more traditional classics. Despite the fact that, strictly speaking, no professional theatre industry exists in Malta yet (as there are no budgets to support it), you are likely to come across one production or another most weekends of the year.

The theatrical calendar runs from October to May, but one of the most loved, long-standing theatrical traditions takes place every July. Courtesy of the Malta Amateur Dramatics Club, one of Shakespeare's plays is performed annually under the stars, and has been for nearly 100 years. The club is the island's oldest drama institution, and was first established by the British stationed here at the end of the 19th century. It now jostles for attention among other leading local theatre companies, including MellowDrama (www.mellowdrama.com.mt), Masquerade (www.masquerade-malta.com), FM Theatre (http://fmtheatre.com) and Unifaun (www.unifauntheatre.com).

Plays in Maltese, obviously written or translated by local authors, have also found their place and are attracting a niche audience. The most popular venue for shows of this kind is the Catholic Institute in Floriana, which was

A variety of costumes on display.

THE MALTESE TENOR

One of Malta's proudest cultural exports is international opera star Joseph Calleja. Elected to the prestigious Board of Directors of the European Academy of Music Theatre in 2015, Calleja has taken the opera world by storm, playing roles such as Rodolfo in *La bohème*, Edgardo opposite Natalie Dessay in *Lucia di Lammermoor*, and the Duke of Mantua in *Rigoletto*, the role in which he made his house debut in 2006. He returns to Malta regularly and gives an annual open-air concert during the summer months. He also co-funded charity organisations that help young children and families in need, as well as talented young classical musicians.

originally built in 1954 as a monument to those fallen in the war. It is also the venue of the annual Choir Festival.

Opera

Despite the fact that Malta lost its opera house to the bombs of World War II in 1942, a love for the art endures. Every March, the Manoel Theatre hosts a lavish opera festival that attracts music lovers from all over Europe. Since 2013, performances have also been held in the Pjazza Teatru Rjal, an open-air theatre built on the site of the ruins of the former opera house in Valletta. Meanwhile, Gozo has become something of a hub for the genre with two active opera houses located in the capital city, Victoria. There is an air of competition between the two, but also one of collaboration. Opera lovers particularly enjoyed productions of Verdi's most popular works, *Aïda* and *Rigoletto* – one at each venue.

Art

The Maltese art scene has always been rich, with a plethora of well-known local names through history that have included Giuseppe Cali, Edward Caruana Dingli and Francesco Zahra.

More recently, the local scene has also boomed, with several galleries opening their doors to showcase local talents. For obvious reasons, seascapes are typical of the islands, while sculpture is also popular. Maltese limestone, the soft yellow stone that is visible almost everywhere, has become a prevalent artist's medium, too.

Ghana and the revival of Malta's music

Another art form that is coming back in vogue is the *Għana* (pronounced "aana"), the foremost form of traditional Maltese music. Often improvised and performed at gatherings for friends and family, it is typically a four-line stanza consisting of eight syllables. Somewhere between a Sicilian ballad and the rhythmic wail of an Arabic tune, you should consider yourself lucky if you happen on an impromptu performance of this kind. It is usually sung by two or more *għannejja* (singers) as a song-duel. Both will carry out a conversation, with a guitar interlude between each stanza. It all involves a lot of comedy and quick wit, with most "duels" lasting for an hour or so.

Other traditional musical forms are also being coaxed back on to centre stage. The search for Maltese instrumental music led to the discovery of Edward Jones's *Maltese Melodies*, consisting of 16 popular folk tunes dating back to the late 18th century. These are the earliest recorded Maltese folk melodies.

Today, the local music community is doing its bit to bring tunes of this type to the fore. Ruben Zahra, for instance, is a local expert and published a book called *A Guide to Maltese Folk Music*. His work often accompanies some of the most dynamic local events, including fashion shows and physical theatre.

As a result, Ghanafest, the Malta/Mediterranean Folk Music Festival, has now become a firm favourite every June. Highlights include workshops on traditional instruments and a special programme for children.

One of the galleries of paintings in the Fine Arts Museum in Malta.

A culture of festivals

With the summer climate so conducive to life outdoors, it is no wonder that a culture of annual festivals has been cultivated in recent years. These unique events have created a boom, by bringing elements of the arts to the masses and putting them out there to be discovered.

Among them, the **Malta Arts Festival** is one of the most popular. For three weeks at the start of July, it aims to showcase the work of local and foreign artists and to present it in the most accessible way possible. It is a bonanza of performances, music and dance, and brings the capital city to life in a way many thought could never happen. The crowds of attendees are proof of this new demand for cultural activities, and whole families can be seen soaking up the exceptional atmosphere.

Similarly, the **Malta Jazz Festival** (held over a long weekend in July) has also made waves across the region. Since it was first introduced in 1990, it has attracted international stars including Joe Zawinul, Chick Corea, Mike Stern, John Scofield and the Brad Mehldau Trio. It is known to be a hub for exchanging musical experience, and the atmosphere really is like no other. Best of all, the magnificent and historic setting at Ta' Liesse Whaft, across from the Grand Harbour, truly sets the scene for something spectacular.

For a twist on the family-friendly Carnival that takes place across the islands, the tiny village of Nadur, in Gozo, hosts a grizzly alternative. With blood, guts, gore and drinking, it is as macabre as it is animated – and great fun!

A dance performance at the Malta Arts Festival.

MALTESE PANTOMIME

If you're here over Christmas, try to secure tickets for the Christmas pantomime – a very Maltese take on a British tradition. Originally introduced by the British who were stationed here, Maltese pantomime mimics the English version in many ways – which in itself mirrors the commedia dell'arte tradition. But the Maltese pantomime has evolved dramatically over the years, retaining British traits, but adding a very local flavour. It is now the Christmas show of choice for adults and children, who individually enjoy different, tailored elements of the same product.

As usual, the show revolves around a fairy tale such as *Sleeping Beauty* or *Cinderella*, and includes singing and dancing. One of the central characters is the "dame" – a bawdy man dressed as a woman who usually steals the show. Contrarily, the leading man is traditionally played by a girl dressed in knee-high boots – and he always gets the princess, of course.

Maltese tang is added in a variety of ways, with politicians and local personalities bearing the brunt of the constant jokes. Elements of Maltese comedy are also injected and the final result, while still spoken in English, feels authentically local.

Today, a second pantomime in English also takes place at the MFCC in Ta Qali, as well as one in Maltese at the Catholic Institute.

Finally, to wrap up the calendar of summer arts festivals, Notte Bianca provides one magical night before the close of the season. Held every October, it injects 24 hours of artistic mayhem into the capital, with a spectacular, night-long celebration of culture and the arts. For one night only, roads and cultural venues come alive with a programme of entertainment designed to feature something to appeal to everyone. It also opens doors to venues that are usually closed, including state palaces and museums, and the streets and squares become locations for open-air concerts. Best of all, all art and musical forms are represented, from classical to pop and contemporary.

A musician pulls out all the stops at the Malta Jazz Festival.

Carnival

Although this new injection of culture has certainly made a difference, national festivals are hardly something new for the islands.

Dating back several hundred years to the 16th century, Malta's vibrant February carnival has long been a celebration of colour and passion in the run-up to Ash Wednesday. And today it is just as energetic and exciting as it always was.

Although things have changed a little to accommodate the developments in Valletta, the capital remains Carnival's home. Everyone gets involved, from tiny children dressed to the nines in crazy costumes, to the grown men who dedicate their lives to crafting the huge floats that meander through the streets. A competition takes place annually, and the winning team is awarded the honour of building "King Carnival" for the following year.

Meanwhile, the rest of the island gets into party mode. Official festivities take place, with dancing and singing through the streets, while, on the final day, a big Carnival parade culminates in the main street of Floriana with an impressive firework display.

HANDMADE MARKET

Bringing Malta's artists further to the fore is a specialised market called Patches, launched in 2010 as a way for individual artisans and those involved with the local contemporary art scene to sell their wares. It really is a treasure trove of beautiful things, bringing together quality, local designs from artists, designers, stylists and craftspeople. Part of the fun of this market is its location, which changes every time. Past editions have been held at the Upper Barrakka Gardens, with the beautiful backdrop of the Grand Harbour, as well as at the eclectic Suq tal-Belt (the Old Market on Merchants Street, Valletta). For details, visit www.patchesmalta.com.

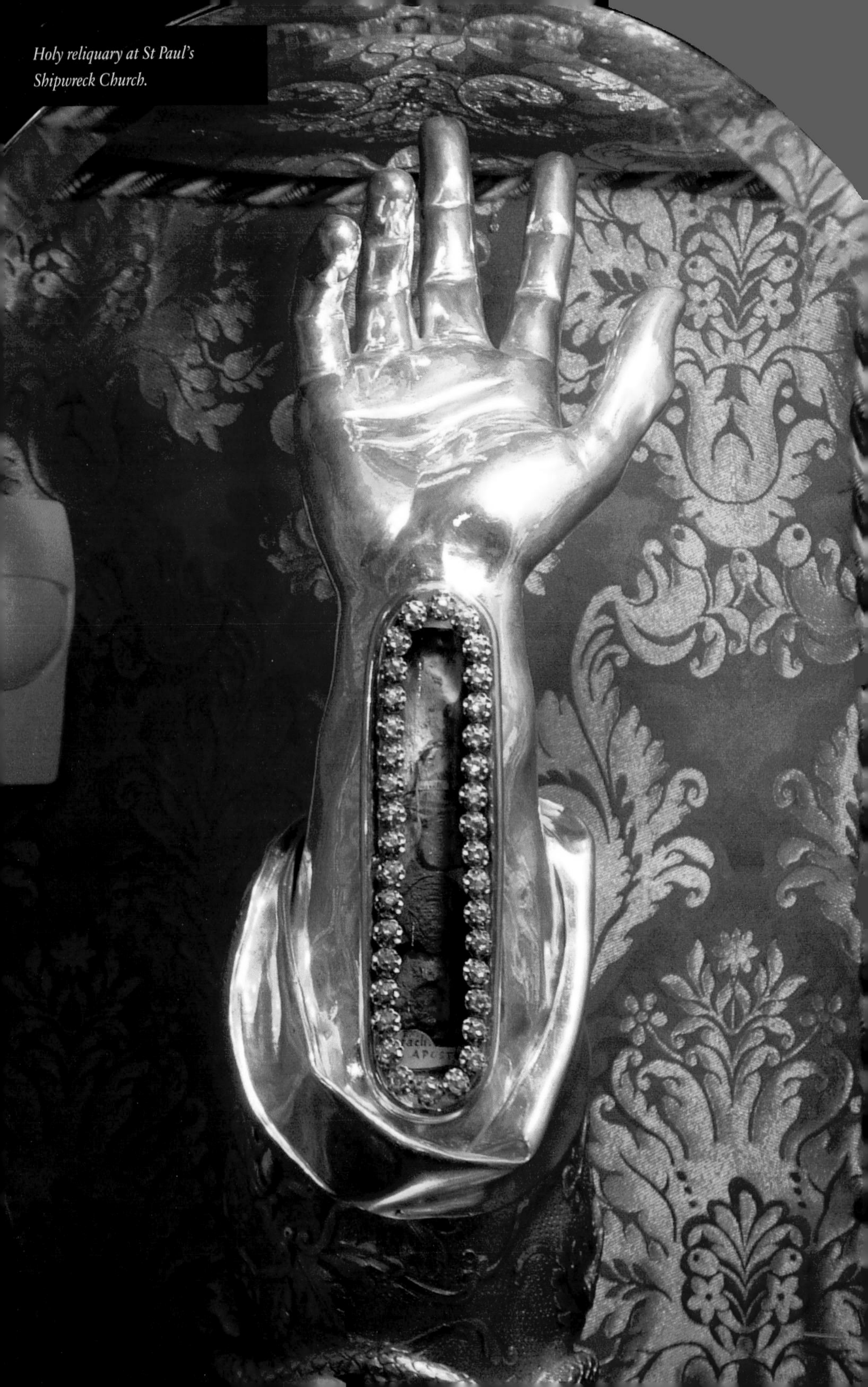

Holy reliquary at St Paul's Shipwreck Church.

SUPERSTITION AND FOLKLORE

Malta is a staunchly Catholic country, yet this is also an island of superstition where pagan symbols are omnipresent and where luck is a way of life.

It is said, with some justification perhaps, that most Maltese are superstitious, and a traditional wariness about things unknown is an important facet of the national character. This may not be so true today, but in days when there were fewer outside influences to distract, such as television, the cinema and the internet, everyone knew what brought good luck or bad luck. This was particularly noticeable away from sophisticated town society but, even there, many a mother would never tempt fate by wearing green the day her child was to sit an important exam.

Saints preserve us

Much superstition is handed down through families and much has a religious slant to it. For instance, university students may make their promises to St Jude, patron saint of students, for luck.

St Rita, St Anthony and the Virgin Mary are equally popular. In Gozo's Ta' Pinu Sanctuary, a corridor is devoted to paintings of shipwrecked sailors saved by the Virgin Mary, as well as macabre remembrances of other miraculous cures after invoking her name – such as gallstones in jam jars, discarded crutches and babies' trusses.

God and the devil

Religious shrines are also commonplace. Until recently, it was the norm for bus drivers to craft a little shrine to their chosen patron saint close to the front seat; the modern fleet doesn't allow for it. Nevertheless, older passengers will still make the sign of the cross before a journey.

Meanwhile, to deter the devil, churches have two clocks in their towers, one real, the other a trompe l'oeil. Tradition says the devil is confused by two clocks and so cannot come to collect departing souls.

Warding off evil in a more overtly pagan manner, many houses in rural communities have bulls' horns tied, points outwards, on the highest corner of a roof or perhaps above the front door. Many, trying to get the best of both

Ta' Pinu shrine.

According to tradition, it is good luck to have a baby on St Mary's Day, which falls during the month of August. In fact, folklore goes so far as to suggest that a baby born on this day will grow up to become a talented horse racer!

protections, attach horns on one corner and a saint's effigy on another.

In the 18th century, young girls in society were given simple coral necklaces to ward off evil and, until recently, many men wore tiny amulets shaped like a horn on a chain around the neck. In the old Latin tradition, many still make the *qrun*, that is, point the fore- and little finger of the hand like bulls' horns, to ward off the evil eye or to wish someone ill.

Maltese folklore suggests that an egg laid on Lady Day (25 March) possesses special healing properties. As a result, they were left to harden until their contents turned into a balsam-like texture that was used to remedy all sorts of wounds.

Tradition and superstitious rituals play a big part in Maltese weddings.

Keeping an eye open

Since bad luck is not confined to humans, the *luzzu* and *dghajsa* – the beautiful, brightly coloured traditional boats, which have been used by Maltese sailors since Phoenician times – have their protection, too. Each boat may be named after a Catholic saint, but each also has, on either side of its prow, the wide-open, ever-alert eye of Osiris, one of the most important of the Ancient Egyptian gods, ready to ward off the worst.

In a similar effort to ward off evil, horses pulling carts, or *karrozin*, often have red tassels or feathers attached to their harness or bridle.

Old wives and young mothers

Many old beliefs have faded away, but old wives' tales still abound. It has always been deemed that the best months for marriage are January, April and August, when bodies are most fertile; that women should not work in fields during menstruation or the produce will be ruined; that black underwear ensures pregnancy, white the opposite; and, if a pregnant woman craves a particular food and does not eat it, her child will have a birthmark in that shape.

Although much less so today, young mothers are especially wary of the evil eye. It may be possessed by a woman who does not know that she has it. And if she should say to a mother, "What a beautiful baby you have", then the next day the child will develop spots, a cold or a squint. The baby has been "given the eye".

Life and death

An enjoyable custom often takes place on a child's first birthday, when the family gets together for what is known as the *quccija*. They assemble a tray of small objects for the child to choose from, varying them slightly for a boy or girl. Among them might be a thimble, pen, rosary, egg, a computer mouse and some money. The object chosen foretells the child's future – as a tailor, clerk, priest, farmer, IT consultant, banker, etc. It used to be said that if you did not carry out this ritual, your child would not succeed in life; nowadays, it is just an excuse for a party.

Another Catholic home ritual mimics the pagan celebration of rebirth. Two weeks before the Christmas crib is assembled, a child is given bowls in which to sow seeds of wheat. The seedlings are kept in the dark and watered every two days. As soon as the shoots begin to sprout, the bowls are put near the figure of the baby Jesus.

On a sadder note, if a family member should die at home, a glass of water or a saucer of salt must be placed near the front door. The spirit must never leave the house thirsty or without salt to flavour its food.

The ever-watchful eye of Osiris brings good luck to luzzus.

FIREWORKS, BANDS AND SAINTS

When petards explode deafeningly overhead it might sound as if war has broken out, but don't worry, it is just another of Malta's many *festas*.

Like Christmas and Easter, the *festa* is one of the most important events in the Maltese calendar. *Festas* used to be celebrated all year round, but recently they have been restricted to the May–September season, when good weather is all but guaranteed. There are some 30 different *festas* celebrated each year throughout the islands.

Once upon a time, the *festa* was exclusively a religious event, but nowadays it is more simply an excuse for a village celebration, with big bands, fireworks and a procession. It has also changed from being a one-day event to a weekend of festivities.

A *festa* literally gets off to a bang with exploding petards, but the real celebrations begin in the evening, when the villagers come out en masse wearing their finery. The local church, too, will be splendidly dressed with red damask hangings, the altar garlanded with flowers and the best silverware on display. Outside, the church will be brilliantly illuminated by hundreds of light bulbs. The streets are also decorated, and vendors sell all sorts of fast foods, from *pastizzi* to hot dogs and chips. Accompanied by more petards and a brass band, the statue of the village patron saint is paraded through the streets. The day ends at around 11pm or later with a superb firework display – both aerial and floor-mounted, and usually to music.

The patron saint is always central to the festivities, and is carried around the town as part of a lively parade.

For the week of its festa, each parish church will be lavishly dressed with twinkling lights and vibrant drapes. Inside is ju as festive, so it's well worth popping in for a peek.

During festa time, the streets are absolutely jam-packed with locals meeting, talking, eating and drinking, while tourists often arrive on buses for the occasion.

Nougat sellers with brass-and-glass stands are a traditional sight during a festa. The great news is you can often try before you buy.

The vibrant fireworks displays, both on the ground and in the air, are usually a festa highlight. Each village will battle it out to try to make their show the very best.

A local band parades through town.

BATTLE OF THE BANDS

Every town and village in Malta, and sometimes even every parish, has its very own brass band – or in some cases, two.

It all started with the British, who imported their military brass bands for displays of pomp and pageantry. When the locals wanted to start their own bands, the British encouraged them, and officials of the band clubs eventually came to wield political, not just musical, power.

Today, bands and their band clubs are highly popular, and during the *festa*, every house and car will be playing their band's marches at top volume. In fact, so great is the pride taken in the prowess of local bands that, occasionally, fights break out in the streets as rival fans and clubs clash. Police and parish priests now monitor the marching routes and try to make bands pass through friendly streets rather than through rival territory. Visitors are definitely encouraged to join in, and will be welcomed into the revelry with open arms, especially if they're swigging from a bottle of local Cisk beer. It's best to wear old clothes, though, as things can get messy!

As the statue is paraded through the streets on the shoulders of selected volunteers, it is heralded by the parish clergy, who ensure that no one forgets this is a religious event.

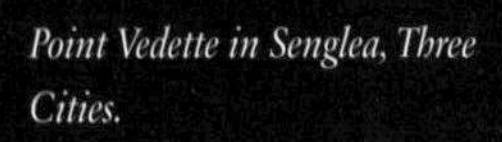

Point Vedette in Senglea, Three Cities.

MALTESE ARCHITECTURE

Look past the cluttered skyline of mishmashed high-rises, to the historic palazzi and charming houses of character at the islands' core.

The Maltese Islands probably reached their architectural peak around 3,000 BC with the erection of the Neolithic temples, which are still regarded to be the oldest free-standing stone structures in the world.

Of course, there have been other highlights. During Roman rule, beautiful temples, town houses, baths and villas were built. Sadly, mere traces remain today.

Into the darkness

The Dark Ages cast a shadow over Malta as they did the rest of Europe; but, while the latter emerged triumphantly out of the torpor to beget the great monuments of the Romanesque and Gothic period, the Maltese islands slumbered on. All through the Middle Ages the islands remained desolate, sparsely inhabited and isolated. At that time Mediterranean shipping tended to hug the continental coastline, shying away from Malta to avoid shipwreck and the pirates that might be lurking in the islands' coves and bays. Outside influences passed the islands by.

Indigenous Maltese architecture of the medieval period is almost non-existent and such buildings as there are were strongly influenced by Arab tradition. In Mdina, Vittoriosa and Gozo's citadel there are surviving late-medieval houses with windows on the first floor of a characteristically Catalan inspiration. They typically feature round-headed double lights separated by an excessively slim colonette. Mdina Cathedral dates from the 13th century but was considerably altered centuries later and has thus lost its medieval character.

Enter the Knights

It was in 1530, at the height of the Renaissance that Emperor Charles V handed over the

Wooden covered balconies in Valletta.

SET IN STONE

Malta isn't blessed with many natural resources; one of its most valuable is its Lower Globigerina Limestone, one of its oldest rock layers.

With a light-yellow tint and soft, mouldable texture, it has been used to construct everything from ancient temples to modern apartment blocks.

The limestone has become increasingly sought after in recent years. Some quarries have reached their limit so older soft-stone, shallow quarries are being reopened for deeper exploitation.

The Limestone Heritage Museum (http://limestone-heritage.com) is run by a family immersed in the construction industry, and is located in an old quarry.

islands to the Order of St John. It was a momentous event, ushering in a long period of building activity that would produce outstanding architectural monuments.

With the arrival of the Knights, Malta was linked once more to international currents and with owners who represented a concentration of wealth combined with an incredible reserve of human resources. The rich aristocratic Knights, particularly the Grand Masters, would in time shower their riches on their new headquarters and endow the islands with fine buildings and works of art. Eminent artists, military and civil engineers, architects and artisans were lured to Malta as the Order was a good paymaster. Painters such as Preti and de Favray, and engineers and architects such as Buonamici, Mederico Blondel and Charles François de Mondion called in at Malta expecting to stay only a few days, but remained much longer to benefit themselves and Maltese posterity.

Typical Maltese architecture.

The Knights chose Birgu as their initial base because its position, straddling a promontory in the Grand Harbour, had deep creeks on either side to provide shelter for their fleet. They were fully aware that their immediate task was security; the new Malta headquarters would become an Ottoman target sooner rather than later.

In fact, their immediate position was untenable; but with the help of some of the foremost military engineers of the day provided by Christian states, walls were built that rendered it sufficiently strong to withstand the great Turkish force sent by Suleiman the Magnificent in 1565.

The building of Valletta

After the Great Siege, the Order decided to build a new fortified town on the higher promontory (Mount Scebberas) that dominates the two main ports of Marsamxett and Grand Harbour. Pope Pius IV sent Francesco Laparelli da Cortona, one of his best engineers and an assistant to Michelangelo at St Peter's, to advise and supervise the project.

The first stone was laid on 28 March 1566 and the city was named Valletta after the heroic

THE REPUTATION OF GEROLAMO CASSAR

The greatest Maltese architect was Gerolamo Cassar (*c.*1520–92), whose influence and legacy was to Valletta what Christopher Wren's was to London. He designed the Grand Master's Palace, the Conventual Church/Co-Cathedral of St John, the *auberges* of the Knights, the Hospital of the Order, the slaves' prison, the Ferreria (arsenal) and several more churches and monastic buildings; many survive today.

Before embarking on his works, Cassar was sent on a short tour of the foremost cities of Italy, and so his buildings rose in a somewhat rigid variant of Italian Mannerism. But his designs, as it transpired, also perpetuated many traditional features that appeared on early buildings in Mdina and Birgu. They set the character of all the buildings in Valletta and influenced all subsequent Maltese building and architectural enterprise.

Cassar's emphasis was strongly horizontal, with huge masses of plain masonry predominating, the whole tied in with "rusticated" corners – that is, with sunken joints and roughened surfaces. These corners became his hallmark. Cassar also believed that all his buildings should echo the fact that they were constructed in a fortified city and have, therefore, a military cast. Even his masterpiece, the (now riotously decorated) Co-Cathedral of St John, was designed to be as severe on the inside as it is on the outside.

siege victor. The massive fortifications that encircle the town were completed in less than five years with a local labour force being augmented by foreign labour from Italy.

When Laparelli left the island, in around 1569, the task of completion was put into the hands of his able assistant, Gerolamo Cassar.

Maltese Baroque

Cassar went on to become the city's foremost architect. His crowning glory was the Co-Cathedral of St John. However, the interior of this landmark building was subsequently transformed, mostly by the Calabrese painter Mattia Preti, into the magnificent Baroque interior we see today.

During the first part of the 17th century, a number of parish churches were built in a style strongly reminiscent of the Italian Quattrocento, with the addition of the occasional element recalling the late-medieval Maltese church. Unfortunately, as parish wealth increased, many were later enlarged and, in the process, ineradicably changed.

One, however, the parish church of Attard, was almost untouched, and is the best example of this period on Malta. Another, Santa Marija, in Birkirkara, is remarkable for the richness and crispness of its carving.

Francesco Buonamici

It was Francesco Buonamici, an architect from Lucca in Italy, who designed the first important Baroque buildings in Valletta. He was the Order's resident engineer between 1634 and 1659, and was primarily responsible for overseeing the extensions to the Order's fortifications (notably those protecting Floriana) as well as the maintenance of all other fortifications.

His designs, in the then-current Baroque style, include the church of St Nicolas in Valletta; the plan of the church of St Paul at Rabat, with the adjoining church of St Publius; part of the facade of the church of St Philip in Zebbug; and several altar retables (the frames enclosing decorated panels behind the altars).

Buonamici's civic buildings include the Jesuit College and Hostel de Verdelin in Valletta, Wignacourt's College at Rabat and, possibly, the facade of the Inquisitor's Palace, Vittoriosa. In the first two facades, Buonamici shows how it was possible to articulate a long front by means of panelling while at the same time retaining the columnless treatment of Valletta's earlier palaces.

By the mid-17th century, Mederico Blondel from France had succeeded Buonamici as

The dome of the Carmelite Church soars above Valletta.

resident engineer. In Valletta he designed the splendid facade of Valletta's church of St Mary of Jesus, and it is quite likely that he was also responsible for the churches of St Rocco and St Francis. In Mdina, the splendid Carmelite Church is his masterpiece. Also active during this period was the great Maltese architect Lorenzo Gafà' .

The 18th century

During the next century, a number of florid Baroque buildings rose in Valletta and Mdina. They were designed by Romano Carapecchia, who worked in Malta for 30 years from 1706, and a Frenchman, Charles François de Mondion, resident engineer from 1715 to 1733.

The major building from this period, however, is the Auberge de Castille, originally designed by Gerolamo Cassar, but remodelled by Andrea Belli in 1741. A Maltese architect who had studied in Italy and travelled through Austria and Germany, Belli designed several other outstanding buildings that give Maltese architecture its authority. His are the Bishop's Seminary (1733) in Mdina (now the Cathedral Museum); the Augustinian Priory in Rabat (1740); the Archbishop's Curia (1743) in Floriana; and in Valletta's South Street, the building that houses the Museum of Fine Arts (1761).

Another architect of note during this period was the Sicilian Stefano Ittar, responsible for the neoclassical Biblioteca – the National Library (1786–96) and the Customs House.

The impressive Auberge de Castille.

LORENZO GAFÀ'

Lorenzo Gafà' (1630–1704) is Malta's greatest Baroque architect. After beginning his career as a sculptor, he turned to architecture and is responsible for many of the splendid churches that have come to typify and symbolise the Maltese islands. His most important works include the church of San Lawrenz in Vittoriosa, Gozo Cathedral and the Cathedral of Mdina. The last masterpiece, set in a dramatic position on the ramparts of the old city, is an unforgettable sight. The encircling walls of the city look like part of the church building itself, and the whole is surmounted by a dome such as only a great Baroque sculptor could have fashioned.

Repairing war damage

Malta's most important recent architectural treasures are well over a century old. In 1833 the church of Santa Marija (also known as the Mosta Dome) was designed by Grognet de Vasse. In 1841, St Paul's Anglican cathedral, designed by William Scamp, replaced the Order's Auberge d'Allemagne. Then, in 1860, the Royal Opera House was designed by Edward Middleton Barry.

Sadly, though, this, along with so many other buildings of architectural importance, were destroyed during World War II, and the opera house has lain in ruins ever since. Fortunately, EU funds have made it possible to finally complete this longed-for project. The rebuilding of the opera house was part of a wider development that gave the entrance to Valletta a "new look". Renowned Italian architect Renzo Piano was selected to lead it all, and the project encompassed a new City Gate, Parliament (in a new building and location) and, of course, the opera house, which is now an open-air theatre.

Piano's designs created plenty of controversy, especially as they are a step away from convention. In fact, his designs show a modern, open-air structure that incorporates the remains of the bombed Victorian building into a new glass creation.

Critics and members of the local arts community had hoped for something different and, possibly, the reconstruction of the theatre to its former glory, but Piano maintained: "…a modern opera, of conventional size, would not fit in this place considering today's requirements for rehearsal, backstage facilities and accessibility, besides generating exorbitant running costs… We strongly believe that, after more than 60 years of controversy, the ruins of the demolished opera have undeniably reached the status of monument, irrevocable witness of history and the dignity of collective memory."

coming of age when it comes to modern architectural decisions, with a more holistic view being taken. Plans are also being made to make the most of what is already available, with many areas of Valletta being pedestrianised to allow those roaming the city better to enjoy the views.

Recent improvements have included St George's Square, opposite the Grand Master's Palace, which has been rejuvenated to entice visitors and now makes the perfect space to sit back, relax and take in the very best of the Knights' architectural accomplishments.

The newly built approach to the City Gates and Parliament building in Valletta.

Building a future

Meanwhile, other projects are under way to give the islands an architectural lift, and many will blend the old with the new. For instance, the highly anticipated Manoel Island development, which will construct residential and commercial spaces around the beautiful old Lazaretto and the majestic 18th-century Fort Manoel, the latter of which has been fully restored. Similarly, Fort Chambray in Gozo combines a centuries-old fort built by the Knights of St John with striking modern additions.

So, after the lacklustre 20th century, when few buildings of long-lasting worth were built, it seems that the islands are finally

ECO-ARCHITECTURE

Like most parts of the world, the islands are becoming more eco-focused. The government has to comply with EU regulations, and local architects are looking at reducing energy use. Traditional houses were built with thick walls, small windows and high ceilings to keep homes cool. During the building boom of the 1950s and 1960s, these methods were forgotten and builders instead chose to use thinner walls, larger windows and lower ceilings, which increased the need for air-conditioning. Today, architects are careful to insulate buildings well, and innovative cooling methods have even made use of the surrounding seawater in some developments.

Gozo octopus in garlic sauce.

A TASTE OF MALTA

Maltese food, embracing simple flavours and techniques that have passed from generation to generation, has seen an upsurge in popularity.

First-time visitors to Malta may be surprised to discover that these tiny islands have a cuisine of their own. And anyone who passed this way before the 1970s will be pleased to know that it's now readily available in eateries that have specialised in its unique flavours and cooking techniques.

Tasty mix

Geographical position has meant that the people have been subject to many culinary influences: from the north, the influence of Sicily and Italy, and from the south, skills picked up along the length of the North African coast, from Tunisia to Egypt, where many Maltese communities were comfortably established until driven out during World War II.

Some of these origins show, but Maltese cooking is governed primarily by the kind of produce found on the islands – which is similar to that of neighbouring Sicily. So, although the likes of asparagus, kiwi fruit and other exotic imported items can be readily found now, this availability is comparatively recent. Truly Maltese dishes are those produced with ingredients that are indigenous to the islands and farmed from local waters.

Typical dishes

Ask the Maltese and Gozitans for the names of the best local dishes and you will hear the same answers wherever you are – even if some profess not to like one or two of these particular dishes themselves. The Maltese repertoire is made up almost entirely of a half-dozen or so favourite dishes, such as *fenek, timpana, minestra, kawlata, mqarrun fil-forn, bragoli* and *torta tal-lampuki*. Two of these, *timpana* and *mqarrun fil-forn*, are baked pasta and, although a large slice of either might seem a meal in itself, here it is considered a starter. Both are made of macaroni layered with meat, eggs and cheese and, in the case of *timpana*, a casing of light flaky pastry, too. They're delicious, if heavy on the carbohydrates. A variation of this recipe is *ross fil-forn*, with rice replacing the pasta. It is baked with minced meat, eggs and lots of bright-yellow saffron.

Pastizzi are popular Maltese pastries.

Pasta is as popular here as in Italy, although it is unlikely that the average family will eat it daily at home as the Italians do. It is not unusual for the spaghetti sauce to be made using the delicious juices from another dish being prepared, such as squid, octopus or rabbit.

Soup and vegetables

A favourite first course is soup, such as *aljotta* (a thin, clear fish broth) in summer, when fish supplies are plentiful, or *minestra* (a chunky vegetable soup) in winter. *Minestra* is Malta's answer to minestrone, although in this soup the vegetables – preferably nine or 10 different kinds – are cut into rough chunks; dried beans, chickpeas, lentils and small pasta shapes are then added. It is a thick, hearty and filling dish, perfect for a cold winter's day.

Other favourite winter soups include *soppa tal-armla* ("widow's soup") and *kawlata*. *Soppa tal-armla* consists of finely chopped white and green vegetables only. When the dish is served, a *gbejna* (a soft, round fresh sheep's cheese) is placed in each bowl. *Kawlata* is a similar vegetable soup, in which either a lean piece of pork or some Maltese sausages have been simmered. The meat is usually eaten separately.

Just add a thick chunk of Maltese bread to any of these soups and you have a nourishing meal in its own right. In fact, soups are staple to every Maltese family, who, with much justification, have a high regard for the basic ingredients – local vegetables. Farms may be small but their richly worked soil produces some excellent vegetables and fruit. Little is done by way of spraying to extend the life of the produce, so vegetables must be eaten within a day or two of purchase.

Because of this organic policy, housewives frequently shop daily for supplies of fresh food and can be seen in the street markets or at the painted trucks, selecting from the piles of seasonal produce.

These include giant cauliflowers, kohlrabies, artichokes, aubergines, green peppers and *qara' bali* (a round, small marrow of the courgette family, best served boiled or stuffed).

Rabbit casserole.

Maltese sausage.

RABBIT AND CHIPS

Malta's national dish is *fenek* (rabbit): fried, casseroled or roasted. Rabbit is often the prize in village raffles and there is even a special outing, known as a *fenkata*, when a family or group of friends get together for a picnic or in a simple village restaurant to enjoy fried rabbit with chips and lots of red wine.

It has been many centuries since rabbits were seen wild and free on the islands, however – though hunters, who have shot them almost to extinction, claim that there are signs of them still on barren coastal stretches. All of the rabbit eaten here is specially bred for the table and is on sale, alive and cuddly, in the markets.

Main meats

One of the simpler pleasures of Maltese cooking is the good old-fashioned roast dinner, usually beef or pork. (Lamb is mostly eaten at Easter.) The meat is placed in a large greased tray, surrounded with chunkily sliced potatoes and onions, liberally sprinkled with herbs, rock salt and pepper and oil; then the tray is topped up with stock and the whole thing placed in the oven for slow roasting. As the stock evaporates, keeping the meat moist, the potatoes and onions pick up the flavours of the juices.

Enjoying a seafood platter in Marsaxlokk.

Unfortunately, this homely skill has not spread to many restaurants. But many are adept at another dish worth trying, *bragoli*. This is not unlike the Italian beef olive, but in this case the sliced topside beef is rolled, stuffed with boiled eggs and bacon, and simmered in red wine.

Fruits of the sea

Rivalling rabbit as the national speciality is *lampuka*, a much more refined dish. *Lampuki* (plural of *lampuka*) are dorado, a fish that migrates past the islands between September and November. A sleek and elegant fish, it has white flesh and a distinctive flavour of the sea. It's a curious fact that *lampuki* have been caught in the same manner by Maltese fishermen since Roman times. As the season approaches, so fishermen cut and gather the large, lower fronds from the island's palm trees, which they plait into flat rafts. These are taken out to sea where they are floated and the *lampuki*, discovering the nice patches of shade that these rafts offer, gather beneath them. Quickly, the fishermen then encircle them with nets. The trick never fails.

Depending on their size, *lampuki* are grilled, fried or made into a wonderful pastry-covered pie with cauliflower, spinach and olives called *torta tal-lampuki*.

Of course, these waters are abundant with other excellent fish, so Maltese fishermen are never short of options. There are tuna (although blue-fin tuna is becoming taboo here, too, now, much like the rest of the world) and swordfish, and smaller fish like sea bass, grouper, amberjack, mullet and skate. And then there are octopus and squid, which the Maltese are adept at turning into something delicious.

Fast food

Pizzas, burgers and Chinese takeaways are readily available in places such as Bugibba and St Julian's, but the islanders also have their own fast food. It might only be a slice or two of bread, but then Maltese bread is surely one of the world's best, good enough to be almost addictive. Made traditionally as a cottage loaf, the sourdough is baked directly on the oven surface. It has a crisp, firm crust, with a soft white centre punctured with random holes that are caused by the sourdough system.

It is full of flavour and is delicious spread with butter. But the Maltese prefer it as *hobz biz-zejt* (literally, bread with oil), which is eaten at any time of the day as a snack. To make it, first slice the bread thickly and then cut in half some ripe, tasty tomatoes. Rub the tomatoes on to the bread until it turns pink. Leave the tomato on the bread and add salt, pepper and capers to taste, then generously add some olive oil. Additional ingredients, according to personal preference, can include basil, onion, tomato purée (the locals love their own sweet version, known as *kunserva*) and/or garlic.

Then there are the gloriously inexpensive *pastizzi*. Baked on trays in special ovens, they are made of flaky pastry into which a pocket of filling is folded. The choice of fillings is cheese (*rikotta*, seasoning and a little egg), mushy yellow marrowfat peas, or, more rarely encountered, anchovy. As the *rikotta* filling is undoubtedly the best, so *pastizzi* came to be popularly translated as cheesecake, but do not be misled – they are always savoury, never sweet. They are remarkably inexpensive and on sale daily most of the morning from bakeries, cafés and bars. Two or three, always eaten warm, fresh from the oven, make a favourite mid-morning snack.

Baking a variety of savoury dishes.

FOODIE FESTIVALS

During summer, look out for the many food festivals that offer the chance to delve into Maltese cuisine and culture at the same time. Most take place in stunning parts of the island, which gives you more reason to explore – with a glass of wine, of course.

Events include the Farson's Great Beer Festival, which combines food and beer from around the world; the Marsovin Wine Festival in Hastings Garden, where you can sample local wines while nibbling tasty Mediterranean specialities; and, for a really authentic flavour, the Siggiewi Agrarian Show, where you can uncover traditional Maltese farm life and try local delicacies including thyme honey.

Something sweet

The Maltese have a very sweet tooth. Shops, cafés and stalls are always laden with all manner of cakes and biscuits, some garishly bright and powerfully sweet, others farmhouse-simple.

One inexpensive favourite is quickly recognised by a delicious aroma that wafts wherever it's on sale – outside Valletta's bus terminal gate is the favourite location (and also in the evenings at *festas*). Called *mqaret*, these are small-flat diamond-shaped pastry cases filled with a soft date mixture that is flavoured with aniseed. Sold by vendors seated at small carts on which there are shallow, bubbling oil friers, *mqaret* are served deep-fried, cooked to order, and eaten piping hot. It's the frying and the aniseed that produce the tempting aroma. Another unusual sweet treat to look out for is *kannoli*, crunchy cylindrical biscuits resembling large cigars, filled with ricotta cheese and candied fruit.

Beware the inferior pixxiplamtu, a member of the shark family, which is often passed off as swordfish. Swordfish has dark, shiny skin, pixxiplamtu does not, so it is served or sold skinned in order to disguise it.

Many families will order a *torta* from a leading confectioner when a special dessert is required: something rich and sweet and preferably with the extravagant use of ground almonds. In the villages, once or twice a week, there are deliveries of the most delightful, simple biscuits, made by local bakeries. Like the produce, many of the most popular Maltese sweets are seasonal.

Holiday specials

For the Carnival weekend that heralds Lent, there is *prinjolata* (a kind of gateau made with pine nuts). During Lent there is *kwarezimal*, a sweet almond biscuit covered with honey and pistachio nuts, which originally conformed to the Lenten rules because it contains no eggs or shortening. And, in the winter months, there is *qaghaq tal-ghasel*, a ring of sweet pastry filled with a mixture of dark treacle, semolina and candied peel. In fact, these are so popular that they can often be found year-round.

The best, however, are *figolli*, an Easter treat. These are biscuity cakes that are shaped into figures then decorated with brightly coloured icing, a small chocolate Easter egg and, the most important part, old-fashioned faces to give them character. In the biscuit there is a layer of sweet almond paste. On the whole, the more expensive it is, the thicker and better is its almond centre.

As final proof of the passion for sweets, there is *qubbajt*, the local nougat sold at every *festa* from decorated stalls, each with a large pair of chrome scales as a centrepiece. There is a choice of hard (dark and brittle) or soft (pale and chewy).

Drinks

The local brews, Hopleaf Pale Ale, Blue Label Ale and Cisk Lager, are all very drinkable and will certainly appeal to older British drinkers. A nice, cool refresher with just a drop of alcohol is Farson's Shandy, a good old-fashioned combination of beer and lemonade that remains popular.

A selection of La Croce wines, produced from grapes grown on the Maltese Islands.

The wines of Malta and Gozo have also gained ground, and viticulture is fast becoming a popular aspect of local life. The two major wineries are Marsovin and Delicata. Meanwhile, perhaps the islands' most distinctive drink is Kinnie, sometimes described as the Maltese answer to Coca-Cola. This splendid soft beverage definitely originates from the cola stable but its bitter-orange tang makes it much more a "grown-up" drink. Well chilled, it makes a perfect midday refresher or evening aperitif.

The Azure Window, on Gozo Island, has been formed by the forces of wind and the sea over time.

SPORT AND SCUBA DIVING

Voted the third-best scuba-diving destination in the world, the Maltese Islands have plenty to offer sport enthusiasts, both above and below the surface of the sea.

For one of the world's smallest nations, Malta has plenty to offer those keen to pack a little action into their holiday – from trotting races, staged on the island since 1868, to computerised tenpin bowling, to beach volleyball, as well as water sports, marathons, golf and tennis.

On the surface

It's likely that the calm, crystal-clear Mediterranean waters around Malta have played their part in attracting you here – and now you can make the most of them thanks to the huge variety of water sports available. Most beaches – sandy or rocky – offer the facilities you'll need to sail, parasail, canoe, snorkel, windsurf, jet-ski or water-ski, and help will be at hand to ease you into the process if you are a beginner.

More than 40 species of fish can be seen around the islands, including grouper, moray, cuttlefish, octopus, flying gurnard, angler fish, barracuda and eagle ray. Sea anemones add their own splash of colour.

To dive for

Having been voted one of the top-three diving destinations in the world, Malta provides the perfect opportunity to grab your aqualungs and head below the surface of the sea. The translucent waters that surround the islands give them special year-round appeal, as nowhere in the Mediterranean can you see so far underwater or discover such a large variety of dive sites, both natural and man-made.

Playing golf on Malta.

While the Mediterranean's sea life may not be as colourful as that of the Maldives or the Red Sea, for instance, its underwater topography and the clarity of its waters rate well above most other places in the world. In fact, underwater visibility is generally 6–20 metres (19–65ft), but can extend to 50 metres, up to 30 metres (164ft, up to 98ft) below the surface. Some of the best diving is found off the southern shore of both Malta and Gozo. In the deep water beneath the sheer cliffs, the spectacular rock formations are a diver's delight – among them are arches, caves, buttresses, drop-offs and tunnels.

Dive schools flourish throughout the islands, with operators offering tuition, arranging accompanied dives and hiring out equipment. And with no tides to worry about, they are rated highly as a "learn to dive" destination. Here newbie divers will usually stay within the 10–25-metre range. Of course, things get more exciting the deeper you go. The islands boast a number of sunken shipwrecks for those divers keen to take on a challenge and explore further. Planning is important, though it's also vital to remember that wind direction here can change at the drop of a hat and strong underwater currents can create the odd issue. As always with scuba-diving, beginners should never be without an instructor, and even the most experienced divers should constantly be accompanied by a buddy.

Taming the seas

Sailing in Malta was given fresh impetus with the revival of the Middle Sea Race for ocean-going yachts. This 1,000km (600-mile) spectacle, staged each October, starts and ends in Malta's Marsamxett Creek; it encompasses the island of Sicily and takes from three to six days to complete, depending on weather conditions.

Sunday best: trotting for glory at Marsa.

TOP DIVE SITES

Whether you're a seasoned scuba diver or are still finding your flippers, the Maltese Islands promise a huge variety of dive sites that are bound to entice you into the water. Depending on your abilities, this is our pick of the must-see spots below the surface:

Cirkewwa

Easily the island's most popular dive site, this whole area is marine-protected. Keep your eyes peeled for barracudas, jacks and tuna.

Um el Faroud

This wreck was sunk following a tragic accident in 1995, and now sits off the southern village of Zurrieq. Only recommended for experienced divers.

Ghar Lapsi

Great for divers of all abilities, immerse yourself among caverns, reefs and caves, and enjoy plenty of typical Mediterranean marine fauna.

Dwejra Point, Gozo

This area's unique limestone formations make it a must for any diver. The water visibility here is probably the best on the island.

Le Polynésien

Nicknamed Malta's "Titanic", this is the wreck of a 19th-century passenger liner that sank at the end of World War I. Not for beginners: only the most experienced deep-sea divers need apply.

Malta's oldest yacht marina is in Msida, near Sliema, matched now by the Cottonera Marina in Vittoriosa in the Grand Harbour, which is deep enough for today's mega-yachts. At St Julian's is a small marina, part of the Portomaso complex, and new marinas are planned for other parts of the island, including on Manoel Island.

Windsurfing

Windsurfing came to Malta in the late 1970s and is now a year-round sport which attracts enthusiasts from far and wide. For those who have yet to tread a sailboard, Mellieha Bay is an excellent place to learn. The keenest windsurfers set their sights on the daily wind direction and then speed off to different parts of Malta and Gozo.

Sea conditions can vary from flat calm to choppy when the prevailing *majjistral* sets in from the northwest or the strong *grigal* blows up from the northeast; races are a real test even for very experienced board sailors.

The open expanse of Mellieha Bay also lends itself to water-skiing, jet-skiing and snorkelling (Comino's Blue Lagoon is another good spot) and a host of family-orientated activities. Parasailing fans should head for Golden Bay, for a bird's-eye view of Malta's fascinating northwestern tip and striking views across to Comino and Gozo.

Trotting treat

Horse racing is Malta's most popular spectator sport – not the thoroughbred gallops you see on British racecourses, but trotting meetings that regularly pull in crowds of 4,000 to Marsa racetrack and are held all year round. Trotting remained for many years staunchly male-orientated, but now the spectacle provides exciting entertainment for everybody.

You can bet on the Tote or with independent on-course bookmakers – the stakes are low and the odds not unreasonable. Make your own way to the racetrack rather than taking an organised excursion, as tour buses have the infuriating habit of leaving halfway through the meeting.

There are 700 registered horses in Malta, most imported from France and Scandinavia; many are stabled close to the 1,000-metre (3,280ft) circuit, which was laid down in 1868 but shortened to meet international standards in 1981. Around 500 races are held each year in meetings staged every Sunday afternoon, on alternate Saturdays and on public holidays. It's a full afternoon's entertainment – trotting cards include up to 12 races and can take up to five hours to complete – though you don't have to stay the distance.

Equestrian sport of a less serious kind altogether takes place during the *Mnarja* festival of St Peter and St Paul in Rabat on 29 June each year. Its bareback horse and donkey races on Saqqajja Hill date from the time of the Knights, and winners receive banners to be used in church as altar cloths.

Windsurfing off the coast of Malta.

If you want to take the reins yourself, you can visit the Golden Bay Horse Riding School (which is signposted just off Golden Bay beach; www.goldenbayhorseriding.com). It caters for all standards of rider and uses a number of panoramic routes around this part of the coast.

Golf on course

Most Mediterranean holiday destinations accept that golf is a big attraction – and Malta is no exception. The island has only the 18-hole Royal Malta Golf Club (http://royalmaltagolfclub.com) course at present, though there are talks of other courses opening in the future.

The Maltese show very little inclination towards playing golf, leaving visitors to pitch in for the best tee-off times. The Royal Malta, retaining British links in its title (though no one recalls when, if ever, royal assent was ever given to the club), is a pleasant 5,091-metre (16,702ft) parkland course that makes few demands on the seasoned club player.

Golf is just one aspect of the Marsa Sports Club complex, Malta's number-one sporting venue, which has numerous tennis courts, squash courts, mini golf, a cricket ground, a billiards room, a freshwater swimming pool and a fitness centre. Sports-minded visitors can take out a temporary membership while they are on holiday in Malta to make full use of the wide-ranging facilities.

The long haul

With its equable winter climate and flat topography, there are two notable long-distance sporting events that attract good international fields to the islands. The Malta Marathon is run each February and attracts high-class athletes, including, in the past, European and Commonwealth champions.

Hiking along the coast, San Blas Bay.

RAMBLE AROUND

Rambling has been popular in Malta for nearly 150 years and today it remains the perfect way to discover the countryside, promising stretches of unspoilt land and tranquil spots that feel as though they've been unchanged for centuries. It is a joy to chance upon dramatic cliffs plunging into waves, rocky scrubland or hidden, lush valleys. In fact, only around one fifth of Malta is built-up – so it's great fun to get out there and explore.

Popular routes include around Delimara Point and Marsascala in the south, Buskett Gardens and Bahrija in the centre, Anchor Bay and Paradise Bay in the north, and Dwejra and Hondoq ir-Rummien.

The other major endurance trial is the Ironman triathlon challenge, which is also gaining popularity in Malta. This contest combines tough courses of swimming, running and cycling, and is not for the faint of heart.

Local favourites

Turn to the sports pages of Malta's newspapers and you will be struck by the amount of space devoted to football – it dominates the sporting scene throughout the year.

The football season only excludes the hottest summer months – July and August. Otherwise, it is a hive of activity and a hot topic of conversation. Malta's Football Association (MFA) is over 100 years old and one of the oldest in

Europe. There are national championships and a national knockout competition (FA Cup), and Malta's national team is active in FIFA's World Cup and UEFA's European Championship, with clubs also taking part in European club competitions. The MFA has a splendid national stadium at Ta' Qali. It will not take very long to gather that most Maltese (male and female) are football-crazy and are well versed in the various fortunes of international clubs.

Meanwhile, relatively new to the scene but fast gaining ground, is the very British game of rugby. Established here in the late 1990s, the Malta Rugby Football Union was formed, and the Maltese team has been present at the Rugby World Cup. It has become a popular sport for spectators, and visitors are always welcome to watch or join one of the clubs.

The Maltese game of *bocci*, derived from a game played in Ancient Rome and similar to the French *boules*, but using wooden blocks instead of balls, gets less publicity but is widely popular and is taken seriously by its devotees. Most towns and villages on the island have their own *bocci* club, which becomes a popular social centre on long summer evenings.

Tenpin bowling is also a serious pursuit and attracts a young crowd to the 20-lane Eden Super Bowl (with fully computerised scoring) at St George's Bay.

The success of Maltese player Tony Drago abroad gave snooker a boost on the island and most sports and band clubs have their own full-size snooker table for patrons.

Finally, and somewhat bizarrely for an island known for its Mediterranean climate, ice-skating has become increasingly popular in recent years. A small ice rink is sometimes installed close to the entrance of Valletta around Christmas time, which, needless to say, is a big hit with the locals.

The Challenge Marathon takes place in Malta every year over three consecutive days.

THE "PASSEGGIATA"

If you're exhausted by the mere idea of all these different sports, why not make like the Maltese and take a walk? The well-loved *passeggiata* is the exercise of choice for many on the island, and the pretty seafront promenades make the perfect place to work your pins in style. It's actually more of a social activity than a form of exercise, as most islanders will wander up and down the stretch between Sliema and St Julian's, or other similar promenades, stopping every couple of metres to chat with friends and neighbours. So why not join in the fun? Stop en route to indulge in a delicious ice cream from one of the nearby *gelaterias*.

Crystal Lagoon, Comino.

GOING TO SEA

Although Malta has relatively few sandy beaches, its blue skies and blue waters are the envy of the Mediterranean. An excellent way of enjoying both is to take to the sea.

The Maltese are understandably proud of their surrounding sea. In contrast to the waters of most other countries in the Mediterranean, those around Malta, Gozo and Comino are clear, blue and unpolluted. In the Blue Lagoon, you don't need a snorkel and mask to watch a coin sink to 30 metres (100ft). The grim sea pollution, annually condemned in other resort areas by the European Union for failing to meet health standards, is still rare here. Jellyfish, on the other hand, do sometimes plague the waters and you should keep your eyes peeled.Understandably, much of Maltese life revolves around the sea, both above and below its shimmering surface.

Visitors in search of boat trips are well catered for in Malta. Things have progressed remarkably since the heady, romantic days when the only way to have a day out was by finding, and bargaining with, a willing fisherman with a *luzzu*.

Grand Harbour cruise

The most popular boat trip, and the one that no visitor to Malta should miss, is the Grand Harbour cruise. From Sliema, the boat crosses Marsamxett Harbour, with Valletta as its backdrop, then passes Manoel Island and the Msida Yacht Marina before heading out to sea and turning through the breakwaters into Grand Harbour. This is the way to see Valletta, Fort St Elmo, Fort St Angelo and the Three Cities as seafarers have done for centuries. In fact, it is only from this perspective that you can truly start to appreciate the scale of Malta's sea defences. Deep within the harbour, the modern dockyards and commercial enterprises bring Malta's maritime history up to date.

The tour is accompanied by a commentary interspersing insightful historical narrative with humorous anecdotes.

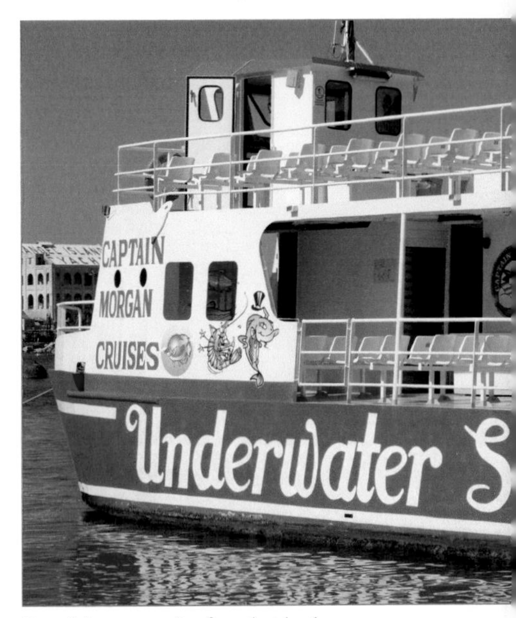

One of the many cruises from the islands.

Days out

The biggest choice of pleasure cruises is to be found along the Strand in Sliema. The largest company is Captain Morgan (tel: 2346 3333; www.captainmorgan.com.mt), with an ever-growing fleet of distinctive red-and-white boats that also operates out of Bugibba. The price of a day cruise generally includes a buffet lunch with local wine, constant refreshments and, should it be required, a door-to-door service by minibus.

The most comprehensive sightseeing trip that you can take is the Round the Islands cruise, which takes in the whole archipelago; alternatively, there is a Round Malta cruise and a full-day Comino cruise. The latter is extremely popular with all the cruise companies, however, this can mean that the lagoon seems overcrowded and short on the tranquil, turquoise charm that it once had. An alternative is the Paradise Diving speedboat (www.paradisediving.com), which picks passengers up from the Paradise Bay Resort Hotel and ferries them over to the island and back every half-hour or so.

Different vessels

Most pleasure cruisers are fairly functional, unremarkable vessels, but there are exceptions. A romantic, schooner-rigged Turkish *gullet* plies the route to Gozo, Comino and the Blue Lagoon.

On the Malta-Gozo ferry.

For an alternative to yachting, hop on board a kayak. The sport is becoming increasingly popular in Malta, and especially so with eco-minded travellers. Try Rugged Coast Adventures on 9999 4592; www.seakayakmalta.com.

Modern rigged catamarans also sail the Maltese waters and, by night, the *Spirit of Malta* turns into a party craft – although, with its reggae music and rum rations, it is actually much more Spirit of the Caribbean.

The most unusual vessel is the *MV Seabelow*. It has a large observation keel below the water line, where passengers eagerly scan the depths for marine life. In truth, there's not a lot to see down here. The most unusual sight is a statue of Christ, placed on the sea-bed in St Paul's Bay in May 1990 to commemorate the visit of Pope John Paul II. His Holiness remained above the waves, sailing by on a high-speed catamaran to bless it.

Plain sailing

Here are a few tips to ensure that you have an enjoyable day out. Firstly, make sure you know where you are going. That may sound silly, but many a round-the-islands excursion has turned into a Blue Lagoon trip at the last moment because of weather conditions, and the passengers are the last to be told. Don't forget your sunblock and sunhat (sunburn at sea is much more likely than on land because of reflection from the water). Finally, if you're not a good sailor, beware the longer cruises, where the swell can be a little rough.

If you only want to dip your toe in the water, metaphorically speaking, try the **Blue Grotto** trip, or Gozo's **Inland Sea** trip. The latter is a surprisingly lively small-scale adventure, particularly good for children.

Serious sailing

The main island of Malta alone has an indented coastline of some 200km (320 miles), with clear water where bays and coves provide secure anchorage for the night. With more than 1,500 sheltered berths on offer, Malta is making its mark as an attractive international yachting centre. The Msida Marina Yachting Centre is the largest facility, though even little Gozo has a marina of its own. Other marinas include Vittoriosa and Portomaso, both with excellent facilities. You can charter craft from here or, for sailing boats, try Nautica (tel: 2134 5138; www.nautica.com.mt); or, for cabin cruisers, Sun Seeker (tel: 2138 5678; www.sunseekermalta.com).

For really serious sailors, the two highlights of the calendar are the Syracuse–Malta and Middle Sea races. The Middle Sea Race in October draws some of the world's fastest yachts. Another strenuous annual event is the single-handed, round-Malta race. The Royal Malta Yacht Club (tel: 2133 3109; www.rmyc.org) on Manoel Island has full details of these and also organises island regattas.

In the winter months, the wind is usually north-easterly *(grigal)*, which causes surges and can reach storm conditions that last an average of three days, the worst occurring in January.

Sailing off the coast of Malta.

Sunset over Victoria, Gozo.

Gnejna Bay.

19th-century facades, Valletta.

GIO. BATTA
TOMMY HILFIGER
MOHANS
GIFT SHOP RETAILERS
308

St. George's Square, Victoria.

INTRODUCTION

A detailed guide to the Maltese Islands, with principal sites clearly cross-referenced by number to the maps.

Investigating the salt pods in Marsalforn.

Malta may only be a tiny country, but it has a never-ending array of beautiful attractions to entice and enthral visitors.

Valletta is one of Europe's smallest capitals, but was once the base of the illustrious Knights of St John. The city is currently undergoing a huge transformation as its rise to international prominence continues, and it readies itself to become the European Capital of Culture in 2018. Nevertheless, its architectural and historical legacy is superb. Any city would be proud to possess such jewels as the Palace of the Grand Masters and the Co-Cathedral of St John.

On the other side of Grand Harbour lies the Three Cities, the original home of the Knights and later the dockyards during the period of British colonial rule. Flattened during World War II, it hides much of its historic pedigree in tranquil streets that see few visitors.

Gun battery at Valletta.

On a plateau in the centre of the island, Mdina, the old capital, is one of the world's finest examples of a medieval walled city that is still inhabited.

Central Malta is dominated by the great dome of Mosta, but this is not unusual as churches are a Maltese speciality, as you will see if you spend time touring this lesser-known area. Meanwhile, Sliema, St Julian's and Paceville have developed into Malta's most important resort area.

The north of the island is also known for its brash newer resorts, Bugibba and Qawra, and a short distance away are the island's scarce but very pleasant sandy beaches.

Further north are the beautiful, and less developed, islands of Gozo and Comino, while the south is where Malta's prehistoric temples are found.

All the sites of interest are numbered on specially drawn maps to help you find your way round. It's a good idea to hire a car, though the island's bus system has been already upgraded.

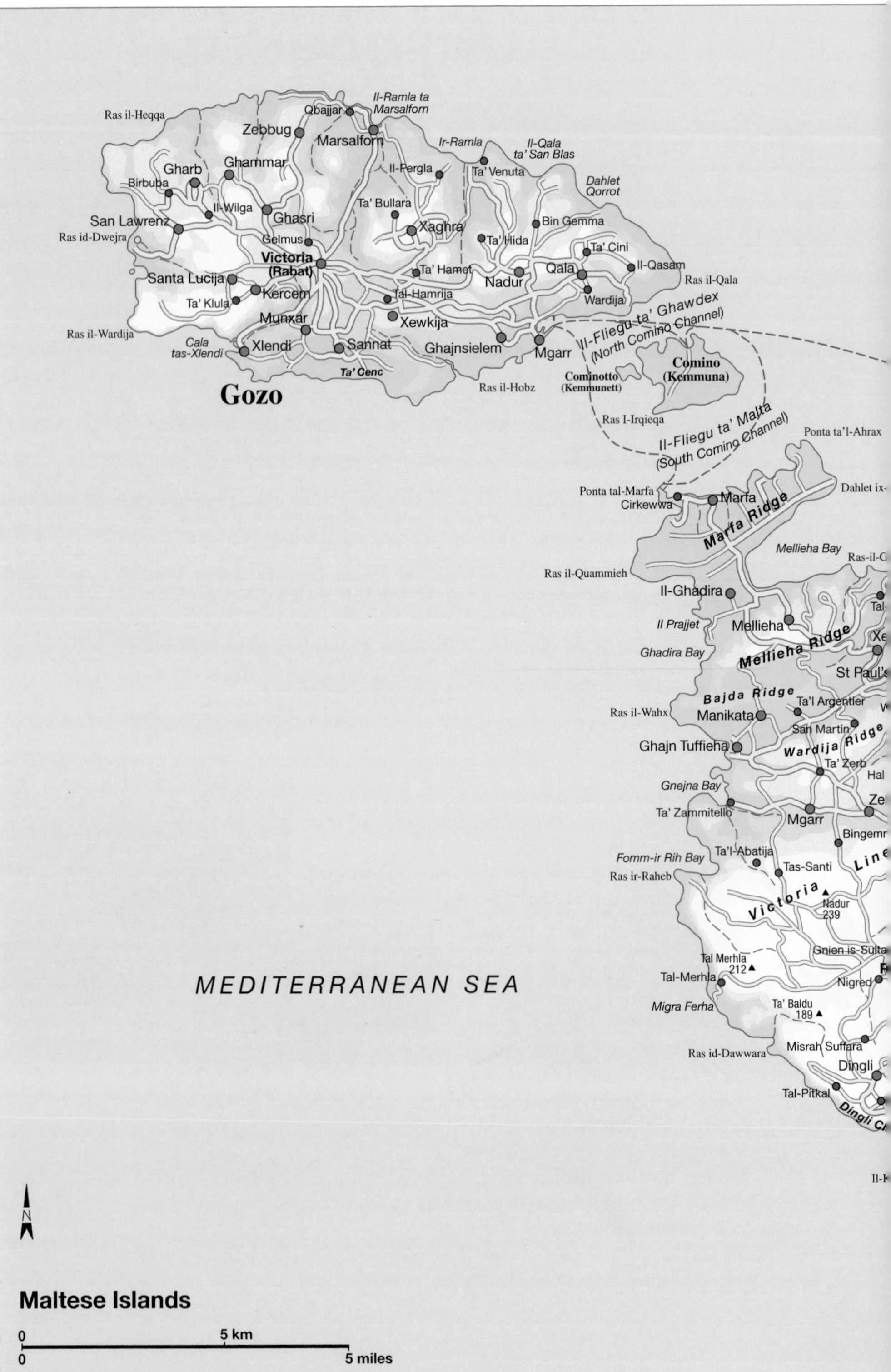
Gozo
Ras il-Heqqa
Qbajjar
Il-Ramla ta Marsalforn
Zebbug
Marsalforn
Ir-Ramla
Il-Qala ta' San Blas
Gharb
Ghammar
Il-Pergla
Ta' Venuta
Dahlet Qorrot
Birbuba
Il-Wilga
Ghasri
Ta' Bullara
San Lawrenz
Bin Gemma
Ras id-Dwejra
Gelmus
Xaghra
Ta' Hida
Ta' Cini
Victoria (Rabat)
Il-Qasam
Santa Lucija
Ta' Hamet
Qala
Nadur
Ras il-Qala
Kercem
Ta' Klula
Tal-Hamrija
Wardija
Il-Fliegu ta' Ghawdex (North Comino Channel)
Munxar
Xewkija
Ras il-Wardija
Cala tas-Xlendi
Xlendi
Sannat
Ghajnsielem
Mgarr
Ta' Cenc
Comino (Kemmuna)
Cominotto (Kemmunett)
Ras il-Hobz
Ras I-Irqieqa
Il-Fliegu ta' Malta (South Comino Channel)
Ponta ta'l-Ahrax
Ponta tal-Marfa
Cirkewwa
Marfa
Marfa Ridge
Mellieha Bay
Ras il-Quammieh
Il-Ghadira
Il Prajjet
Mellieha
Ghadira Bay
Mellieha Ridge
Bajda Ridge
Ta'l Argentier
Ras il-Wahx
Manikata
San Martin
Ghajn Tuffieha
Wardija Ridge
Ta' Zerb
Gnejna Bay
Ta' Zammitello
Mgarr
Fomm-ir Rih Bay
Ta'l-Abatija
Tas-Santi
Ras ir-Raheb
Victoria
Nadur 239
Tal Merhla 212
Tal-Merhla
Migra Ferha
Ta' Baldu 189
Misrah Suffara
Ras id-Dawwara
Dingli
Tal-Pitkal
MEDITERRANEAN SEA
N
Maltese Islands
0
5 km
0
5 miles

MEDITERRANEAN SEA
Corse (France)
Roma
ITALY
Tirana
MONTE-NEGRO
KOSOVO
MACE-DONIA
ALBANIA
Napoli
Sardegna
GREECE
Palermo
Reggio di Calabria
MEDITERRANEAN SEA
Sicilia
Catánia
Siracusa
Tunis
ALGERIA
TUNISIA
MALTA
0 100 km
0 100 miles
Pozzallo, Catánia
Ras il-Qawra
Salina Bay
Qawra
Bugibba
Ras il-Qrejten
Bahar ic-Caghaq
Ras I-Irqieqa
Burmarrad
Wied il-Ghasel
Victoria Lines
Madliena
Il Ponta tad-Dragunara
Paceville
Gharghur
Il-Ponta Ta'San Giljan
St Julian's
San Pawl tat-Targa
Naxxar
Sliema
Ta' Glorni
Mosta
Msierah
Il-Ponta Ta'Dragut
Gzira
Lija
Birkirkara
Valletta
Balzan
Tal-Mirakli
Floriana
Gwardamanga
Vittoriosa
Kalkara
Xghajra
Ta'Qali
Santa Venera
Senglea
Madliena
Attard
Hamrun
Wied is Sewda
Cospicua
San Leonardo
MALTA
Qormi
Hal Muxi
Zabbar
Zonqor
Zebbug
Ghammieri
Paola
Bulebben Iz-Zghir
Hal Mula
Marsaskala
Marsaskala Bay
Hal Dwin
Tarxien
Il-Gzira
Wied Qirda
Luqa
Tas-Sienja
Ponta tal-Mignuma
Wied il-Kbir
Zejtun
St Thomas Bay
Siggiewi
Gudja
Bir id-Deheb
Tal-Munxar
Mqabba
Misrah Strejnu
Ghaxaq
Ta' Haxxluq
Marsaxlokk
Il-Ballut
Tal-Providenza
Il-Hofra z-Zghira
Kirkop
Borg in-Nadur
Qrendi
Safi
Tal-Bajjada
Zurrieq
Marsaxlokk Bay
Delimara
Birżebbuġia
Ghar Lapsi
Bubaqra
Ras il-Hamrija
Ta' Ghammer
Kalafrana
Ponta ta'Delimara
Wied iz-Zurrieq
Hal-Far
Benghisa
L-Artal
Ponta ta'Benghisa

A street view in Valletta, showing the traditional gallerija that many homes in the capital have.

VALLETTA

The Knights of St John founded Valletta in the 16th century, creating the finest fortified city in Europe. Having been ravaged during World War II, it is now being restored to its former glory.

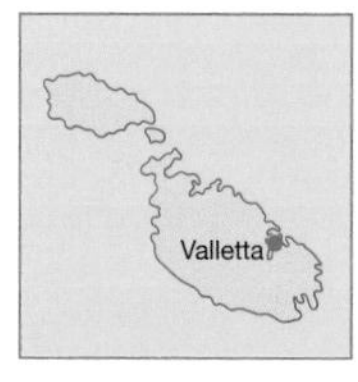

Main Attractions
- Triq Ir-Repubblika
- St John's Co-Cathedral
- Valletta Living History
- The Palace of the Grand Masters
- St George's Square
- Manoel Theatre
- The Malta Experience
- Valletta Waterfront
- Upper Barrakka Gardens
- Lascaris War Rooms

Emerging bloodied but unbowed after the heroic Great Siege of 1565, the Knights and the other inhabitants of Malta realised that in order to be ready for a second Islamic invasion, they had to build a new and better fortified city on Malta.

The site chosen was virgin territory across from what was then called the Great Harbour (now the Grand Harbour). The high, barren, uninhabited rocky peninsula known as Mount Sceberras, with the tiny fort of St Elmo at its tip, both commanded the entrances to the harbours and dominated the lands on either side. It was from this unguarded superior position that the Turks had managed to rain down their fire with such devastation. The Knights would not make the mistake again of leaving such a strategic position accessible to the enemy.

A planned city

After much political argument and discussion, plans by the Vatican architect Francesco Laparelli were accepted. One of the most important planned towns of the Renaissance would now be built. Laparelli's Valletta would be a city laid out in a rigid grid plan – that is, with all roads running straight and crossing each other at right angles. There would be main squares and secondary squares.

To make the city beautiful, there would be uniformity of house design. Noxious trades would be zoned together to protect the residential quarters. Laparelli designated a vast space for a Grand Masters' palace to be built "as large as Palazzo Farnese in Rome", and there would be excellent sites for a conventual church and hospital, as well as for eight *auberges* for the different *langues* that formed the Order.

On the morning of 28 March 1566, with great pomp, the foundation stone was laid. There, where the chapel of

The Carmelite Church, a Valletta landmark.

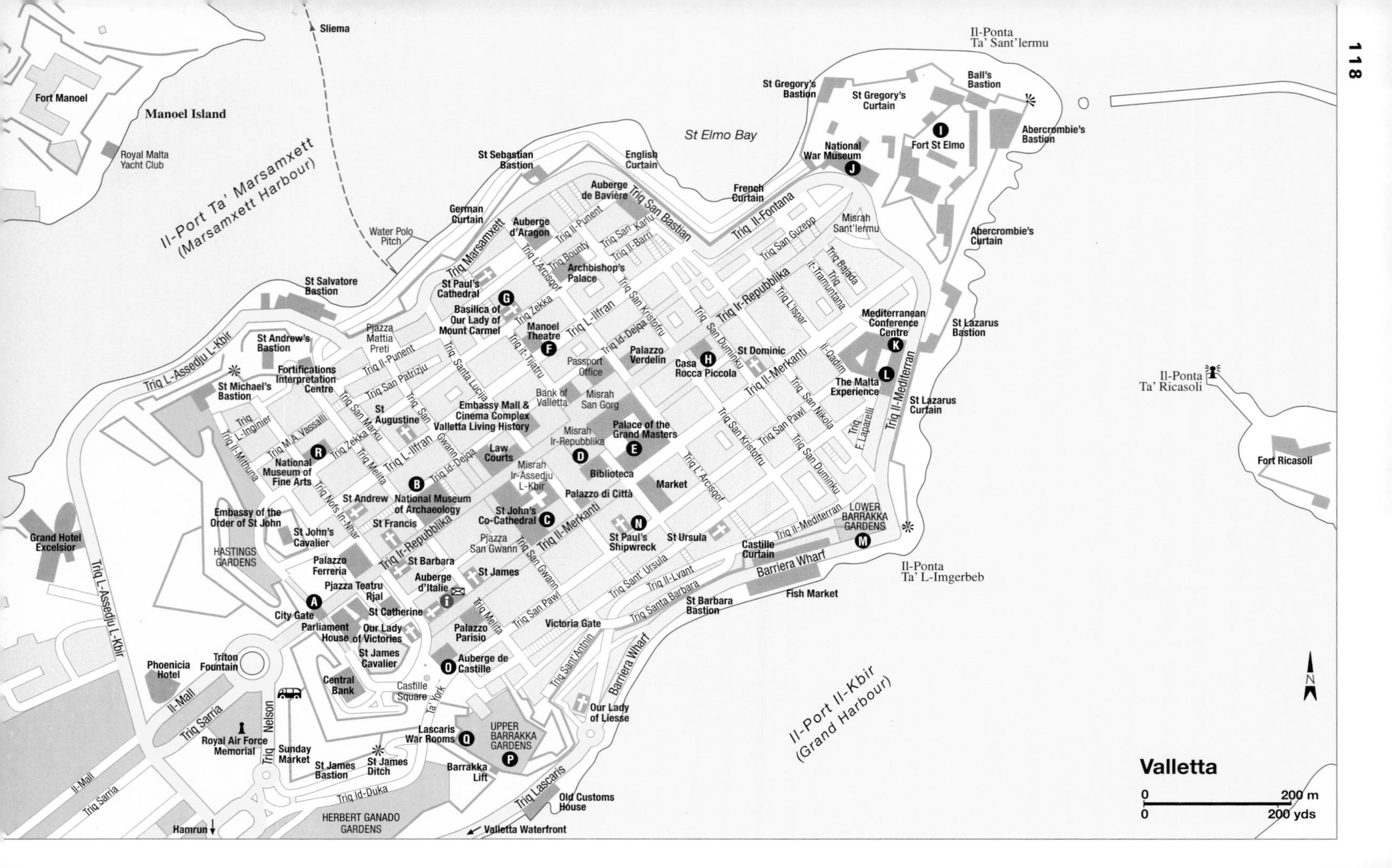

Valletta
0
200 m
0
200 yds
N
Sliema
Fort Manoel
Manoel Island
Royal Malta Yacht Club
Il-Port Ta' Marsamxett (Marsamxett Harbour)
Water Polo Pitch
St Elmo Bay
Il-Ponta Ta' Sant'Iermu
St Gregory's Bastion
St Gregory's Curtain
Ball's Bastion
Fort St Elmo
Abercrombie's Bastion
National War Museum
Abercrombie's Curtain
St Sebastian Bastion
English Curtain
French Curtain
German Curtain
St Salvatore Bastion
St Andrew's Bastion
St Michael's Bastion
Fortifications Interpretation Centre
Triq L-Assedju L-Kbir
Auberge de Bavière
Triq San Bastian
Triq Il-Fontana
Misrah Sant'Iermu
Triq San Guzepp
Triq Bajada
Triq it-Tramuntana
Triq L'Ispar
Triq Ir-Repubblika
Auberge d'Aragon
Triq Marsamxett
Triq Il-Punent
Triq San Karlu
Triq Il-Barri
Triq Bounty
Triq L'Arcisqof
Archbishop's Palace
St Paul's Cathedral
Basilica of Our Lady of Mount Carmel
Triq Zekka
Manoel Theatre
Triq L-Ilfran
Triq it-Tijatru
Triq Id-Dejqa
Triq San Kristofru
Palazzo Verdelin
Casa Rocca Piccola
St Dominic
Triq San Duminku
Triq Il-Merkanti
Il-Qadim
Mediterranean Conference Centre
The Malta Experience
Triq Il-Mediterran
St Lazarus Bastion
St Lazarus Curtain
Il-Ponta Ta' Ricasoli
Fort Ricasoli
Pjazza Mattia Preti
Triq San Patrizju
Triq San Marku
Triq Santa Lucija
Passport Office
Bank of Valletta
Misrah San Gorg
St Augustine
Triq San Gwann
Embassy Mall & Cinema Complex
Valletta Living History
Palace of the Grand Masters
Misrah Ir-Repubblika
Triq San Pawl
Triq San Nikola
Triq F. Laparelli
Triq L-Inginier
Triq M.A. Vassalli
Triq Il-Mithuna
National Museum of Fine Arts
Triq Melita
Law Courts
Misrah Ir-Assedju L-Kbir
Biblioteca
Market
National Museum of Archaeology
St Andrew
Triq Nofs In-Nhar
Embassy of the Order of St John
St John's Cavalier
St Francis
St John's Co-Cathedral
Palazzo di Città
St Paul's Shipwreck
St Ursula
LOWER BARRAKKA GARDENS
Castille Curtain
Il-Ponta Ta' L-Imgerbeb
Grand Hotel Excelsior
HASTINGS GARDENS
Palazzo Ferreria
St Barbara
Pjazza San Gwann
St James
Triq Sant' Ursula
Triq Il-Lvant
Triq Santa Barbara
Barriera Wharf
Fish Market
St Barbara Bastion
Auberge d'Italie
Pjazza Teatru Rjal
City Gate
St Catherine
Parliament House
Our Lady of Victories
Palazzo Parisio
Victoria Gate
Triq Sant'Antnin
St James Cavalier
Auberge de Castille
Phoenicia Hotel
Triton Fountain
Central Bank
Castille Square
Ta' York
Il-Mall
Triq Sarria
Triq Nelson
Royal Air Force Memorial
Sunday Market
St James Bastion
St James Ditch
Lascaris War Rooms
UPPER BARRAKKA GARDENS
Barrakka Lift
Our Lady of Liesse
Il-Port Il-Kbir (Grand Harbour)
Triq Lascaris
Old Customs House
Triq Id-Duka
HERBERT GANADO GARDENS
Hamrun
Valletta Waterfront
A
B
C
D
E
F
G
H
I
J
K
L
M
N
O
P
Q
R

Our Lady of Victory would be built, a richly decorated altar was set up and High Mass celebrated in honour of Santo Spirito. The new city that would rise was christened Valletta after Grand Master Jean Parisot de la Valette, who had been the Great Siege commander and led the Order to victory.

In spite of the enthusiasm and urgency, work was slow and laboured. Hard rock had to be turned into a plateau before building could begin. After a few years Laparelli returned to Rome and the work passed into the hands of a Maltese architect, Gerolamo Cassar.

Lasting glory

Cassar, then in his late forties, had worked with Laparelli and, during the Siege, while only a boy, had helped repair fortifications and invent war weapons. He had studied in Rome at the expense of the Order. Slowly but surely, the city began to take shape.

Today, although much restored after the damage of World War II, and masked by a plethora of modern shop fronts and advertising hoardings, the city remains a delight, combining Laparelli's original designs and Cassar's magnificent architecture. The dramatic Valletta outline, with its superb bastion walls wrapped protectively around it, and its skyline of rectangular masses varied only by a cupola or church spire, remains one of Europe's great cityscapes.

The changing face of the capital

The gracious Royal Opera House, one of the first sights a visitor would encounter within the city walls, was one of the many buildings destroyed by World War II bombing. It lay in ruins for decades until 2010, when plans were laid out for the complete rehabilitation of the entrance to the city. Fast-forward to the present, and the entrance to Valletta may well look a little different to visitors who haven't been for a while: the capital has been given a much-needed face-lift by the **City Gate** Ⓐ project, led by renowned Italian architect Renzo Piano. The project involved the remodelling of the entrance, together with the construction of a

TIP

Parking space in the city is limited. All cars are charged for time spent – the times are recorded by cameras and car-hire companies then informed. A Park and Ride service is sign-posted in Floriana.

New Valletta City Gate walkway.

FACT

Look down as you pad through St John's Co-Cathedral and note that the terracotta and white marble chequer-board floor is actually a series of plaques remembering the dead.

new parliament building, a piazza and a new performing space. The most controversial aspect of the project was the demolition of the old Victorian City Gate, built by the British, and replace it with a modern structure, which has been compared by some people to the ancient Egyptian temple of Edfu. The new **Parliament House,** designed by Renzo Piano and officially inaugurated in 2015, also provoked criticism for allegedly being unnecessary, ugly and too expensive. The environmentally friendly building consists of massive, porous blocks connected by bridges to allow the view of the fortifications of St James Chevalier from the Republic Street. On the site of an old opera house now stands an open-air theatre, **Pjazza Teatru Rjal** (http://pjazzateatrurjal.com), which offers an interesting cultural programme. It is also the venue for the Valletta International Film Festival.

The **European Capital of Culture Valletta 2018** programme includes some serious infrastructure projects, such as the regeneration of areas such as the covered market at is-Suq l-Antik tal-Belt and Strait Street, together with the construction of the new Valletta Design Cluster in the old civil abattoir and the new approach to the art in the MUZA project. All these projects are due for completion before 2018.

It is becoming harder and harder to bring cars into the city, as residents' parking has taken up all the available space. Thankfully, as a result of the recent public-transport reform, it is now easy to get to the city by bus, and most routes will drop you off right outside the entrance.

The main thoroughfare

Immediately ahead of City Gate is **Triq Ir-Repubblika** (Republic Street), the city's main artery, leading from the City Gate all the way down to Fort St Elmo at the tip of Valletta's promontory. It is not only the historical focus of the city, but also the main shopping street, with popular boutiques, small shopping malls and a selection of indoor and open-air cafés.

After about 200 metres/yds, on the corner of narrow Triq Melita (Melita Street), is the imposing **National Museum of Archaeology** Ⓑ (tel:

Nighttime in lively Paceville.

ISLAND NIGHTLIFE

For a capital city, Valletta has never really had a strong reputation for attracting night owls. Today, it is mostly popular with the island's cultural crowd, who meander into the tiny wine bars, such as Trabuxu (http://trabuxu.com.mt), Leglegin or Bridge Bar, after an evening of theatre, music or fine art.

If you have something more exuberant in mind, head to the resort areas of St Julian's, Paceville or Bugibba. St Julian's is the most upmarket, with several luxury hangouts that include the ultra-chic Tiffany at Portomaso (www.tiffanymalta.com). Here you can sip on champagne cocktails while enjoying the backdrop of the marina below.

Paceville tends to attract a very young crowd, and is overflowing with international students during the summer months. They head straight for clubs such as Havana, Plush (www.plush-lounge.com) and Footloose (http://footloosebar.com), which are all open until the early hours. Wild nights often follow on from the many drinks offers available at these bars.

Bugibba, meanwhile, is somewhere in the middle of the two. It attracts crowds of expats, who love the British pubs and karaoke bars. There's a great atmosphere to be enjoyed here, though, even if pubs and clubs aren't your thing. Simply walk along the promenade soaking up the lively feeling in the air.

2122 1623; http://heritagemalta.org; daily Jan–Feb 9am–5pm; Mar–Dec 9am–6pm). This was one of the original Knights' *auberges*, the Auberge de Provence. It contains collections of prehistoric pottery, sculpture and personal ornaments recovered from the megalithic temples that dot the island, including Malta's famous "Fat Ladies" – statues of overweight women that have been discovered in the island's temples and are thought to be a symbol of fertility. There are also some typical examples of tomb furniture of the Punic and Roman periods.

St John's Co-Cathedral

To the right, continuing along Republic Street, is **St John's Square** (Pjazza San Gwann), with **St John's Co-Cathedral** ❸ (tel: 2248 0400; http://stjohnscocathedral.com; Mon–Fri 9.30am–4.30pm, Sat 9.30am–12.30pm, Sun for services only). Although its frontage is somewhat plain, the interior is awe-inspiring in its wealth and detail; it is rightly regarded as one of the most important and remarkable monuments on the islands.

Work was begun on the Conventual Church dedicated to St John the Baptist (the patron saint of the Order) in November 1573. Its design and construction were entrusted to the Order's chief architect, the aforementioned Gerolamo Cassar. Originally, it was planned to be sited in lower Valletta, close to the Holy Infirmary, but, realising that the ringing of the bells would disturb the sick, the Grand Master changed the site to its present position at the heart of the city.

The fortress church of St John's

Cassar's training in military architecture explains the austere lines of the facade, which has been described accurately as that of a fortress-church and a continuation, in conception, of Valletta's fortified lines.

The two western towers, quite rare in Renaissance Italy, set the pattern for future Maltese church architecture, and there is hardly a church on the island without the characteristic twin bell towers on its front.

Exterior of St John's Co-Cathedral.

Interior of St John's Co-Cathedral.

FACT

The St John's Co-Cathedral crypt houses the remains of 12 Grand Masters, including the hero of the Great Siege, Jean Parisot de la Valette. Due to its restoration, the crypt is not currently open to the public.

But if the facade of St John's is bleak, the interior is an unqualified triumph.

As you leave the sunlit square and walk through the main portal into the semi-darkness of the cathedral, the sense of contrast is striking. The rigid, plain lines of the exterior change, as if by magic, into a dazzling blaze of colour and decoration, which made Sir Walter Scott exclaim with delight in 1831: "This is the most magnificent place I saw in my life."

The richly painted vault, arabesque carvings covering every inch of the walls, and multi-coloured marble slabs stretching from one end of the floor to the other, may initially be overwhelming, but a sense of harmony does prevail.

Building St John's

The building was completed in 1577, but important additions were made well into the 18th century. The plan of the church is simple: a vast rectangular chamber with an apse at its eastern end, a slightly pointed barrel vault, originally coffered, and chapels at the sides behind high arches. Cassar, obviously uncertain of the structural and statical potential of the local limestone, used extra-thick walls between the side chapels as supports for the heavy buttresses above, thus counteracting the enormous lateral thrust of the huge vault.

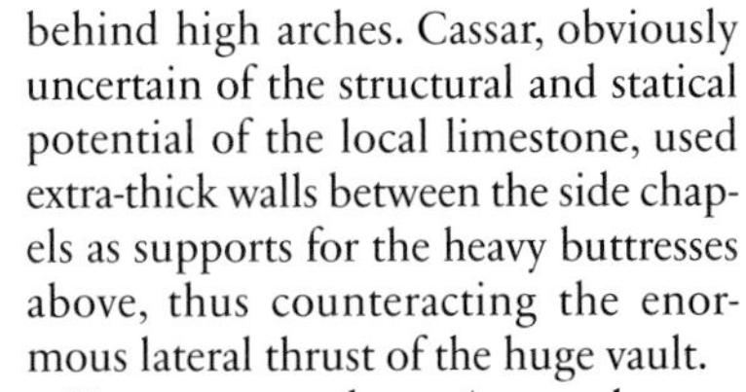

Very narrow doors (opened years after the church was completed) lead from one chapel to the other, each small enough not to interfere with the stability of the supporting walls. The vault is divided into six bays by wide ribs, each resting on the pilasters between the arches of the side chapels. In each bay, an oval window gives light, although the light is somewhat restricted owing to the presence of the buttresses outside.

Decorating St John's

For more than 70 years after its completion, St John's remained a vast cavernous stone structure barren of all decoration. Then, in 1661, Grand Master Rafael Cotoner commissioned Mattia Preti to decorate the ceiling. Known as *Il Cavalier Calabrese*, Preti was one of the most outstanding artists of his age.

The frescoed ceiling of St John's Co-Cathedral by Mattia Preti.

ON THE ROAD AGAIN

As in many cities, the idea of a hop-on, hop-off bus tour has really taken off in Malta and numerous companies are now vying for business. Great when the weather is good as you can sit on the top deck and admire the view as you are ferried around top sights including Valletta itself, the temples, the Mosta Dome and Mellieha. The main service providers are the Malta Sightseeing Buses (tel: 2169 4967; www.maltasightseeing.com) and Pink Sightseeing (tel: 2148 9991; www.pinksightseeingbus.com), and both offer detailed commentaries in several languages. Additionally, Bedford buses can often be spotted picking up tourists and driving them around. As yet, no proper system is in place for this, but details are expected to be released soon – so keep your eyes peeled!

Born in Taverna, Calabria, in 1613, he studied in Rome and Naples, where he came under the influence of the art of Caravaggio and the Venetian masters of the 16th century, whose main traits characterise all his artistic works.

Preti divided each of the six bays of the vault into three sections by means of painted architectural devices such as balustraded balconies, cornices and elaborately decorated archways, thus creating 18 spaces in which he depicted episodes from the life of John the Baptist – from Zachary in the Temple, to John's Birth, his Encounter with Christ in the Desert, Christ's Baptism, John's Preachings in the Wilderness, the Reproval of Herod, the Dance of Salome and the final episode of the Beheading. Figures of saints and heroes of the Order, dramatically illuminated on each side of the oval windows, are considered among the best of Preti's work.

The two Cotoner brothers, Grand Masters Rafael (1660–63) and Nicolas (1663–80), under whose rule the decoration was brought to fruition, are given a place of honour in the large lunette over the main door.

Preti completed his masterpiece in less than five years, while working concurrently on the preparation of drawings for the elaborate full-relief sculptures of the nave and aisles. The plain stone surface of the pilasters, arches, walls and ceilings of the chapels (perfect material for the carver's chisel) was transformed into a riot of gilded flowers, scrolls, shells, winged angels and escutcheons – all the design motifs that are characteristic of Baroque ornamentation.

Using surprisingly skilful illusionistic effects, considerable dexterity in the use and combination of colours and, above all, absolutely perfect draughtsmanship, Preti turned St John's Co-Cathedral into his own personal artistic triumph.

The chapels of the langues: right aisle

Each of the eight *langues*, or national sections of the Order, had its own chapel where the Knights prayed and attended Mass. The chapel nearest the entrance on the right is that of Castile, León and Portugal, dedicated to St James. The Portuguese Grand Masters Antonio Manoel de Vilhena (1722–36) and Manuel Pinto de Fonseca (1741–73) are commemorated in two splendid monuments.

The next chapel, dedicated to St George, is that of the *langue* of Aragon, Catalunya and Navarre, whose altarpiece and paintings are also by Preti. The chapel contains two of the most beautiful Grand Masters' mausoleums in St John's: those of Nicolas Cotoner (1663–80) and Ramón Perellos (1697–1720).

The **Chapel of Auvergne**, with an altarpiece depicting a variety of scenes from the life of St Sebastian, comes next. The monument commemorates Grand Master de Chattes Gessan (1660), who died only four months after his election.

The chapels of the langues: left aisle

At the end of the left aisle is the **Chapel of the Holy Relics**, with an altarpiece

Details from the interior of St John's Co-Cathedral.

Details from the interior of St John's Co-Cathedral.

FACT

Running parallel to Republic Street is Strait Street, a landmark for anyone who served in Malta during World War II. Known then as "The Gut", it comprised of nothing but ever-open bars, dancehalls and brothels. Today, these establishments have disappeared and the street is enjoying its second lease of life and offers several pleasant dining options

of *St Charles Borromeo*. Next to it is the **Chapel of Provence**, with a contemporary copy of Guido Reni's *St Michael*, and the mausoleums of the two Provençal Grand Masters, de Paule (1623–36) and Lascaris Castellar (1636–57).

Next is the **Chapel of France**, dedicated to St Paul. This chapel was shorn of Preti's sculptural decoration in the 1840s by a short-lived iconoclastic movement that introduced motifs representing the British Crown, the fleur-de-lis and the eight-pointed cross. The mausoleum of Grand Master de Rohan (1775–97), which was also adversely tampered with, and that of Adrien de Wignacourt (1690–97) are both located here.

Adjoining the Chapel of France is the **Chapel of the Langue of Italy**, with an altarpiece of the *Mystic Marriage of St Catherine*, one of Preti's finest works in Malta. The chapel contains the monument of Grand Master Carafa (1680–90), with a marble relief of the Battle of the Dardanelles fought in 1656 by the galleys of the Order of St John, with Carafa as the Captain-General of the fleet.

Queen Victoria statue, Republic Square.

The last chapel is dedicated to the **Three Kings of the Langue of Germany**, with the monument of Grand Master Zondadari (1720–22), a splendid mausoleum made of bronze and black marble. All these chapels have undergone major restoration over the last six years.

Artworks in St John's

The chancel and choir, and indeed the whole of St John's, is dominated by a magnificent marble group representing the *Baptism of Christ* by Giuseppe Mazzuoli (1644–1725), with a gilt-bronze *gloria* as background, the work of Giovanni Giardini (1646–1721), an Italian sculptor and silversmith. The high altar, certainly the richest in Malta, is made of lapis lazuli and precious marbles and is enriched by a relief of The *Last Supper*, also in gilt bronze, at its centre.

The Beheading of St John by Caravaggio (1573–1610), the renowned Italian painter, is found in the cathedral museum and is undoubtedly the most famous painting in St John's – and, indeed, in the whole of the Maltese Islands. A crucial landmark in the history of European art, it was one of Caravaggio's last works, and certainly considered one of his best. Another of the artist's masterpieces, *St Jerome*, hangs close by.

The museum's other principal treasures are a magnificent set of 14 Flemish tapestries by De Vos, made after cartoons by Rubens and Poussin, which portray scenes from the Life of Christ and religious allegories. During June (the festival month of John the Baptist), they are hung in the nave of the church. There are future plans to build separate museums to house tapestries and Caravaggio's works, as well as silver artefacts from the Bartolott Crypt.

The history of the Order, its Knights and admirals, its warriors and heroes, is emblazoned on marble tombstones that cover the floor of the nave, aisles and oratory.

Heart of the city

Return to Republic Street and further along, to the left, are the **Law Courts**, a modern, post-war building complete with massive pillars. Beyond are the two grand squares that give the city its centre.

A detour here, left on Triq Santa Lucija (St Lucy Street), leads to the, Embassy cinema, with its audiovisual show **Valletta Living History** (tel: 2122 2225; http://embassycomplex.com.mt; daily with regular shows between 10am–3.15pm). This fantastic film promises to help you see the city in a whole new light, and is entertaining for all ages.

Next is **Republic Square** **D** (Misrah Ir-Repubblika), until recently known as Queen's Square. Its landmark is a nicely refurbished statue of Queen Victoria, which is surrounded by lovely open-air cafés.

Caffè Cordina (www.caffecordina.com) is Valletta's best-known café and has a fine reputation for the quality of its food and coffee, even if service can be leisurely. In addition to being popular with tourists, its gilded interior is the meeting place of local businessmen and lawyers, who collect in the late morning beneath the painted ceilings, standing and talking around the bar.

To the left of the square is the flank of the Grand Master's Palace, but lending its imposing presence as a backdrop is the **Bibliotheca**, the National Library (tel: 2123 6585; www.maltalibraries.gov.mt; mid-Jun–late Sept Mon-Sat 8.15am–1.15pm; Oct–mid-Jun Mon–Fri 8.15am–5pm, Sat 8.15am–1.15pm; free). Dating from 1786, it was the last building of importance erected in Valletta by the Order of St John. There are said to be more than 300,000 books and documents in the building, including, in the archives, more than 10,000 priceless manuscripts dating from the 12th to the 19th century. Among the letters is the signed bill and accompanying letter in which Henry VIII proclaimed himself the head of the Church of England.

The Palace of the Grand Masters

However, while the surroundings could be better, nothing can diminish

A Caravaggio in the cathedral.

Republic Square, Valletta.

A view of the Palace of the Grand Masters.

the inner splendour of the **Palace of the Grand Masters** **E** (tel: 2124 9349; Mon–Wed and Fri 10am–4pm, Sat–Sun 9am–5pm; armoury daily 9am–5pm;), where visitors can tour the Armoury and Royal Apartments.

Work on the palace started in 1571, under Grand Master La Cassière, with the architect Gerolamo Cassar (1520–92) entrusted with its design and construction. From the time it was completed, a few years later, until the end of the Order's stay in Malta in 1798, the palace was used by all successive Grand Masters, and after that, until 1964, by the British governors. Since 1976, it has housed the offices of the President of the Republic.

The Palace's facade and interior

The main facade of the palace, which opens on to Republic Street, is plain and generally disappointing, and was even more so before the addition of its only decorative elements, the two Doric gateways and the long wooden balconies that were constructed during the time of Grand Master Emanuel Pinto de Fonseca (1741–73). Corner pilasters with ponderous rustications, so characteristic of 16th- and 17th-century Valletta, raise the height of the building, giving it a visual impression of strength.

The sumptuous interior of the palace more than makes up for the unprepossessing aspect of the facade. All state rooms, as was usual in important buildings of the period, are located on the first floor, while the ground floor was reserved for stables, coach houses, kitchens, servants' quarters and stores.

Some fine masonry work in local limestone – the groined cross vaults, saucer domes and plain vaulting supported on massive walls – can be seen in most of the ground-floor rooms and corridors, especially in the older sections of the building. An open corridor runs round the main **Neptune Courtyard**; its balustraded arcading, subtropical trees, a small flower garden with a bronze statue of Neptune and a sculptured marble and stone fountain bearing the coat of arms of the Aragonese Grand Master, Ramon Perellos (1697–1720), make it one of the finest ensembles of its kind in Malta.

Breastplates on display.

The Armoury

Two large vaults at the rear of the palace contain the Armoury, which has one of the most important collections of arms and armour in the world.

The Armoury was, from the time of Grand Master Pinto, originally housed in a long hall in the upper floor of the palace, but was transferred to its present location in 1976, when the hall was converted into the Chamber of Parliament. On permanent exhibition are splendid suits of armour (some of them elaborately engraved), rapiers, swords, daggers, halberds, pikes and lances, flintlocks, arquebuses, pistols, mortars and small ordnance. A limited number of Turkish arms and trophies completes the impressive collection.

At the back of another courtyard, named after Prince Alfred to commemorate the first visit to Malta by the second son of Queen Victoria in 1858, stands a high bell tower with a clock that has been chiming the hours since 1745. Four bronze figures, representing Moorish slaves, strike three gongs with a hammer every quarter of an hour. Its four dials variously show the hour and minutes, the phases of the Moon, the month and the day.

The Grand Master's apartments

The first floor is reached by a winding marble staircase with unusually shallow steps, said to have been purposely constructed for the benefit of old and gout-ridden Knights and Grand Masters. The newel (the staircase's centre pillar) is a hollow masonry cylinder with balustraded openings, while a handrail is carved into the wall. The barrel-vaulted ceiling, which follows both the curvature and slope of the stairs, is a rare masterpiece of masonry work and a tribute to Malta's ancient craft of stoneworking.

The first floor, or *piano nobile*, contains the main apartments built round wide corridors overlooking the Neptune Courtyard. The highlights are the **Council Chamber**, also known as the Tapestry Chamber, and the **Supreme Council Hall** (also called, until a few years ago, the Hall of St Michael and St George). Both halls have superb timber ceilings, with decorated wooden

Armoury on show in the Palace of the Grand Masters.

Watching the world from a gallerija.

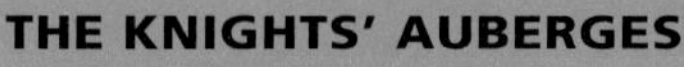

THE KNIGHTS' AUBERGES

Of the eight *auberges* in Valletta designed by Gerolamo Cassar for the various *langues* of the Knights of the Order (see page 40), five still stand. The most famous and most imposing is the Auberge de Castille, now the office of the prime minister. The others are the Auberge d'Aragon (a government ministry) in Pjazza Independenza, the Auberge d'Italie (Malta Tourism Authority or MUSE) in Merchant's Street, the Auberge de Provence (the National Museum of Archaeology) and the Auberge d'Angleterre et de Bavière, used as government offices, but currently awaiting new designation. Three *auberges* have disappeared. The d'Allemagne was demolished to make way for St Paul's Anglican Cathedral and two were destroyed in World War II. The Law Courts stand on the former site of the d'Auvergne, while the faceless headquarters of the General Workers Union occupies the site of the old Auberge de France.

The *auberge* with public access, the National Museum of Archaeology, has been gutted and much altered over the centuries so there is little to remind you of its former function or atmosphere. But if you want to see inside a relatively little-changed *auberge*, make the short trip to Vittoriosa where the Auberge d'Angleterre there now functions as the local public library.

FACT

The wide marble-paved corridors of the palace have a decorated ceiling of canvases painted in 1724 by Nicolo Nasoni (1664–1730) and a vast array of lunettes recalling naval engagements between the Order and the Turks.

beams of red Sicilian chestnut resting on carved supporting brackets designed to reduce the span. Richly painted and gilded cross beams, placed at frequent intervals, provide an elaborate coffered effect.

The Council Chamber

The senior members of the Order met regularly in this room to discuss the day-to-day administration of the island. The tradition was continued by the Maltese Parliament, which held its sittings here from 1921 until 1976. It later relocated to the former Armoury, and then again in 2015 to the new Parliament House.

The most striking feature of the room is a set of **Gobelin tapestries**, donated to the Order by Grand Master Ramón Perellos in 1710. Known as *Les Tentures des Indes*, they depict in vivid colours (subdued by age) jungle scenes recalling the hunting expeditions of a German prince in Brazil, the Caribbean Islands, India and tropical Africa, undertaken between 1636 and 1644.

Above the hangings around the four walls of the chamber is a frieze made of rectangular panels showing galleys of the Order in action against the Turkish fleet. The frieze incorporates allegorical figures representing Faith, Charity, Fortitude, Virtue, Manhood, Vocation, Providence, Munificence, Victory, Hope and Justice. At one end is a large painted crucifix on which Grand Masters and members of the council took solemn oaths during their deliberations by extending their hand towards it.

The Supreme Council Chamber

The Grand Master summoned his Supreme Council, consisting of the 16 most senior members of the Order, whenever important decisions on domestic affairs or on foreign relations had to be made. Gianbattista Tiepolo (1693–1770) immortalised one of the sessions of the Supreme Council held in the Supreme Council Chamber with a superb painting that hangs in Udine, Italy.

The main chamber frieze depicts the Great Siege of 1565. At the end of the hall is a modified version of the original throne used by the Grand Masters

Inside the Palace of the Grand Masters.

and, later, during the colonial period, by governors representing the British monarchs. At the opposite end of the hall is a singers' gallery, previously in the private chapel of the Grand Master, decorated with scenes from Genesis, said to have been brought by the Order on their flight from Rhodes.

The State Dining Hall

Adjacent to the Supreme Council Chamber, the State Dining Hall is a room of beautiful proportions in which the Grand Masters, and later the British governors, gave sumptuous dinners in honour of important visitors and local dignitaries.

The hall originally had a timber ceiling like all the state rooms of the palace, but this was unfortunately destroyed during the extensive aerial bombardment suffered during World War II and replaced by a concrete roof that was painted with a copy of the original design.

Paintings of British royalty adorn the walls, including: King George III, during whose reign Malta became a part of the British Empire, George IV, Victoria, Edward VII, Alexandra, George VI and Elizabeth II.

The Ambassador's Room

On the other side of the Supreme Council Chamber is the Ambassador's Room, also known as the State Room, where Grand Masters received the credentials of envoys to Malta, a practice retained to this day by the President of the Republic when accepting the credentials of new ambassadors accredited to the islands.

A new space in the city

Back on Republic Street, take the time to enjoy **St George's Square** (Misrah San Gorg). This was recently transformed from a car park into a welcoming outdoor space, with benches and dancing fountains – it makes the perfect spot from which to admire the facade of the palace in more detail and watch the Changing of the Guards. At night the square takes on a magical aura, and you can enjoy dinner here at the perfectly positioned Malata Restaurant (www.malatarestaurant.com). The best time to visit the square is during the Valletta Green Festival.

Stone lion guarding the palace courtyard.

An oppulent hallway at the Palace of the Grand Masters.

Meanwhile, if the need takes you, head to the swanky public convenience just a few doors down on Strait Street. And while you may not think of it as the obvious spot to enjoy a bit of culture in the capital, it is. Opened in 2010 as an innovative project spearheaded by the Valletta Local Council, it transformed the city's previously uninspiring conveniences into something altogether a little more exciting. Now, following on from the success of this one, other arty toilets are opening their doors, all of which will be exhibiting pieces of cultural importance.

Continue your journey on the opposite side of Palace Square and there is the Main Guard. This elegant building once housed a ceremonial guard, but originally was part of the Chancellery of the Knights. Above its Doric portico is a royal coat of arms, carved in limestone, which was erected by the British and has an inscription dated 1814 recording in Latin the covenant between Malta and Britain. To the right of the building, behind the trees, is the Italian Cultural Institute (www.iicvalletta.esteri.it).

The people's theatre

A short distance from the Palace, on **Old Theatre Street** (Triq It-Tijatru), is the **Manoel Theatre** **F** (the box office tel: 2124 6389; www.teatrumanoel.com.mt), an 18th-century gem with gilded boxes rising in tiers to the ornate ceiling. It is reputed to be the second-oldest theatre still in use in Europe. Built in 1731 by Grand Master Manoel de Vilhena, mostly with money from his own pocket, it was opened "for the honest recreation of the people".

The theatre was a great success for well over a century, but with the opening of the Royal Opera House (able to accommodate far larger audiences), the Manoel fell into disrepair. In time, as its fortunes changed, it became cheap lodging for beggars, a dancehall and, more recently, a cinema. Then, in response to a public appeal, the theatre was bought by the nation and, after delicate restoration, has been officially declared Malta's National Theatre. It stages plays performed in both Maltese and English.

You don't have to attend a performance at the theatre to get a glimpse inside. Tours generally operate Mon–Fri

The Carmelite Church.

THE GREAT SIEGE FRIEZE

The main chamber frieze in the Supreme Council Hall is by Matteo Perez d'Aleccio (1547–1628), painter, engraver and probably a pupil of Michelangelo. Painted between 1576 and 1581, the work is unique in being the only reliable pictorial depiction of the famed Great Siege of 1565. The event was vividly described to the painter by eyewitnesses.

You can follow the dramatic episodes of the arrival of the Turkish armada in May, the landing of the Turkish troops in Marsaxlokk Bay, the epic month-long siege of Fort St Elmo, and its fall on the eve of St John's Day. The assault on Fort St Michael and the Posts of Castille and Allemagne at the Borgo, with Grand Master La Valette wounded at the head of his troops, is graphically illustrated with evident feeling. Perez d'Aleccio completes the pictorial history of one of the major events of Malta's history with a vivid panorama of the entire war, the arrival of the Little Relief and later of the Great Relief (sent from Sicily) and the final withdrawal of the Turkish army on 7 September. Separating the Siege panels are allegorical female figures that represent Justice, Happiness, Prudence, Fortitude, Temperance, and the three theological virtues of Faith, Hope and Charity. Perez d'Aleccio also painted the fine frieze in the Yellow Room.

10am–4.30pm, Sat 10am–12.30pm, and include entry to the theatre's interesting small museum. Concerts are also given in the theatre's recital room (for more information, tel: 2223 3523).

Adjacent to the theatre, just after the intersection with Old Mint Street (Triq Zekka), is the landmark domed **Basilica of Our Lady of Mount Carmel G**. Also known as the Carmelite Church, Cassar's original building (1570) was destroyed during World War II, but was superbly rebuilt and completed in 1958. Its mighty dome is a feature of the Valletta cityscape from wherever it is viewed.

War and peace

Return to Republic Street and, still on Palace Square, on the other side of the Main Guard, is the impressively proportioned **Palazzo Verdelin**, also known as Hostel de Verdelin or Casa delle Colombe, which houses an elegant restaurant (www.michaels.com.mt) and a police station.

After sitting through the newsreels of Stuka bombers and island devastation on show here, walk a little way along Republic Street and soothe your nerves at the **Casa Rocca Piccola H** (tel: 2122 1499; www.casaroccapiccola.com; Mon–Sat 10am–4pm). Not a museum, the house is still lived in and has withstood the ravages of time extremely well. The owners are very amiable and give a lively guided tour behind the scenes of the only patrician house in Valletta open to the public.

Fort St Elmo

At the very tip of the peninsula, **Fort St Elmo I**, first built in 1488, played a pivotal role in the defence of the islands during the first Great Siege. Unfortunately, because of the high ground that overlooked it, the Turks were able to breach its defences and the Knights suffered devastating losses. With the exception of a handful of Maltese who were able to swim to safety across the harbour, its complement of 600 brave defenders was slaughtered. Look carefully at its outer walls and you can still see the scars of 1565.

With the creation of Valletta, the land bordering St Elmo was levelled and the fort was repaired and enlarged to form a classical star-shaped fort as

The Grand Master's seat of power in the Throne Room.

The saluting battery in Valletta.

FACT

The splendid silver plates on which patients were fed at the Sacra Infermeria were mostly looted by Napoleon and melted down to pay for his Egyptian campaign. However, some pieces survived and are on display at the National Museum of Fine Arts.

part of the defensive bastion walls that encircle the city. During World War II, its bastions were manned by the coastal and anti-aircraft batteries of the Royal Malta Artillery. It is therefore appropriate that, today, part of the fort is devoted to the **National War Museum** ❶ (tel: 2123 3088; daily 9am–6pm, last admission at 5pm).

The items on display in this interesting museum document the island's resistance during World War II, and the most treasured exhibit is the actual George Cross medal conferred in 1942. This was awarded by King George VI in recognition of the "heroism and devotion" of Malta's people during the siege. The cross is woven into the design of Malta's flag.

Whilst walking around Valletta Bay at sea level, you can cross the new red pedestrian bridge, which links both sides of the St Elmo breakwater together, and is lit up at night. The old Victorian bridge was damaged during the war.

More information about the fortifications can be found at the **Fortifications Interpretation Centre** at St. Mark street (tel: 2122 8594; http://thefortressbuilders.weebly.com; summer Mon, Wed, Fri 9am–1pm, Tue, Thu until 4pm, winter Mon, Wed, Fri 10am–4pm, Tue, Thu until 7pm, Sat 9.30am–1pm).

Sacra Infermeria

Just a two-minute walk away, along Triq Il-Mediterran, is the **Mediterranean Conference Centre** Ⓚ (tel: 2124 3840/6; www.mcc.com.mt) – an uninspired name for such a fascinating place. For more than two centuries this landmark was the Sacra Infermeria (the Holy Infirmary) of the Order of the Knights of St John of Jerusalem. Work on the foundation began in 1574 and extensions were added over the next century.

Not only was the nursing that was provided of the highest standard, it also featured the world's longest hospital ward, the Long Hall, which, in 1666, was described as one of the "grandest interiors in the world". By 1787 the hospital had a complement of 563 beds, which could be increased to 914 in times of emergency. Patients were fed generous portions of food from silver plates. In November 2015, the centre housed the Valletta Summit on Migration.

The Upper Barrakka Gardens.

Today, there is public access to two parts of the building (separate entrances). The most popular is **The Malta Experience** **L** (tel: 2552 4000; www.themaltaexperience.com; shows each hour Mon–Fri 11am–4pm, Sat–Sun 11am–2pm, Jul–Sept no show at 2pm on Sun). This is a dramatic audio-visual show encapsulating the main events in the islands' history using the latest projection techniques. It also offers tours of La Sacra Infermeria (combined tickets with the show). The other exhibition area is devoted to the **Knights Hospitaller** (tel: 2141 7334; Mon–Fri 9.30am–4.30pm, Sat–Sun until 4pm), which explains the hospitaller aspects of the Knights' work through a series of tableaux. Admission to this exhibition will also enable you to see the Long Hall, as long as no commercial exhibitions are taking place.

Gardens with a view

Continue along Triq Il-Mediterran to the **Lower Barrakka Gardens** **M** for the fine sea views, a neoclassical monument to the first British governor of Malta, Sir Alexander Ball, and the Siege Bell. The last is dedicated to the victims of the second Great Siege of World War II and was unveiled by Queen Elizabeth II in 1992.

On Triq Il-Mediterran turn inland up the street of steps and then left on to Triq San Pawl to find the church of **St Paul's Shipwreck** **N**. Often described as Valletta's hidden gem, it has an ornate Baroque interior and claims to possess the wristbone of St Paul and half of the column on which he was beheaded in Rome.

Afterwards, return to the cafés around Republic Street for light refreshment, or head down towards the relatively new **Valletta Waterfront** development which is located on the Valletta side of Grand Harbour and provides a lively place to visit for lunch or dinner. Numerous eateries line the waterway, and the pretty painted doorways of 18th-century vaults provide the backdrop. Dating back more than 250 years, the original facade of the project was part of Grand Master Pinto's Baroque wharf.

Today it is has been completely renovated to bring something new to the city – seaside dining, with views across to the Three Cities or of the cruise liners

St Paul's Shipwreck Church.

The Auberge de Castille.

FACT

The Valletta Waterfront development is part of plans to regenerate areas of the island that have lain in ruins since the end of World War II.

as they come and go. It's a great spot for lunch or dinner, as well as shopping and strolling. The best way to get there is to take the winding walkway down from near Castille Palace, or the lift down to the bottom floor of the central MCP car park. The newest addition is a 58-metre high lift connecting the Grand Harbour with the Upper Barrakka Gardens and the city, which costs just €1 to ride. The new lift is built on the same site as the elevator that operated between 1905 and 1973, but which was dismantled in 1983 for safety reasons.

Castille and the Grand Harbour

One of the city's most handsome and most photographed buildings is the **Auberge de Castille** ⓿ that greets you if you enter the city by car. A wonderful example of Baroque architecture, it was redesigned under the instructions of Grand Master Pinto in 1741 by Andrea Belli, a Maltese architect from Zejtun. The high doorway, flanked by a pair of cannons, is approached by an elegant flight of steps. The exterior is magnificently decorated with carved stone, and inside there is a particularly fine staircase and an attractive paved courtyard. The restoration of the palace was completed in 2014. Today this is the prime minister's office and, unfortunately, is rarely open to visitors.

From here head for the spectacular views from the **Upper Barrakka Gardens** ⓟ. These gardens were recently made over, and are now a delightful place to relax and take in the views. This is the highest point on the 16th-century bastion walls that the Knights of the Order of St John built, and it provides a magnificent panorama of Grand Harbour. The harbour is often busy, with a steady stream of boats and the Mediterranean's best cruise liners making their way in and out. Tours of it depart regularly from the Strand at Sliema.

Just outside the Upper Barrakka Gardens entrance is another of Malta's audiovisual shows, Sacred Island (tel: 2122 2644; www.mecmalta.com/StPaulsSI.html; shows every 90 mins daily 10am–5pm), which takes a religious perspective on the archipelago. Close by, signs point to the **Lascaris War Rooms** ⓠ, which are burrowed into the solid

Grand Harbour, Valletta.

 Map on page 118

rock below the gardens. This underground complex (tel: 2123 4717; www.lascariswarrooms.com; daily 10am–5pm) is a honeycomb of map rooms and planning rooms where Malta's defensive strategy during World War II was plotted. It is a fascinating secret place, well interpreted with models, dioramas and a lively headphones tour. At the site you can book a two-hour tour to the War HQ Tunnel (Mon–Fri 10am and 1pm).

Near Castille Place in Merchants' Street (Triq Il-Merkanti), just around the corner, is the old **Palazzo Parisio**, now the Ministry of Foreign Affairs. When Napoleon Bonaparte took Malta he used the Palazzo Parisio as his quarters. Opposite is the former post office, which was also a former Knights' *auberge*. Stop by at **St James Cavalier** (tel: 2122 3200; www.kreattivita.org; Mon–Tue 9am–5pm, Wed–Fri 9am–9pm, Sat–Sun 10am–9pm, Jul–early Sept 9.30am–1pm, Sat–Sun 10am–1pm; free), the national centre for creativity. A great cultural space to explore, it offers art galleries, an art-house cinema and an intimate theatre space.

Museum of Fine Arts

Continue from Castille Place into South Street (Triq Nofs In-Nhar), across Republic Street to the **National Museum of Fine Arts** R (tel: 2122 5769; http://heritagemalta.org; daily 9am–5.15pm), an elegant building that began life as a private palace but was taken over in British times and turned into Admiralty House. Lord Louis Mountbatten, as Admiral of the Fleet, had his headquarters here. In the museum are Italian and Maltese paintings. The museum is due to close in September 2016 as part of the new city project (MUZA) and will be relocated to the Auberge d'Italie, on Merchants Street, under the authority of the European Capital of Culture Valletta 2018 initiative. This means that the museum will occupy the same place it did back in 1924. The idea is to convert it into a community-oriented, interactive, national museum, presenting four different stories and histories (Mediterranean, European, Colonial and Artistic) through objects and displays.

Illuminated manuscript from the museum in St John's Co-Cathedral.

Valletta Harbour.

MFC-6631

THE BRITISH INFLUENCE

The British may have left decades ago, but their influence is still clear today through a variety of quirky touches.

The Maltese Islands came under the protection of the British Crown in 1800. For the best part of 200 years, the islands were British and adopted many of Britain's customs and laws. Today, wherever you go there are affectionate reminders of those days.

Most people in Malta speak English, cars travel on the left, unlike in the rest of continental Europe, British street furniture abounds, and almost every football fan follows the fortunes of British clubs – especially Manchester United – even if they also have allegiances to Italian teams such as Juventus or AC Milan. British newspapers are even printed locally now.

Food and drink, too, shows a British influence. Not only do supermarkets stock all the big British brands, many cafés do a plate of sausage, egg and chips. Several of the islands' older bars have a pub-like feel, serve archetypal British beers and drinks such as pale ale and shandy, and go under British-style pub names.

The British armed forces may have moved on (their barracks are often now used as government housing estates), but as returning visitors they are always welcome. In the old days, *dghajsas* (water taxis) would ply Grand Harbour, offering to ferry servicemen across to Strait Street, Valletta's red-light district. Today, British expats are still welcome, and thousands have made the islands their home.

A striking salute to the days of the British, some red telephone boxes have been retained.

The Pub, in Valletta, was Oliver Reed's last drinking spot before he died. It now pays homage to him, as well as to pub life in general.

Recently refurbished, Victoria Gate in Valletta is the city's oldest gate. It was designed by Emanuel Galizia and named after Queen Victoria.

Bingemma Fort.

THE VICTORIA LINES

The wall known as the Victoria Lines was built by the British between 1870 and 1899 along a natural fault that runs 12km (8 miles) across Malta from Kuncizzjoni in the west to Madliena. Its purpose was to protect Valletta and the south from a land invasion from the north, just as Hadrian's Wall in Britain was built by the Romans to prevent an invasion from the north.

The Victoria Lines links four forts and a number of artillery batteries, but some sceptics still cast doubt as to whether the wall ever really had any military significance. One cherished theory is that it was built simply to keep the British armed forces occupied. In the event, British naval power was such that the defensive line was never tested.

These days, the wall is one of Malta's best-kept secrets. In the cool months it offers walkers some of the best vantage points for enjoying views over the island's threatened open countryside. In 1988 the Maltese government submitted the Victoria Lines for consideration as a Unesco World Heritage Site, and numerous protective efforts have taken place to safeguard them since.

Cruise liners have largely replaced Royal Navy ships, but their occasional visits are greeted with enthusiasm.

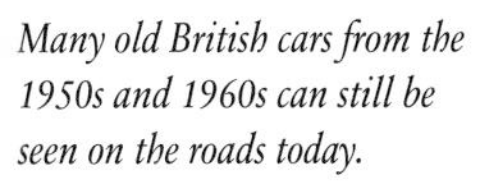

Many old British cars from the 1950s and 1960s can still be seen on the roads today.

Boats in Dockyard Creek, in front of the Maritime Museum.

THE THREE CITIES

Once home to the Knights, and later to the great dockyards that kept the British Mediterranean Navy afloat, today the Three Cities remains one of Malta's most atmospheric areas.

Main Attractions
- Inquisitor's Palace
- Pjazza Vittoriosa
- Malta Maritime Museum
- Fort St Angelo
- Fort Rinella

When Charles V of Spain gave Malta to the homeless Order of St John, they settled in the area known as Il Borgo, which was the home of a small but nevertheless flourishing community. Set deep in the safe reaches of the harbour, its creeks provided shelter for the Knights' galleys.

This spread of land, around the bay from Valletta, consisted of two promontories with dividing flat ground; Birgu (now Vittoriosa) and Isola (now Senglea with Bormla (now Cospicua) in between. Jutting out from Vittoriosa was Fort St Angelo, the only means of defence. Curiously, to this day, the Maltese living in this area cling to the old names handed down from the days of the Knights and call the Three Cities, respectively, Birgu, l'Isla and Bormla. Today's road signs, as if designed to confuse rather than aid, use either.

During the Knights' tenure, considerable sums were spent creating the kind of buildings the Order required, and the whole was wrapped in impregnable defensive bastion walls. Later, the British garrison made its own additions.

Docklands

Above all, this is the location of Malta's famous dockyards, the target of most of the bombing in World War II as the Axis partners persistently tried to destroy the docks and the ships undergoing essential repair work. Cospicua and Senglea suffered considerable damage during this time. Houses and streets were reduced to rubble and families were evacuated. Since then the whole district has been totally rebuilt, but much of it rather hastily. The small amount of historical or architectural interest that remained after the conflict is now masked by post-war building and development.

Religious statue.

A statue at Inquisitor's Palace.

Unfortunately, it is much neglected and in need of restoration and rehabilitation, but nonetheless remains an intriguing place.

Cospicua took the brunt of the bombardment in World War II but has since been re-established as a commercial centre around the dockyard. Its huge church of the **Immaculate Conception**, built in 1637, narrowly escaped total destruction and is worth a look inside. For a general visit, however, Cospicua is the least worthwhile of the Three Cities.

Vittoriosa

Vittoriosa, the least damaged and most fascinating of the Three Cities, is not yet a place for the average tourist. But as there are a few cafés and restaurants on the waterfront and some tiny local shops to serve the neighbourhood, for independent explorers, this is all to the good.

The whole entrance to Vittoriosa has recently undergone refurbishment works, so the area is looking in fine form and is ready to welcome curious visitors.

The Inquisitor's Palace

Start your visit on Triq Il-Mina Il-Kbira (Main Gate Street) at the **Inquisitor's Palace** Ⓐ (tel: 2182 7006; http://heritagemalta.org; daily 9am–5pm), a 16th-century *palazzo* that once housed the court, residence and prison of the Office of the Inquisition.

As the Pope's delegate, the Inquisitor was accommodated in style. Though its role was to combat heresy and protect the Catholic faith, this office was not quite as dogmatic when it was first established as the infamous Spanish Inquisition. It was only as the Inquisitor's power base grew stronger that it took on a more ruthless role. Two Inquisitors went on to Rome to become popes – Alexander VII (1655–67) and Innocent XII (1676–89). The office also provided 25 cardinals.

If the exterior is unprepossessing, inside there are fine murals, and the ceiling of the main hall features coats of arms of the 62 Inquisitors carved from wood.

The dreaded Judgement Room is a reminder of the brutal power that the Inquisition so ostentatiously wielded.

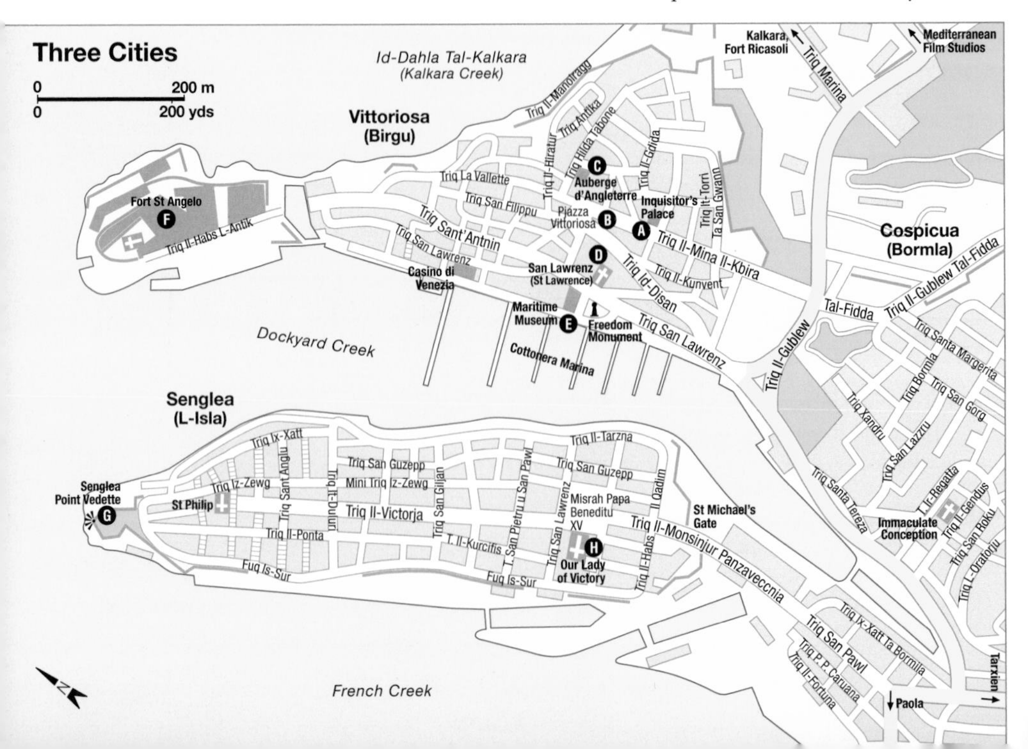

Map on page 142

Its door was made deliberately low so that each prisoner was forced to bow to the presiding Inquisitor on entering the room. Directly below here are a honeycomb of cells where victims were kept prisoner.

The palace is now home to the Museum of Ethnography, which focuses on popular devotions and religious values.

Pjazza Vittoriosa

Further down the road is **Pjazza Vittoriosa** **B** (Victory Square), the heart of Vittoriosa, with its balconied band-institute building and its inevitable Victory monument.

Just off here, turn right into Triq Hilda Tabone/Britannic Street. This was once the headquarters of the Knights and several *auberges* (Knights' inns) once graced this and surrounding streets. Name plaques recall former sites but the only surviving *auberge* is the **Auberge d'Angleterre** **C** on North West/Mistral Street, just off Triq Hilda Tabone. Today, this handsome honey-coloured building houses Birgu Local Council (open to the public Mon–Fri 8am–12.30pm, 1.15–4.45pm, Sat 8am–noon).

The Knights' church of San Lawrenz

The church of **San Lawrenz** **D** (St Lawrence), located on the waterfront overlooking the yacht marina and facing Senglea, is one of the highlights of any Three Cities tour. This was originally the conventual church of the Order of St John and contains many relics of the Knights.

Built in 1723 to replace a smaller church erected by Count Roger the Norman, it is a magnificent building in a picturesque corner. This was where momentous ceremonies took place. In front of it stands the **Freedom Monument**, erected in 1979 to commemorate the withdrawal of the British forces, while behind is the Church Museum containing the sword and hat of the most heroic Grand Master, Jean Parisot de la Valette (officially open daily 9am–noon but often closed, so enquire at the tourist office in Valletta before making a special journey).

FACT

The Freedom Monument marks not only the site of the British withdrawal, but also the very spot where Nelson's representative landed in 1799 to claim the island for Britain.

The church of San Lawrenz.

Shopping in Malta

Shopping has taken off in Malta in recent years, with backstreet boutiques and open-air markets providing all manner of delights

Not so long ago, well-to-do locals would not have dreamt of purchasing much more than their daily requirements from Maltese vendors – they preferred to jet off to somewhere more on-trend such as Paris, Rome or London.

Today, though, much of the islands has come to resemble an identikit international high street, with many of the same brands and products. If this is the sort of thing you're after, then Sliema should be your first choice. Here, global chain shops line every main street. It is also home to the Plaza, which was the island's first proper mall, as well as to the newest Point complex further along the road in Tigné. Just across the water, Valletta has become a shopping capital, too, and the products available tend to mirror those in Sliema. Meanwhile, designer labels have started to pop up around the upmarket Portomaso region, which attracts a steady stream of wealthy visitors.

Local glasswork.

There are more authentic options, however. For instance, Santa Lucia Street in Valletta is best known for jewellery, and tens of little shops line the road vying for business. In Gozo, the paths that lie parallel to Republic Street and the square are also good for netting local bargains in family-run boutiques.

If you're on the hunt for bits and bobs to take back home to a loved one, you'll find that most shops in the resort areas stock souvenirs – but few of them will be authentically Maltese. If it is local crafts that you want, the Ta Qali Craft Centre is a good place to start looking, as everything here is made on-site. The Mdina Glass factory (www.mdinaglass.com.mt) has become a stalwart of the area, as well as a popular local brand. Pop inside to watch the glassblowers at work, and then wander round the expansive showroom, which stocks everything from tiny glass figurines and Christmas decorations, to huge lamps and table sets. Items here have become very desirable, which has pushed prices up. Other local crafts include silverware, lace and pottery.

Food

Meanwhile, much like in Italy, food shopping has been taken to a whole new level. Aside from sprawling supermarkets, delis and specialised shops have become the order of the day. For local produce try Ta' Mena in Gozo (www.tamena-gozo.com), which is family-run and focused on selling only organic produce. Here you can pick up a bottle of local wine, goat's cheese or delicious honey, all of which will travel back with you brilliantly. Alternatively, the White Sheep on Rue d'Argens in Gzira (www.thewhitesheep.eu) promotes the exact opposite – a great range of scrumptious international treats, including cheeses, wines and sauces. Locals love it, and you'll find numerous pre-packaged items that can be transported away easily.

Markets

Of course, if you really are a bargain hunter, then you can't do better than one of the many open-air markets that set up shop to flog everything from fruit to fancy items for the home. The best ones include It-Tokk (www.it-tokk.com), which takes place daily in the main square of the Gozitan capital of Victoria, as well as the popular Merchants Street market in Valletta – although both have become increasingly commercial in recent years. Contrarily, the lively Marsaxlokk Sunday market remains as traditional as it always was. It is well-loved by locals, who swing by here to purchase the freshest fish for their family Sunday lunch.

Along the waterfront

Now walk through the grand entrance arch to the old dockside that forms the crowded Cottonera Marina, and to a splendid colonnaded building that once housed the old naval bakery. It is home to the **Malta Maritime Museum** Ⓔ (tel: 2166 0052; http://heritagemalta.org; daily 9am–5pm; charge), which features collections of model ships, actual Maltese boats and many exhibits dealing with the maritime history of the Maltese Islands, from the Phoenicians to the British occupation. The cafés and restaurants along here are popular with the yachting community as well as with locals, and provide the perfect spot to stop and enjoy the spectacle of the flourishing marina, with Grand Harbour and Valletta as its backdrop. The next building is known as Scamp's Palace.

Fort St Angelo

A short walk on the promontory jutting into the harbour leads to the **Fort St Angelo** Ⓕ, which is currently undergoing a major renovation that was partially finished before the meeting of the Commonwealth Heads of Government that took place here in November 2015. Acclaimed as a masterpiece of military architecture, it has a long and illustrious past. According to the records, the fortress was originally established AD 828 by the Arabs. Before that a Phoenician temple stood here until it was replaced by the Romans, who built a new temple to the goddess Juno. In 1090 Roger the Norman, Count of Sicily, erected a small chapel dedicated to the Blessed Virgin on the spot.

In 1530, when the Order arrived, Grand Master de l'Isle Adam set about converting this high ground into a fortress and during the first Great Siege, St Angelo was the Knights' impregnable command centre and pivot around which the battles were fought.

In 1912 the fortress became HMS St Angelo, headquarters of the British Navy, and received another severe pounding during World War II. Today, it is not open to the public. The chapel and cordoned-off buildings are the domain of the Sovereign Military Order of St John in Malta.

TIP

If you visit Vittoriosa by car, it is best to park around the Main Gate area and walk in along the marina.

MALTA AS FILM SET

In the days of the Order, Fort Ricasoli had a complement of 2,000 soldiers. Today film sets are built here, including those for *Gladiator*, *Troy* and *Agora*. The area around the fort is now the location of the Mediterranean Film Studios (www.mediterraneanfilmstudios.com), which offer film-makers two of the world's largest water tanks, both overlooking the sea and positioned in such a way as to give the cameras natural sky as their backdrop. One tank is a specially designed deep-water photography tank where scenes can be shot underwater in controlled conditions. Malta has become a popular film location as the local government offers various incentives to moviemakers. Recently, it provided the backdrop, as well as hundreds of extras, for Brad Pitt's blockbuster *World War Z* and the *Games of Thrones* series

A guard at Fort Rinella.

Where the Knights' galleys once tied up, now huge container ships drop anchor.

Senglea

On the opposite side of the water to Vittoriosa, Senglea is named after Grand Master de la Sengle, who fortified the promontory and founded this community in 1554. Despite the massive destruction that rendered it uninhabitable during World War II, it has regained a picturesque charm. Once, during Malta's boom period of the 1970s, it had all the makings of becoming an artists' colony when foreign painters, writers and sculptors moved into the houses and apartments overlooking the harbour. Now, with just a sprinkling of emigrés, it has returned to familiar local life.

Senglea's appeal stems from its excellent view over Grand Harbour. The harbour may not be as busy as it once was, but from the gardens, with its famous **Senglea Point Vedette** **G** sentry post at the tip of its promontory, both Valletta and Fort St Angelo look absolutely superb, particularly when floodlit at night. Carved on to the vedette are an oversized eye and ear, symbols of vigilance.

Below, ringing Senglea at the water's edge, is a pleasant walkway that heads towards Cospicua. In the cool of the evening, the still waters in the creek take on the appearance of a tranquil lagoon. The imposing 17th-century parish church of **Our Lady of Victory** **H** was rebuilt here after the war. The statue of Our Lady of Victory is paraded through the streets on 8 September – Victory Day – one of Malta's five national holidays.

Kalkara to Fort St Rocco

From Vittoriosa the road winds around Kalkara Creek to **Kalkara**. Many of Malta's traditional boats are repaired here or are wintered alongside the few craftsmen who still build the traditional *dghajsa* that was once used to ferry passengers to and from ships berthed in Grand Harbour.

Beyond is **Fort Ricasoli**, built in 1670 to guard the entrance to Grand Harbour. A short distance away is **Fort St Rocco**, one of the many small forts created by the Knights as part of Malta's coastal defence, and **Fort Rinella** with its daily costumed re-enactment of life in the fortress and the firing of its Victorian howitzer.

The Phoenician vedette overlooking the Grand Harbour.

Gallerijas in Three Cities.

Narrow street in Mdina.

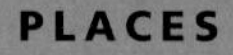
Map on page 150

MDINA AND RABAT

The Silent City of Mdina is a time capsule of medieval palazzi and a world unto itself, while beneath neighbouring Rabat lie fascinating underground discoveries.

The Romans called their town Melita, the Arabs Medina, and in the early days of the Knights it was known as Città Notabile. When the Knights completed the building of the new city of Valletta, the old capital was rechristened Città Vecchia (Old City) to distinguish it from the new. The Maltese, however, corrupting the Arabic, preferred Mdina and that is the name that stuck.

A strategic location

Because of a commanding position on a high ridge that runs along the southwest of the island, there have been settlements here since the Bronze Age. At over 150 metres (500ft) above sea level, the area has always been easy to defend, while below, it is surrounded by fertile fields able to produce abundant vegetables and fruit to satisfy a growing population.

After the Aghlabite Arabs had invaded and taken Malta, AD 870, these new conquerors began to extend the city's perimeter walls along the plateau ridge to encompass a suburb of dwellings they would call Rabat. Then, in 1090, when Roger the Norman, Count of Sicily, conquered the islands, he decreed that a cathedral would be built within the walls to make the city fit for Christians. It was erected on the ruins of a small sanctuary where the house of Publius, the first Bishop of Malta, had once stood.

Mdina's Golden Age

As the years passed and Malta fell into different hands, so the city flourished. Beautiful palaces gave the city a remarkable patrician air. In 1429, when the Saracens attempted to conquer Malta, Mdina stood firm because, as legend has it, St Paul appeared riding a white charger and brandishing a flaming sword to exhort the Maltese defenders. In recognition of this

Main Attractions

- Main Gate
- Palazzo Vilhena
- Mdina Dungeons
- Mdina Experience
- Carmelite Church & Priory
- Palazzo Falson
- Domus Romana
- St Paul's Catacombs
- St Agatha's Catacombs

A medieval cathedral overlooking Mdina.

Detail from Mdina Gate.

bravery, Alfonso V of Aragon, into whose hands the islands had now passed, gave the city the sobriquet of *Città Notabile* ("Noble City").

Over a century later, during the first Great Siege, the city once again acquitted itself with honours and possibly changed the whole fate of Christendom. Its cavalry garrison attacked the Turkish base camp just when victory looked to be within enemy grasp. The Turks pulled back and the tide of war was turned.

The Silent City

As the capital, Mdina was the seat of power of the ecclesiastical, military and civil authorities of medieval Malta. It was – and still is – the home of the oldest families in Malta. Within its boundaries are grand palazzi, monasteries, churches, cathedrals and museums.

For many years it was known as the Silent City because its narrow streets were unsuitable for traffic and its use had been purely residential. But nowadays Mdina is not so silent since residents with permits may drive in with cars, and restaurants, bars, cafés and tourist attractions have been opened in the historical buildings.

The streets were built deliberately narrow and angled so that the limited space would be used to best advantage

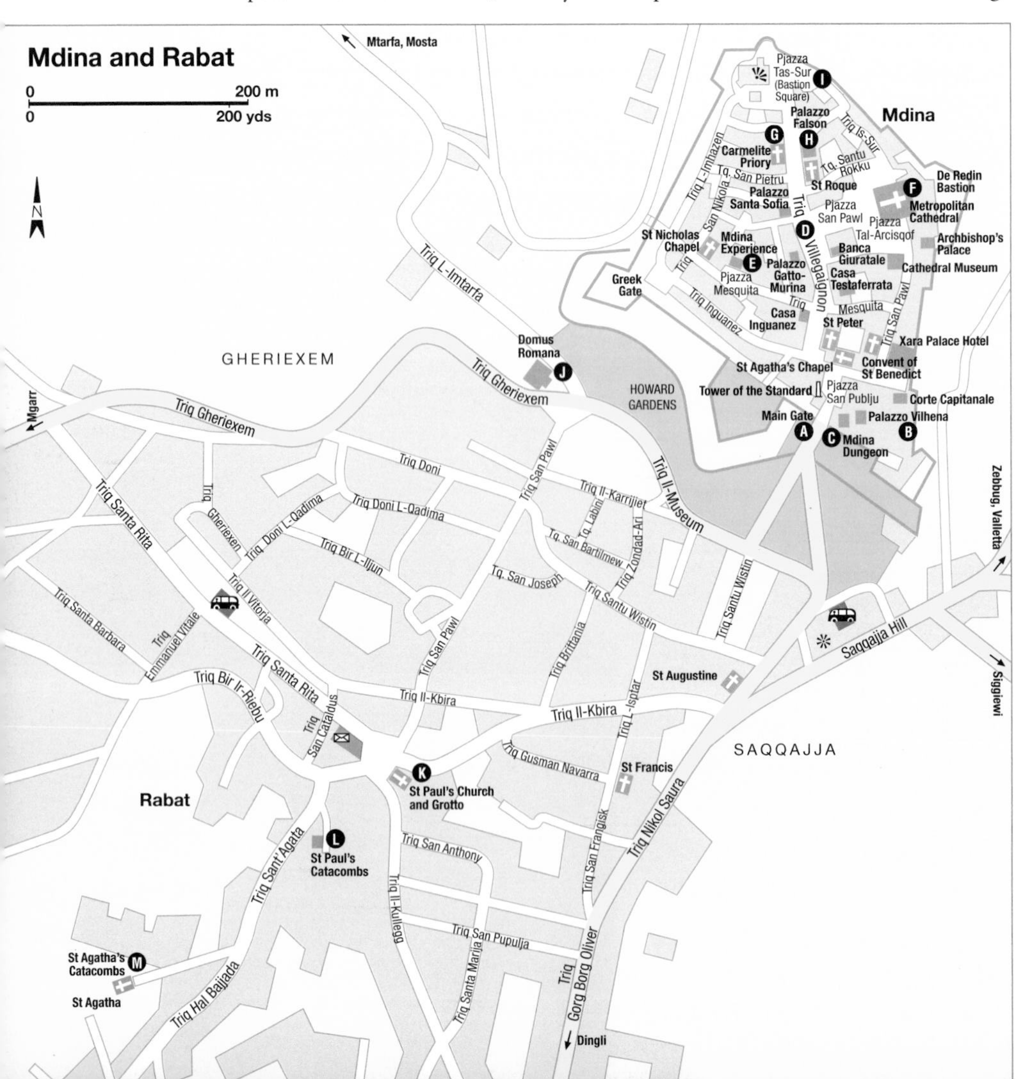

and cooling draughts of air would be circulated. The tall stone buildings cast cooling shadows on each other in the hot summer.

The city walls

Mdina is one of the world's finest examples of a medieval walled city that is still inhabited. The city's fortifications were completed after the Great Siege, and as the Order built Valletta, so they repaired Mdina and gave it the bastion walls that ring it today.

There are three entrances to the city. The Main Gate leads from Howard Gardens in Rabat outside the walls; the Greek Gate opens below into the dry moat's wide ditch and takes its name from the colony that lived in that area; and the "Hole in the Wall", which is exactly that. It was cut into Mdina's walls when Malta's steam railway was in operation and the citizens demanded easier access to the station below on the road leading to Mtarfa.

Entering the city

The **Main Gate** Ⓐ was constructed in 1724 on the instructions of Grand Master de Vilhena. A Baroque triumphal archway with imposing pillars, rich carving and an ornate superstructure, it was reached by drawbridge across a dry moat. This gate replaced an earlier, simple gate still visible in the outside walls to the right. On the inside are the arms of Antonio de Inguanez, which were removed during the short occupation by French forces in 1798 and replaced by a statue of Liberty. The present arms were placed there in 1886 by order of the British governor.

Inside, to the left of the plaza (St Publius Square), is the **Tower of the Standard**, currently the police station but dating back to the 16th century. It was on the top of this tower that bonfires were lit to warn the population that corsairs had landed or that the island had been invaded.

Facing the tower is the Magisterial Palace, the **Palazzo Vilhena** Ⓑ, dating from 1733. Now it houses the worthy but dull National Museum of Natural History (tel: 2145 5951; http://heritagemalta.org; daily

The Mdina Experience provides an opportunity to learn about the city's history.

Mdina Gate.

Antique doorknocker, Mdina.

9am–5pm), with its collection of stuffed animals and birds, as well as rocks and minerals.

Opposite here, the **Mdina Dungeon** **C** (tel: 2145 0267; www.dungeonsmalta.com; daily 10am–4.30pm) is anything but dull. It occupies a real dungeon and offers a grisly trawl through the horrors of sickness, death, torture and executions that plagued the islands in medieval times. It's best left to sensation-seeking teenagers and is definitely not for young children.

Triq Villegaignon

Straight ahead and to the left is Mdina's main thoroughfare, **Triq Villegaignon** **D** (Villegaignon Street). Along its length are Malta's finest houses, preserved by the island's ancient families. Many have private art treasures that would be warmly welcomed by museums in any country. At No. 6, **Casa Inguanez** dates to 1350 and has been in the family's possession since then. The Inguanezes are the oldest of the Mdina families; the Governorship of Malta was held by a Baron Inguanez until supplanted by the Order of St John in 1530.

On the corner of Casa Inguanez is Triq Mesquita, leading to Triq Gatto Murina and the **Palazzo Gatto-Murina.** The building has grace and style and is a fine example of 14th-century workmanship. Continue along Triq Mesquita to the **Mdina Experience** **E** (tel: 2145 4322; http://themdinaexperience.com; daily 10am–5pm), a multimedia extravaganza that combines an opportunity to learn about the history of the city with a chance to examine a Maltese patrician's house.

Return to Villegaignon Street and turn left to St Paul's Square, the spacious forecourt to Mdina's **Metropolitan Cathedral** **F** (www.mdinacathedral.com; Mon–Fri 9am–2pm, Sat 9am–1pm).

Mdina Cathedral

There were other churches on this site but the first documented cathedral dates back to the late-12th to the early 13th century. It is depicted

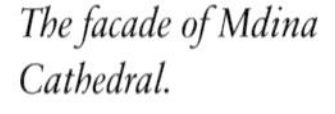

The facade of Mdina Cathedral.

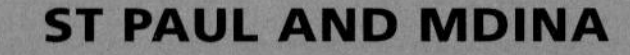

ST PAUL AND MDINA

The closing years of the 17th century heralded a new and exciting architectural period for the island. Self-assured and vital, the approach was Baroque in nature, Italian and Sicilian in origin, but with a character distinctly its own. Mdina Cathedral is probably the finest example of this unique Maltese Baroque style.

The site on which the cathedral was built, is, according to hallowed tradition, the site of the house of Publius, the chief man of the island, who, as related in Acts: XXVIII, lay sick with fever and was healed by St Paul, AD 60. He later became first Bishop of Malta. St Luke, who was travelling with St Paul, is said to have painted the icon of the Virgin that hangs in the side chapel dedicated to the Blessed Sacrament.

Map on page 150

in two frescoes painted by Matteo Perez d'Aleccio in the Palace of the Grand Masters in Valletta and appears to have been built in the south Italian Romanesque style, with a single nave, a high-pitched timber roof and a squat bell tower to one side.

In January 1693, the old cathedral was destroyed by a great earthquake that shook the whole of the central Mediterranean. Only the apse at the back of the cathedral survived, a credit to the renowned Maltese architect Lorenzo Gafà' (1639–1702) who, while working on the cathedral a few years earlier in 1681, had decided to strengthen its structure.

Gafà's masterpiece

Gafà' was again commissioned to design and supervise the new building, which he commenced in 1697. He was then 58 and, having benefited from the work of other Maltese pioneers and with a wealth of experience in church building behind him, he had reached the height of his architectural skill.

The monumental facade, with its interplay of balanced vertical and horizontal lines in the true spirit of the Roman Baroque, is constructed with two superimposed orders, the Corinthian in the lower level and the composite above. The central feature projects a little forward and carries a fine square-headed portal surmounted by a broken pediment containing the crest of the head of the diocese and the Maltese national emblem in heraldic symbols of red and white. It is flanked by the coats of arms of Grand Master Ramón Perellos (1697–1720) and of Bishop Cocco Palmieri (1684–1713). The slightly recessed side bays carry two towers with richly ornamented spires containing six bells, the oldest of which was cast in Venice in 1370.

The plan of the cathedral is in the form of a Latin cross, with a central vaulted nave and two aisles with small side chapels. The transepts, chancel and choir are of generous proportion, while the two small chapels on each side of the chancel are small gems of architecture. The floor is a superb

FACT

Mdina Cathedral is officially, in ecclesiastical terms, the Metropolitan Cathedral, while St John's in Valletta is the Co-Cathedral, the "co" meaning conventual as it forms part of a religious community.

Interior of Mdina Cathedral.

A shutter on a small window in the Carmelite Priory.

patchwork of inlaid multicoloured marble slabs, some macabre, some gaudy. They commemorate leading Maltese ecclesiastics, bishops, prelates, monsignors and canons, as well as prominent laymen, most of whom belonged to the Maltese nobility.

Decorating the cathedral

For decoration, the cathedral has a frescoed nave ceiling dating from 1794 featuring scenes from the life of St Paul, to whom the cathedral is dedicated. It was executed by the two Sicilian brothers, Antonio and Vincenzo Manno. The interior of the dome was painted as recently as 1955.

Mattia Preti (1613–99), who is responsible for much of Malta's glory, is the creator of the altarpiece of the choir, the apse above and the two lateral panels, all depicting various episodes in the life of Malta's patron, St Paul. The royal arms of Spain take pride of place in the centre of the arch surrounding the apse and recall the munificence of Holy Roman Emperor Charles V, who donated the islands to the Order of St John in 1530.

Two interesting relics that survived the earthquake that demolished the earlier cathedral are the marble baptismal font (1495) and the Irish oak sacristy door – a marvel of woodcarving (1520). Both bear the national emblem – a shield divided vertically in the traditional Maltese colours of red and white.

Gafà's architectural masterpiece, however, and the culmination of all his artistic work, is undoubtedly the cathedral's magnificent Baroque dome. Bold and dynamic, more sculptural than architectural, seen from a distance it rises high above the hill of Mdina and dominates the surrounding countryside for miles. The striking profile of the old city's skyline is one of the island's most famous.

The Cathedral Museum

Not to be overlooked is the fine **Cathedral Museum** housed in the former seminary (tel: 2145 4697; www.mdinacathedral.com; Mon–Fri 9.30am–4.30pm, Sat until 3.30pm). In addition to the usual ecclesiastical objects, it holds Italian and Maltese paintings,

Mosaic floor left by the Romans at Rabat.

several fine engravings (some produced by Goya), and a comprehensive collection of woodcuts by Albrecht Dürer. Other highlights are Byzantine enamel miniatures for celebrating Mass on ships and magnificent 11th-century illuminated hymnals.

Back to the main street

Continuing along Triq Villegaignon, other buildings of note include: the **Banca Giuratale**, built by Grand Master de Vilhena to house the university; the **Palazzo Santa Sofia**, on the corner of Holy Cross Street, reputed to be the oldest house in Mdina, with its ground floor dating from the 13th century; and the Carmelite Church, with a fine interior, built in 1659. The plundering of the Carmelite Church by French troops in 1798 was the final straw for the islanders and triggered their uprising against Napoleon.

The adjacent **Carmelite Priory** G (tel: 2702 0404; www.carmelitepriory.org; daily 10am–5pm) has opened its doors to the public, and developed into a fascinating space. The museum offers insights into the way of life of the cloistered Carmelite friars of the 17th century and fully showcases the impressive architecture of the priory. It is the only priory in Malta to be open to the public, but remains a functioning one, with the Carmelite friars living on the second floor.

A few yards further along from the Carmelite Church is **Palazzo Falson** H, also known as the Norman House (tel: 2145 4512; www.palazzofalson.com; Tue–Sun 10am–5pm). Originally built in the 14th century, and added to in the 15th century, it has been beautifully restored to reflect the domestic style of Mdina's 16th-century Golden Age.

Triq Villegaignon ends at Pjazza Tas-Sur, much better known as **Bastion Square** I, where there is a magnificent view of almost the whole of northern Malta. The great dome of Mosta appears a mere stone's throw away. By far the best way to take in the panorama is relaxing at a table at either of the two cafés that sit on the ramparts. The cakes at the Fontanella (http://fontanellateagarden.com) are excellent.

EAT

For a true taste of Malta, head to Crystal Palace, just opposite the Domus Romana in Rabat. Try the traditional ricotta or pea-filled *pastizzi*, washed down with a glass cup of sweet tea.

A fountain at Palazzo Falson.

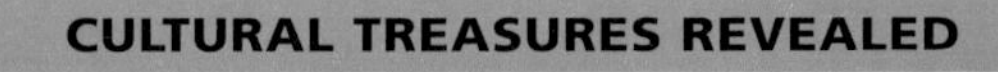

CULTURAL TREASURES REVEALED

The old capital has always been a very cultural space, but with the refurbishment of two important sites – Palazzo Falson and the Carmelite Priory, both on the main street – there is now even more to see and learn within the walls. Palazzo Falson is the former home of Capt Olof Frederick Gollcher OBE (1889–1962). A rather eccentric individual, his home is a treasure trove of items and artefacts that make for very interesting viewing. In 2001, *Fondazzjoni Patrimonju Malti* (Maltese Heritage Foundation) entered into an agreement with the Gollcher Foundation, and proceeded to restore the *palazzo* and all its contents to their former glory. Today run by a very capable curator, the museum has blossomed, and often holds talks on local antiques and other historical items – they are well worth attending if your visit is timed right (for more information, visit www.palazzofalson.com).

Meanwhile, directly opposite is the Carmelite Priory, a truly tranquil space that was closed to the public for centuries. Now open to visitors, you can explore it in earnest, taking in the old kitchen, friar's bedroom and stunning refectory. If you are lucky, you may be in Mdina on a day when the Priory hosts one of its classical lunch-time concerts – in which case, be sure to stop by, before enjoying lunch at the popular in-house café.

FACT

There is a theory that St Paul was held captive in the grotto in Rabat that bears his name. The holes in the wall are said to have held securing rings for chains and irons.

Rabat

Immediately outside Mdina's fortified walls is the suburb of Rabat, now separated from the city to which it was attached in Roman times. The Arabs, who wanted to give wealthy Mdina more strategic protection, first made the distinction. They cut a ditch into the plateau to isolate the city and shaped its outer perimeter to make scaling its walls a hazardous venture and deter potential assailants. Centuries later, the Knights built the dry moat and the steep impregnable bastion walls that still ring the city. Nowadays, Rabat is the commercial centre of this rural part of the island, with banks, offices, shops, a market and inexpensive restaurants.

On the perimeter road that separates Rabat from Mdina is the most important of the Roman remains found in this area. Once the house of a wealthy citizen, today it is **Domus Romana** ❶ (Museum of Roman Antiquities; tel: 2145 4125; http://heritagemalta.org; daily 9am–5pm), also called the Roman Villa (though in fact it was never a villa).

Its foundations were discovered in 1881 and above its mosaic flooring is a charming small museum of Roman antiquities, with a collection of the relics and statuary that have been found nearby.

For great views of Rabat and its surroundings, hop on board the **Melita Trackless Train**, (www.transport.gov.mt) which leaves from outside the Domus Romana daily on the hour. The tour takes you around St Paul's Cathedral in Rabat, the catacombs of St Agatha and St Paul's and onwards to Ghar Barka and the heart of Mtarfa.

Remembering St Paul

From the Roman museum, Triq San Pawl (St Paul's Street) leads straight into the heart of Rabat, to **St Paul's Church**, which is reputed to be the first recognised parish church on the Maltese Islands. Below it is **St Paul's Grotto** ⓚ, where the saint is believed to have spent some time after his shipwreck. Legend has it that its walls have miraculous properties and that scrapings from them will cure the sick if kept by their beds. For centuries,

St Paul's Catacombs.

visiting pilgrims have scraped pieces off the walls and yet (miraculously?) the grotto has stayed the very same size. In 1990, Pope John Paul II came to the church and grotto to pay his respects to St Paul.

The church itself was built in 1675 at the expense of a noble woman, Cosmana Navarra, and above its high altar is a painting of St Paul's famous shipwreck by Stefano Erardi. The adjoining **Church of St Publius** was built as an act of piety by Giovanni Beneguas, a Spanish nobleman who lived for some time as a hermit in St Paul's grotto.

The crypt contains a marble statue of St Paul and traces of frescoes. In the inner room are a marble statue given by Grand Master Pinto, lamps donated by Pope Paul VI and a Christian temple with an *agape* table (on which food was prepared by Christians in remembrance of the Last Supper).

Down to the catacombs

In Roman times it was customary for the bodies of the dead to be cremated, and burial on open ground was forbidden throughout the Roman Empire. In Malta, particularly, burial would have posed a genuine problem, due to the lack of topsoil. Elsewhere in the empire, Palestinian Jews, who did not believe in cremation, adapted to the laws without sacrificing their beliefs by introducing burial in subterranean vaults, and this practice was adopted by Christians. Soon these catacombs would also serve as refuges in times of persecution: places where Christians could hold their religious services in comparative safety.

It is believed that underground churches and catacombs abound in Malta, some known but buried under later buildings and others, so it is said, currently in use, with tiled floors and whitewashed walls, as modern household cellars. Beneath the streets of Rabat alone there are said to be several miles of catacombs, and in St Agatha Street two are open to visitors. Both comprise eerie, vaulted tunnels with stone-cut tombs, niches displaying ornaments or statues, canopies and *agape* tables.

Catacombs of Mdina and Rabat

St Paul's Catacombs Ⓛ (tel: 2145 4562; http://heritagemalta.org; daily 9am–5pm) were in use until the arrival of the Arabs, but were discovered only in 1894. The tunnels are very dark and, unless you have a torch, can be disconcerting. Ask for a map before you enter this mini-labyrinth.

A few yards along the street are **St Agatha's Catacombs** Ⓜ (tel: 2145 4503; http://stagathamalta.com/catacombs.html; daily 9am–4.30pm). Local tradition holds that St Agatha was in Malta and hid in Rabat's catacombs but later returned home to Sicily only to be tortured and die a martyr rather than marry the Roman governor of Catania. The principal feature of the catacombs are its many superbly coloured frescoes, most of which are medieval, but some date to before the Arab invasion. Sadly all have been defaced. Above the catacombs is the church of **St Agatha** and a small museum.

St Agatha, above the catacombs in which she sought sanctuary.

Cloisters at St Paul's Church, Rabat.

CENTRAL MALTA

Lots of things can be found in the centre – churches, crafts, gardens and a splendid palazzo – so do make the effort to journey to this slightly more undiscovered part of the island.

Main Attractions

- Mosta Dome
- Palazzo Parisio
- San Anton Palace Gardens
- The President's Kitchen Gardens
- Ta Qali Crafts Village

The best view of Malta, and particularly of the central part of the island, is from a helicopter. If you imagine it as a dartboard then the bull's-eye is the great dome of the church of **Mosta** ❶ (http://mostachurch.com). If you cannot get up this high then a good substitute is the bastion walls of Mdina, from where the immensity of this great building can also be appreciated.

The miracle of Mosta

Mosta Dome or, to give it its correct title, the Church of Santa Marija Assunta, can be seen from almost any vantage point in Malta. The islanders take great pride in its impressive scale. At 40 metres (130ft) in diameter, it "outdomes" St Paul's Cathedral in London by 6.7 metres (22ft), and is reputed to be either the third- or the fourth-largest unsupported dome in the world, surpassed only by St Peter's in Rome, Hagia Sophia in Istanbul and (though Mosta Dome officials are not much amused by this recent addition) the church at Xewkija in Gozo. Controversy still rages on this issue and unless you are prepared for an argument, it is best not to get too engaged in such local disputes.

Whatever its size ranking, the Mosta Dome is a remarkable church with an elegant interior, built amid great controversy to the design of Giorgio Grognet de Vasse that creates a round church rather than a church shaped like a Latin cross. The first stone was laid in 1833, and the church took 27 years to complete. Its generous size came about because it was erected around a church already existing on the site. The original one had become too small for the growing parish but could not be demolished until an alternative was available.

During the heavy bombardments of World War II, a bomb pierced the dome while the church was crammed full of parishioners sheltering from the air raid. It skidded across the floor but, miraculously, did not explode. A replica is on display in the church.

The geometrically patterned interior of Mosta Dome.

Naxxar

Just north of Mosta, and now virtually connected to it by continuous strip development, lies the town of **Naxxar** ❷ (pronounced "Nash-shar"). Like Mosta, it has a parish church of prodigious size: Our Lady of Victory was completed in 1616 by Tomasso Dingli, a prolific boy-wonder architect who distinguished himself with several notable churches in this part of the island. It is certainly worth a visit, if you can negotiate the traffic screaming all around it.

Opposite is the **Palazzo Parisio** (tel: 2141 2461; www.palazzoparisio.com; daily 9am–6pm; free access to the gardens). This is named after the same Parisio family whose principal house in Valletta was commandeered by Napoleon. The Naxxar house was rebuilt to its present state in 1898 for banker and philanthropist Giuseppe Scicluna, though he only enjoyed it for a year before his death in 1907.

The Palazzo Parisio is an outstanding example of a Maltese stately home, and the finest of its kind open to the public. It is said that its construction and furnishings set new standards for the island, and certainly its carved Lombardy furniture, stucco friezes, painted ceilings and Carrara marbles are remarkable. The great marble coping stone over the balustrade is the longest single piece on the island. It is said to have been transported by countless mules, and the full story is excellently explained in the audioguide.

Today the palazzo is still in family hands, and is run by the vibrant mother-daughter team of Christiane Ramsay Scicluna, Baroness of Tabria, and her daughter Justine Pergola. They have successfully transformed it into a thriving business – between the museum and the charming Luna Collection (a beautiful café, fine-dining restaurant and lounge bar), there is always a reason to visit. The gardens are also spectacular, and considered some of the best in the country.

The Three Villages

From Naxxar take the road to **Balzan**, which, along with **Lija** and **Attard**, make up the "Three Villages". Despite the promising olde-worlde title, don't expect to see villages in the conventional

DRINK

Malta's centre has become popular for its wine bars, often located in old town houses, and locals flock to them for a true taste of tradition. A favourite is Cellini Wine n'Dine (www.cellini-winedine.com; Mon–Sat 7pm–midnight), just across from the parish church in Naxxar, which serves gorgeous meat and cheese platters, as well as an ample selection of wine.

A peaceful corner of San Anton Palace Gardens in Attard.

FACT

For centuries, the Three Villages has been a very desirable address. Property prices are constantly high and there are superb patrician houses dating back to the 17th century.

sense. Indeed, you will be hard pressed even to distinguish one community from the other. In recent years the three have grown into one virtually amorphous mass, with their boundary lines known only to the residents.

Attard

The area is exclusive and the president's official residence is in Attard, at San Anton Palace. This elegant and stately house was the country residence of the Grand Masters from the early 17th century. Grand Master Antoine de Paule (1623–36) was the first to install himself and indulged in the decadent type of lifestyle that was to become the Knights' hallmark after the first Great Siege. In the British colonial era it was used as the governor's residence, and it has been occupied by the Maltese president since 1974. The palace is closed to visitors but the **San Anton Palace Gardens** ❸ are open daily, dawn to dusk (free).

The gardens are a favourite of expats and older visitors, and feature a surprising variety of subtropical plants. There are aviaries and some nice statuary to add interest but, the gardens' famous camel departed some while ago, along with other residents of its so-called zoo. There is a café inside the gardens, and beside the gate furthest away from the palace you will find the Melita Garden (www.melitagardensmalta.com), a gracious old house and garden that is popular for its bar facilities and its pizzas.

The **President's Kitchen Garden** (tel: 2122 6226; daily 9am–7pm; free) has supplied the palace with vegetables since medieval times, but is now a great option for families. Located just behind San Anton Palace, this stunning space has been opened to the public for the first time, and includes spacious grounds to wander through, as well as a lovely café.

In the centre of Attard is the Renaissance jewel of the church of **Santa Marija**, designed by Tomasso Dingli. The detailed carvings in the stonework repay a close look, and it is interesting to note that since the temple-like facade could not support a tower, in 1718 a bell tower was placed above the northern transept.

There is little else of sightseeing interest in the Three Villages, though

PARISH CHURCHES

The central region of the island features some of Malta's largest parish churches. The first of these, built to accommodate the fast-growing populations of expanding parish boundaries, were St George at Qormi and St Philip at Zebbug. They were erected to show village wealth as much as the visible face of the Church. But it is Attard's parish church, dedicated to Santa Marija, that heralds the splendours to come. It was designed by Tommaso Dingli (1591–1666) in 1613, when he was just 22 years old.

This young man went on to become one of the island's most prolific architects and is probably best known for his work on the parish church of Santa Marija in Birkirkara, a triumph of indigenous design and sculpture, and a fine example of a Maltese Renaissance church. Later, he went on to design the parish churches of Naxxar, Gharghur, Gudja and Zabbar. Not that they all remain, as Attard's does, as he envisaged them. As the parishes grew, alterations were made since many proved too small for their congregations. In fact, Dingli's Birkirkara church was never completed because even then they knew it would be too small. Our Lady of Graces in Zabbar was not only expanded but also given a new dome as the original was damaged by French cannon fire.

Our Lady of Victory, Naxxar.

if you are in the area on 6 August, Lija is renowned for the celebrations and superb fireworks at its *festa*.

Birkirkara

From San Anton Gardens it is a five-minute detour to the densely populated town of **Birkirkara** ❹ (road signs abbreviate this to B'kara). It's worth the trip to see the church of **St Helena**, an outstanding example of the Maltese Baroque style. The church was designed by Domenicho Cachia (1710–90) and replaced Tomasso Dingli's earlier church. The Knights so liked Cachia's powerfully proportioned design and his rich interior of frescoes, paintings and carvings that they awarded him the commission for Valletta's prestigious Auberge de Castille – a task that he fulfilled magnificently.

Two winding steps lead up to the platform on which the church stands. Aside from the twin-towered facade, the aisle screens and the entablature are striking features of a building that has been described as the finest parish church on the island.

Ta' Qali Crafts Village

Just outside Attard there are signs to **Ta' Qali Crafts Village** ❺ (Mon–Fri 8am–4pm). Built on the old World War II airfield, it is not the most attractive of places, with many of the corrugated Nissen huts and workrooms clearly still dating from this era. But if you want to see people making a wide variety of Maltese crafts then this is probably still the best place to come. Visit early or late to avoid the coach tours.

Pottery, lacemaking, weaving, silver working and glass-blowing are just some of the indigenous skills on show. Mdina glass (www.mdinaglass.com.mt) is the best known and largest business of its kind, and it is fascinating to watch the glass-blowing and -forming processes.

Nearby, the Malta Fair and Conventions Centre (www.mfcc.com.mt) has been a popular addition and has built its name as a venue for concerts, shows and trade fairs. Meanwhile, the **Ta Qali Family Adventure Park** (tel: 2292 8000; daily 6.30am–11.30pm; free), with its climbing frames and rope structures, is also within easy walking distance.

The Maltese Islands are famed for lace production.

A glass-blower at work at Ta' Qali Crafts Village.

Religious architecture in Sliema.

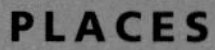

SLIEMA AND ST JULIAN'S

Building sites and coast-road traffic may mask the fact that this is a prime resort area, but the clear sea, smooth-rock beach, cafés and restaurants more than make up for that.

There has been a shift in the centre of tourism in recent years, away from the long-established resort areas of Sliema and St Julian's, to the newer purpose-built resorts of Bugibba and Qawra in the north of the island. Nonetheless, this large holiday conurbation, which runs from Msida, just outside Valletta, to St George's Bay, retains a great appeal for many visitors and is still the island's most popular hotspot.

The shaping of Sliema

Sliema is not only Malta's major holiday area, it is also the main residential area. This is where prestigious apartments sell to the upwardly mobile at what, by local standards, are exorbitant prices. It is also where Malta's wealthy middle classes reside, where children can walk safely to and from friends' houses in the evenings, and where there are many fashionable boutiques in which to shop. There may be a plethora of hotels, lively bars and crowded restaurants in the vicinity, but the core of the area remains residential.

Sliema was originally planned as a small resort for the residents of Valletta to escape to. With its pleasant coastline indented with small coves and its beaches of smooth white rocks facing the clear blue sea, this was where they would come in summer to relax, swim and take the fresh air. Indeed, there used to be a little fishing community, some smallholdings and a military presence in Fort Tigne, which was built in 1761 by Grand Master Pinto.

Gradually, as the wealth and size of the population within the city of Valletta increased, so Sliema began to take shape. Families moved out of the city to take advantage of what was on offer; villas and refined houses were built, land was developed, and Sliema became an established and desirable place to live.

Main Attractions

- The Strand
- Qui-Si-Sana Gardens
- Triq It-Torri
- Bisazza Street
- The Front
- Balluta Bay
- Spinola Bay

Small craft in Spinola Bay.

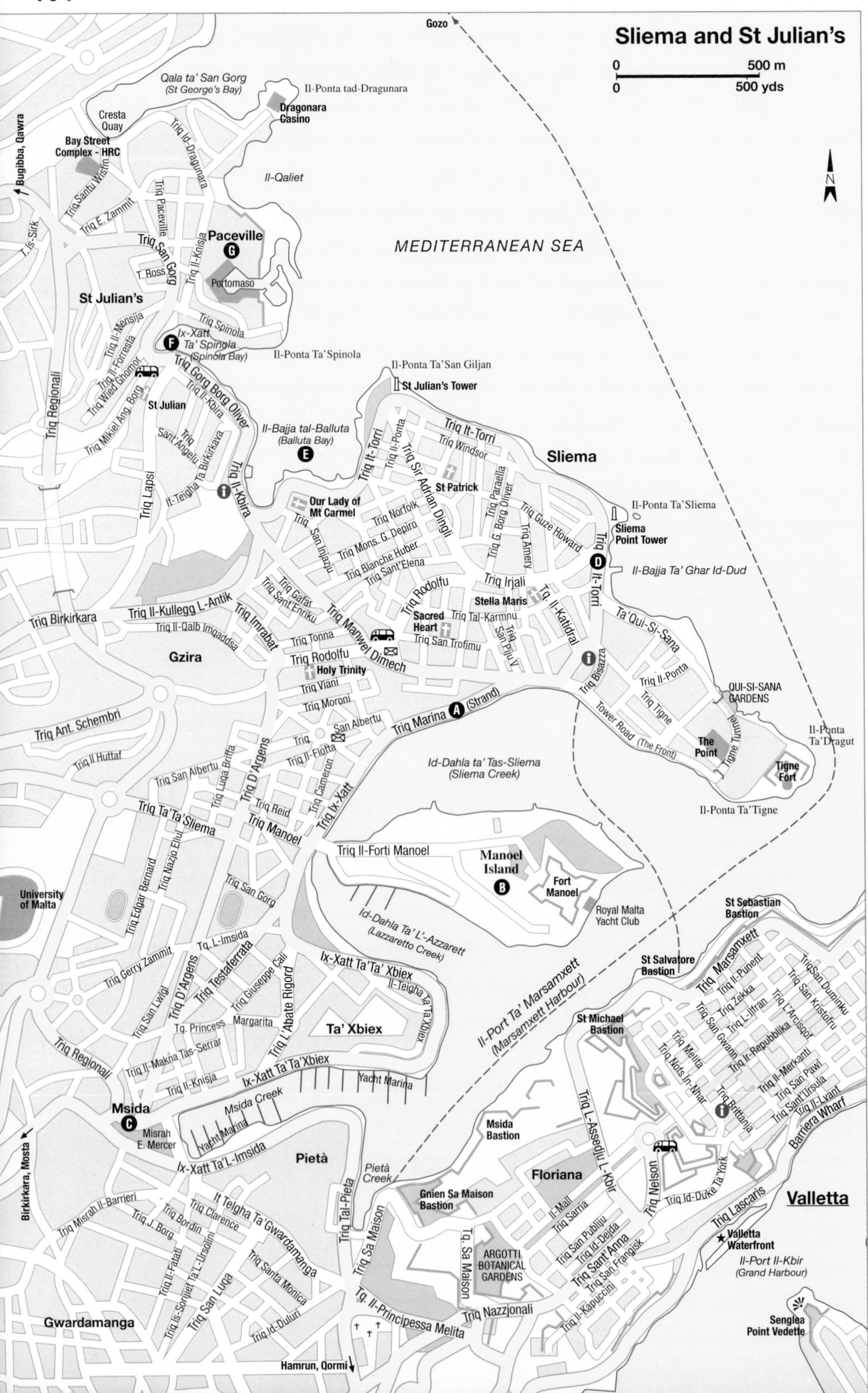
Sliema and St Julian's
0 500 m
0 500 yds
MEDITERRANEAN SEA
Gozo
Qala ta' San Gorg
(St George's Bay)
Il-Ponta tad-Dragunara
Dragonara Casino
Cresta Quay
Bay Street Complex - HRC
Bugibba, Qawra
Il-Qaliet
Paceville
Portomaso
St Julian's
Ix-Xatt Ta' Spinola
(Spinola Bay)
Il-Ponta Ta'Spinola
Il-Ponta Ta'San Giljan
St Julian's Tower
St Julian
Il-Bajja tal-Balluta
(Balluta Bay)
Sliema
Our Lady of Mt Carmel
St Patrick
Il-Ponta Ta'Sliema
Sliema Point Tower
Il-Bajja Ta' Ghar Id-Dud
Stella Maris
Sacred Heart
Holy Trinity
Gzira
Ta'Qui-Si-Sana
QUI-SI-SANA GARDENS
The Point
Tigne Fort
Il-Ponta Ta'Dragut
Il-Ponta Ta'Tigne
Id-Dahla ta' Tas-Sliema
(Sliema Creek)
Manoel Island
Fort Manoel
Royal Malta Yacht Club
Id-Dahla Ta' L'-Azzarett
(Lazzaretto Creek)
University of Malta
Ta' Xbiex
Il-Port Ta' Marsamxett
(Marsamxett Harbour)
St Sebastian Bastion
St Salvatore Bastion
St Michael Bastion
Msida
Misrah E. Mercer
Msida Creek
Yacht Marina
Pietà
Pietà Creek
Msida Bastion
Floriana
Gnien Sa Maison Bastion
ARGOTTI BOTANICAL GARDENS
Valletta
Valletta Waterfront
Il-Port Il-Kbir
(Grand Harbour)
Senglea Point Vedette
Gwardamanga
Birkirkara, Mosta
Hamrun, Qormi
Triq Regionali
Triq Birkirkara
Triq Il-Kullegg L-Antik
Triq Il-Qalb Imqaddsa
Triq Imrabat
Triq Manwel Dimech
Triq Rodolfu
Triq Marina (Strand)
Tower Road (The Front)
Triq It-Torri
Triq Sir Adrian Dingli
Triq Il-Forti Manoel
Ix-Xatt Ta'Ta' Xbiex
Ix-Xatt Ta'L-Imsida
It Telgha Ta'Gwardamanga
Triq Gorg Borg Olivier
Triq San Gorg
Triq Spinola
Triq Ta'Ta'Sliema
Triq D'Argens
Triq Manoel
Triq Ix-Xatt
Triq Ant. Schembri
Triq L-Assedju L-Kbir
Triq Nelson
Triq Marsamxett
Triq Ir-Repubblika
Triq Il-Merkanti
Triq Lascaris
Barriera Wharf
Triq Nazzjonali
Tq. Il-Principessa Melita
Triq Sa Maison
Triq Tal-Pieta
Triq San Luqa
Triq Sant'Anna
Triq Id-Duke Ta'York
Triq L'Abate Rigord
Triq Testaferrata
Triq Gerry Zammit
Triq Lapsi
Triq Il-Kbira
Triq Bisazza
Triq Tigne
Triq Il-Ponta
Triq Irjali
Tq. Il-Katidral
Triq Guze Howard
Triq Windsor
Triq Paceville
Triq Id-Dragunara
Triq Santu Wistin
Triq E. Zammit
T. Is-Sirk
T. Ross
Triq Il-Knisja
Triq Il-Mensija
Triq Il-Forrestа
Triq Wied Ghomor
Triq Mikiel Ang. Borg
Triq Sant'Angelu
Triq Ta'Birkirkara
It-Telgha Ta'Balluta
Triq San Ignazju
Triq Norfolk
Triq Mons. G. Depiro
Triq Blanche Huber
Triq Sant'Elena
Triq G. Borg Olivier
Triq Amery
Triq Paraella
Triq Tal-Karmnu
Triq San Trofimu
Triq San Piju V
Triq Gafar
Triq Sant'Enriku
Triq Tonna
Triq Viani
Triq Moroni
San Albertu
Triq Il-Flotta
Triq Cameron
Triq Reid
Triq San Albertu
Triq Luqa Briffa
Triq Il Huttaf
Triq Nazju Ellul
Triq Edgar Bernard
Tq. L-Imsida
Triq Giuseppe Cali
Tq. Princess Margarita
Triq San Lwigi
Triq Il-Makna Tas-Serrar
Triq Il-Knisja
Il-Teigha Ta'Ta'Xbiex
Yacht Marina
Triq Misrah Il-Barrieri
Triq J. Borg
Triq Bordin
Triq Clarence
Triq Il-Fatati
Triq Is-Sorijiet Ta'L-Ursolini
Triq Santa Monica
Triq Id-Duluri
Tq. Sa Maison
Il-Mall
Triq Sarria
Triq San Publiju
Triq Id-Dejqa
Triq San Frangisk
Triq Il-Kapuccini
Triq Melita
Triq Nofs In-Nhar
Triq San Gwann
Triq Il-Punent
Triq Zekka
Triq L-Ifran
Triq L'Arcisqof
Triq San Duminku
Triq San Kristofru
Triq Brittania
Triq San Pawl
Triq Sant'Ursula
Triq Il-Lvant
Tigne Tunnel

By the early 20th century, fine domestic architecture in cream limestone gave Sliema a subtle grace and elegance of its own. While Valletta remained the capital and business centre, those families who had not already decamped to the desirable residences of the Three Villages, now moved to new, attractive Sliema. A Sliema address implied a certain social status.

Sliema today

Although much remains the same, there have been significant changes, designed to accommodate the new wealthy Maltese, as well as the tourist or expat. Today's generations have begun to settle in the villages outside Sliema. Seafront apartment prices in central Sliema are some of the highest on the islands and many of the younger Maltese generation cannot afford the newly built apartments.

But, for every person ready to move out, there are two or more people ready to move in: people for whom the status of being able to say they live in Sliema really counts. This attitude has led to people on the south of the islands referring to people who live in Sliema as *tal pepe*, "the snobs".

Sliema is, as locals and returning visitors will confirm, not the place that it once was. In a matter of a few recent years, the wonderful seafront houses that created an elegant vista and made the promenade what it was have gone. In the creation of such an idealised vista, the land on which they stood became increasingly valuable and coveted. In their place now are towering, faceless blocks of flats and large hotels.

Holiday Sliema

Of course, none of this will be evident to first-time visitors. The main focus of activity in this area is the **Strand** **A** (Triq Marina), where a ferry connects to Valletta and boat cruises set off around Grand Harbour, and head further afield to the smaller islands of Comino and Gozo. The front buzzes with cafés serving snacks such as *pastizzi* or *timpana*, cream cakes, ice cream, cold drinks and cappuccinos. There are some good restaurants along here, too.

Most visitors to St Julian's and Sliema have come to Malta for guaranteed sunshine.

Sliema promenade.

TIP

Lots of outdoor spaces offer free Wi-fi, including the garden beneath Tower Road.

The tip of the Sliema peninsula is known as **Tignè**, home to the historic Tignè Fort. The area has recently undergone massive transformation into a thriving commercial centre and massive apartment complex. The development was not without controversy, though, as many locals believe it has changed the face of Sliema even more – especially when viewed from Valletta's bastion walls. Apartments here are some of the most expensive on the island, not least because of their stunning, unobstructed views of the capital.

Meanwhile, the three-storey shopping mall has decentralised Sliema, taking people away from the traditional shopping streets. **The Point** (www.thepointmalta.com) has attracted big-name international brands, including various high-street and designer labels, as well as a supermarket. Some Sliema store owners have argued that this is unfair competition, but it has proven quite popular – providing a cool, air-conditioned haven in the summer and a space to get away from the rain in winter. You will also find a variety of food outlets for when you have finished shopping, including familiar international franchises.

On the waterfront is the Fortina hotel (www.hotelfortina.com), which provides a classic view of Valletta, with the Carmelite Church rising like London's St Paul's Cathedral at the centre of a truly unforgettable cityscape.

Along **Qui-Si-Sana** waterfront (its name means the "healthy place") there are beach concessions with pools, bars and changing facilities.

Qui-Si-Sana Gardens

Sliema has undergone a huge transformation in recent decades, turning it from a simple resort into a sprawling concrete jungle. So, making the whole area more attractive has been something of a priority and the local council has striven to create more outdoor spaces. The results include **Qui-Si-Sana Gardens**, which boast lush lawns, play areas and lovely fountains.

Along the seafront

Opposite the ferries, a road-bridge connects the Strand to **Manoel Island** ❽.

Sliema viewed from above.

The Knights' quarantine hospital used to be located here and Fort Manoel was built in 1730 to protect the harbour. During World War I, the Knights' hospital was revived to care for the many wounded soldiers, earning Malta the nickname of "Nurse of the Mediterranean".

Today, the island, home to the Royal Malta Yacht Club, has a somewhat forlorn air about it, but this is destined to change; like Tignè before it, it is undergoing a transformation into an up-market housing complex and extended yacht marina.

The road continues around Lazzaretto Creek to Ta' Xbiex (pronounced "*tash-b-yesh*"), an exclusive residential quarter where many embassies are based, and on to **Msida** ❸. This is the biggest marina in Malta, capable of holding over 1,000 vessels at a time. Situated on the quay is the *Black Pearl*, once a star in the film *Popeye* now a restaurant (www.blackpearlmalta.com).

Along The Front

From the Strand, **Triq It-Torri** ❹ (Tower Road) cuts a congested swathe through to the other side of the Sliema peninsula. At the top of the hill it meets **Bisazza Street**. Together, these are Sliema's two major shopping streets.

As part of Sliema's transformation, Bisazza Street was pedestrianised a few years ago to encourage people to explore the area by foot, admiring fountains, artwork, plants and energy-efficient lighting. The monument to three of Malta's best-loved actors – Gemma Portelli, Charles Clews and Victor Apap – who sit on three chairs facing one another, creates a photo opportunity for visitors, encouraging them to sit in the fourth chair while their friends snap away. Sadly, vandals have targeted the monument several times, smashing the head of the late Charles Clews statue and damaging the statue of Victor Apap. In spite of this, the monument has stood its ground, and has become something of a central attraction on this busy street.

Along **The Front** – as locals refer to this stretch of Tower Road – there are more hotels, restaurants and

Sliema has churches to see as well as sunbathing opportunities.

Marsamxett Harbour, near Valletta.

TIP

St Julian's isn't known for its sandy beaches, but St George's Bay is a good option if you like the feel of sand between your toes. The facilities are good, though it does get very crowded. Just beyond it is the Bay Street Mall, another shopping centre with lots of great restaurants.

(public) rocky beaches, where both Sliema locals and tourists can enjoy a swim. In the evening it becomes a busy promenade. Generations of Maltese have enjoyed the traditional *passeggiata* here, walking, talking and socialising. This is where friends meet to catch up and where boy meets girl. All along The Front, there are ice-cream sellers, soft-drinks kiosks and market stalls selling jewellery and other trinkets (do bear in mind, though, that these are probably not made in Malta).

Balluta Bay

The road continues along the seafront to **Balluta Bay** E, passing some very well-tended gardens. Pop down to them if you have time; they make for a wonderful space for children to play and live-music events are often held in the summer months.

The coastline here is a stretch of smooth, flat rocks, which make excellent sunbathing platforms. The sea is clear and the shore alive with crabs and other marine life. Children will have great fun with the snorkels. Balluta Bay is also home to one of the island's best water-polo teams, Neptunes (www.neptuneswpsc.com), whose club and poolside lido are on The Front.

St Julian's

Balluta Bay runs almost seamlessly into St Julian's, and at **Spinola Bay** F (Ix-Xatt Ta' Spinola) the road reaches its busiest junction. This was once a simple corner where fishermen would land their catches in the evening – some still do – but now it is where most people head for a night out.

This is certainly one of Malta's most picturesque corners and features a clutch of fine waterside restaurants which enjoy a romantic setting.

Look out for the infamous Love statue, too, which was designed by renowned Maltese architect Richard England. It may spell "love" inside-out (the idea being that the sun's rays will shine through at certain points of the day, and magically make the word appear on the pavement) but it didn't exactly make

Many watersports are on offer in the area.

 Map on page 164

locals fall head over heels when it was first installed. Thankfully it has now grown to become a respected landmark in its own right.

On The Front, the San Giuliano and the Caffè Raffael (www.stjuliansrestaurants.com) occupy the former boathouses of the **Spinola Palace**. The palace, built in 1688, is still standing, set in lovely grounds on the hill directly above.

Paceville

At this point you are entering the heart of the package-holiday and nightlife part of St Julian's, with bars and restaurants coming thick and fast. This area comes alive only at night, when the epicentre of the action is the quarter known as **Paceville** ❻. During the summer, impatient traffic jams build at 2 or 3am, while a surging mass of bodies packs the streets, overflowing from the high-decibel bars and clubs that are the lifeblood of this tawdry area.

Uncomfortably close to Paceville, but tucked quietly away, are five-star hotels such as the Corinthia San Gorg (www.corinthia.com) and the Westin Dragonara (www.westinmalta.com), with their beach clubs (open to day visitors) and the Dragonara casino (www.dragonaracasino.com). Within walking distance is the Portomaso complex, with its high-rise tower, 10 restaurants, yacht marina and Hilton hotel (www3.hilton.com).

Portomaso has also become a local hotspot and residents flock here to enjoy the good-quality food, lovely setting and tranquil haven away from Paceville's busiest streets. The project won the Best Marina Development Category of the 2005 International Property Awards, which thrust it into the spotlight and helped to sell many of the 420 upmarket apartments.

Next door, the Portomaso Business Tower has also attracted a lot of attention – especially as, at 23 storeys high, it was the very first skyscraper to appear on the island's skyline. Now, though, it is home to many top local and international firms, as well as a luxurious casino and ultra-chic bar on the top floor.

Sunbathing in St Julian's.

HIDDEN GEMS

There isn't much architectural importance in the Sliema/St Julian's area, but there are some gems to look out for. For instance, the Balluta Buildings, just up from Balluta Bay, are a gorgeous example of the Art Nouveau style. The block may look a little run down, but it is reminiscent of some local architects' brief infatuation with that architectural era, and it lives on in their memory. Meanwhile, if the high-rises are stifling you, take a wander through Sliema's backstreets, where you will get a far more authentic feel for the town. Here, typical town houses still stand proudly, a local variant of Georgian-style architecture. Keep your eyes peeled for their traditional wooden balconies, which are often painted in beautiful, bright colours.

Restaurants on the seafront at Balluta Bay.

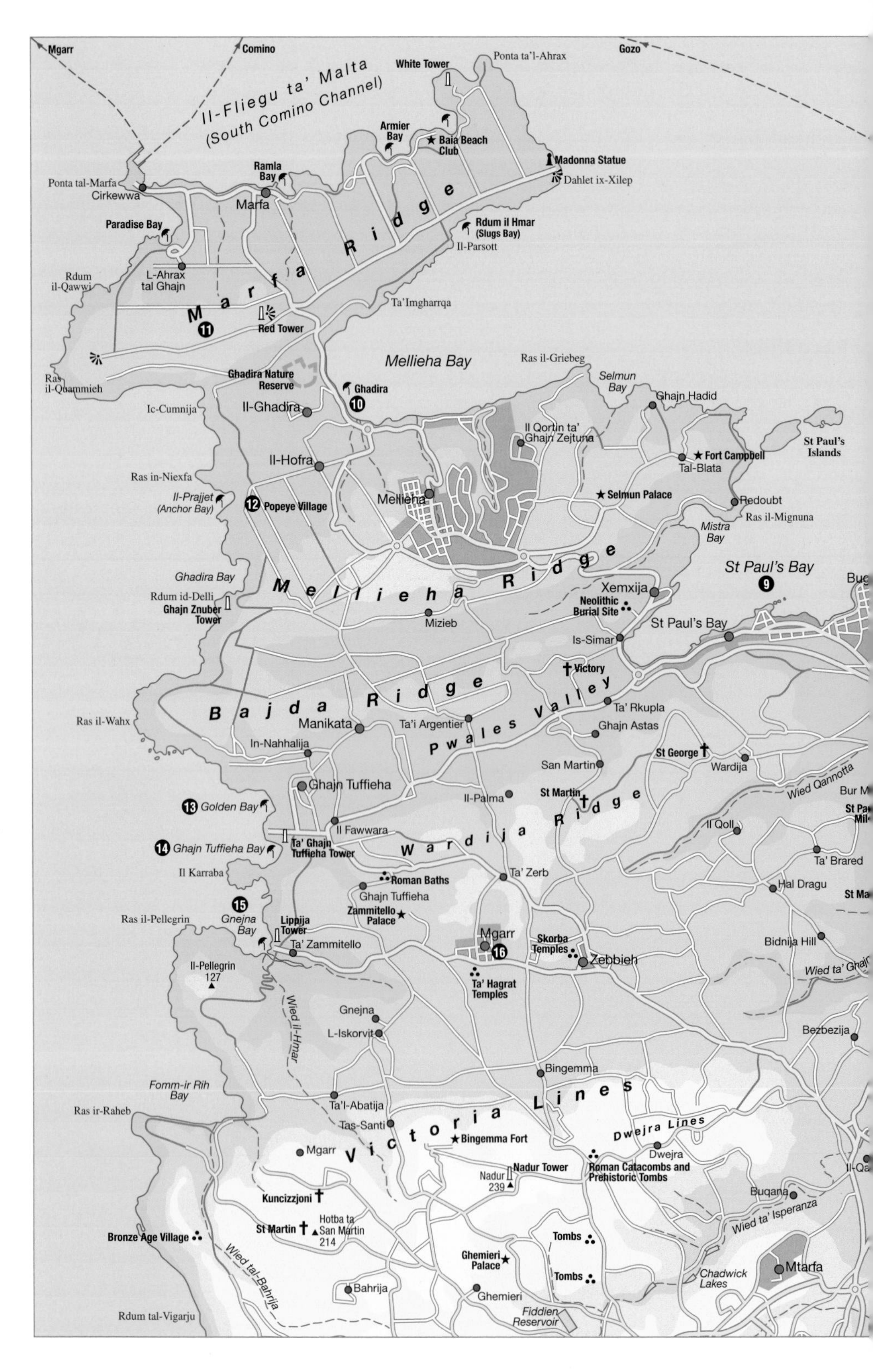

Mgarr
Comino
Gozo
Il-Fliegu ta' Malta
(South Comino Channel)
White Tower
Ponta ta'l-Ahrax
Armier Bay
Baia Beach Club
Madonna Statue
Dahlet ix-Xilep
Ramla Bay
Ponta tal-Marfa
Cirkewwa
Marfa
Marfa Ridge
Paradise Bay
Rdum il Hmar (Slugs Bay)
Il-Parsott
L-Ahrax tal Ghajn
Rdum il-Qawwi
Ta' Imgharrqa
Red Tower
Mellieha Bay
Ras il-Griebeg
Ras il-Qammieh
Ghadira Nature Reserve
Ghadira
Selmun Bay
Ghajn Hadid
Ic-Cumnija
Il-Ghadira
Il Qortin ta' Ghajn Zejtuna
St Paul's Islands
Fort Campbell
Tal-Blata
Il-Hofra
Ras in-Niexfa
Selmun Palace
Il-Prajjet (Anchor Bay)
Popeye Village
Mellieha
Redoubt
Ras il-Mignuna
Mistra Bay
St Paul's Bay
Ghadira Bay
Mellieha Ridge
Xemxija
Rdum id-Delli
Ghajn Znuber Tower
Neolithic Burial Site
Mizieb
St Paul's Bay
Is-Simar
Victory
Bajda Ridge
Pwales Valley
Ras il-Wahx
Manikata
Ta'i Argentier
Ta' Rkupla
Ghajn Astas
In-Nahhalija
St George
Wardija
San Martin
Ghajn Tuffieha
Il-Palma
St Martin
Wardija Ridge
Wied Qannotta
Golden Bay
Il Fawwara
Il Qoll
Ghajn Tuffieha Bay
Ta' Ghajn Tuffieha Tower
Ta' Brared
Il Karraba
Roman Baths
Ghajn Tuffieha
Ta' Zerb
Hal Dragu
Ras il-Pellegrin
Gnejna Bay
Lippija Tower
Zammitello Palace
Mgarr
Skorba Temples
Zebbieh
Bidnija Hill
Ta' Zammitello
Il-Pellegrin 127
Ta' Hagrat Temples
Wied il-Hmar
Gnejna
L-Iskorvit
Bezbezija
Bingemma
Fomm-ir Rih Bay
Victoria Lines
Ras ir-Raheb
Ta'l-Abatija
Tas-Santi
Bingemma Fort
Dwejra Lines
Dwejra
Mgarr
Nadur Tower
Nadur 239
Roman Catacombs and Prehistoric Tombs
Kuncizzjoni
Buqana
Wied ta' Isperanza
St Martin
Hotba ta San Martin 214
Bronze Age Village
Tombs
Ghemieri Palace
Tombs
Chadwick Lakes
Mtarfa
Wied tal-Bahrija
Bahrija
Ghemieri
Fiddien Reservoir
Rdum tal-Vigarju

The North and the Centre
0
1 km
0
1 mile
N
MEDITERRANEAN SEA
Ras il-Qawra
Salina Bay
Ras il-Ghallis
Ghallis Tower
Ghallis Rocks
Qawra
Salt Pans
Il-Hotba
Annuncia
Ta' Hammud
Qalet Marku
Ras il-Qrejten
Qalet Marku Tower (St Mark's Tower)
Il Blata I-Bajda
Mediterraneo Marine World
Splash & Fun Water Park
Madliena Tower
Ras I-Irqieqa
St Michael
Bahar ic-Caghaq (White Rocks)
Maghtab
Wied il-Faham
Ta' San Pietru
Wied il-Ghasel
Victoria Lines
Madliena Fort
Madliena
St George's Tower
Il Ponta tad-Dragunara
Paceville
St Catherine
Mosta Fort
Catacombs
Gharghur
Il-Mielah
St Julian's
Spinola Fort
Il-Ponta Ta'San Giljan
St Julian's Tower
San Pawl tat-Targa
Palazzo Parisio
Tal-Mejda
Il-Bajja tal-Balluta
Sliema Point Tower
Naxxar
Cart Tracks
Tal-Balal
Ta' Giorni
Sliema
L-Iklin
Msierah
Mosta
Ta' Raddiena
Gzira
Id-Dahla ta' Tas-Sliema
Manoel Island
San Gwann tal-Gharghar
Lija
Id-Dahla Ta' L-Azzarett
Birkirkara
Balzan
Ta' Xbiex
St Helena
Il-Port Ta' Marsamxett
Valletta
Gozo
San Anton Palace Gardens
Is-Swatar
Ta' Qali
Tal-Mirakli
Malta Fair and Conventions Centre (MFCC)
Santa Marija
Attard
Santa Venera
Msida
Gwardamanga
Floriana
Ta' Qali Crafts Village
Wied il-Hemsija
Ta' Qassati
Il-Hotob

Playing volleyball, Golden Bay.

THE NORTH

A mixed bag of busy entertainment spots and areas of complete tranquillity, the north is loved by holiday-makers of all sorts.

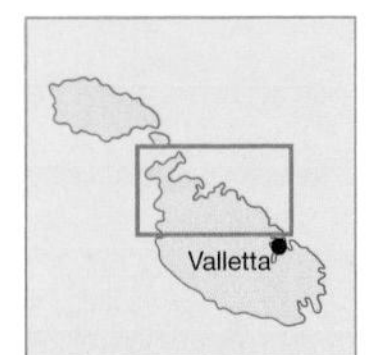

The road sweeps north from Sliema, out of the crowded suburbs and heading for the beaches and coastline of the north. But a beach to a Maltese sun-seeker doesn't necessarily mean a nice bit of sand, or even a foreshore of pebbles or stones. It can mean any stretch by the sea that gives access to the water and if it comprises great slabs and boulders of rock just a metre or two from a busy main road, then this is "beach", too.

It is this coast road, from Sliema to Qawra, that the Maltese find particularly appealing; at weekends they will drive from miles away to park their cars in one long ribbon, from end to end. Then they will stay until late at night, picnicking and barbecuing, and the return journey south can be excruciatingly slow.

Family fun

The road meets the coastline again at **Bahar-ic-Caghaq**. As this is a bit of a tongue-twister for most visitors (it is pronounced "bah-har i tchark"), it is better known as **White Rocks** ❻. Sharing a site here are three family attractions: the **Splash and Fun Water Park** (www.splashandfunmalta.com; daily summer only 9am–8pm); **Mediterraneo Marine World** (www.mediterraneopark.com); and a dinosaur-themed playground (daily; free). Splash and Fun claims to have the largest seawater swimming pool on the island, and its newest attraction is the death-defying Black Hole. It's best to come early in the day, however, as it is only a small facility and soon gets extremely busy.

Mediterraneo Marine World is also a small-scale park, although it does manage to put on reasonably entertaining dolphin and seal displays. The dolphins hail from the Black Sea and were rescued from a bankrupt water park in the former

Main Attractions
- Splash & Fun Water Park
- Mediterraneo Marine World
- Bugibba
- Mellieha Bay
- Paradise Bay
- Popeye Village
- Golden Bay

Ghajn Tuffieha Tower.

FACT

At Bur Marrad, 2km (1½ miles) south of Bugibba, is the Church of San Pawl Milqi, which means "St Paul welcomed". The Apostle is believed to have spent his first few days on Malta here. The present church dates from the 17th century and is now a museum.

Soviet Union. For a price, you can even swim with the bottlenose dolphins – a truly incredible experience.

Alongside the complex are the white rocks that give this area its name. Add a bright red-and-yellow parasol to the deep-blue Mediterranean background, and it's not to hard to see why so many Maltese families like this stretch of coast.

Qawra and Bugibba

After another 3km (2 miles) is **Salina Bay**, named after the local saltpans that have been worked since the days of the Knights. You will probably smell them before you see them, although plans are underway to regenerate the area and turn it into a working museum. The bay marks the start of the largest purpose-built tourist complex on Malta, which was completed in just under 10 years.

Straight across the bay is **Qawra** ❼ (pronounced "Ow-rah") with its impressive Seashells Resort at Suncrest and lidos facing on to Salina Bay. This is the quieter, slightly more up-market part of the development. The road continues around the peninsula, marked at its end by Qawra Tower, before it turns into St Paul's Bay. Once, this stretch of coast was fortified by the Knights, but there is nothing of historical or cultural interest here today.

Bugibba ❽ is the main town of the area. To impartial viewers it may look like a faceless sprawl of concrete, but to many thousands each year, this is holiday heaven. There is no beach (although a "perched" sandy beach has been constructed on a stretch of rocks), but it's a popular resort with both visitors and the Maltese themselves, and at weekends the latter pack out the local restaurants and the Oracle Casino.

St Paul's Bay

The most attractive part of Bugibba is its jetty, where pleasure boats make an enjoyable trip around **St Paul's Bay** ❾. Out here are **St Paul's Islands**, the site of the Apostle's legendary shipwreck, AD 60. It has been remarked that if this happened

SLUGS BAY

If you're feeling adventurous, why not incorporate a spot of rambling into your adventure. Harder to get to than most beaches, *Slugs Bay* (Rdum il Hmar), further along the rough road leading to the eastern tip of Marfa Ridge, faces Mellieha rather than the Gozo Channel. Because it is so difficult to get to, and access is restricted, little to no development has taken place here, which means it is still in impeccable condition.

To clamber down to it, there is a winding footpath whose small entrance is concealed in a car park and picnic area among the acacia and eucalyptus trees. Try to park your car where it can be seen from the main track, no matter how tempting it is to leave it in the cool shade of the trees on a hot day: unfortunately, cars are often broken into here.

The shore is starkly pretty, with room for just a few people on the patch of sand in its tiny bay. Many people prefer to swim off the flat rocks around the entrance, although most are sharp, which can make getting out of the water difficult, so be sure to exercise caution at all times. It is a remote and private place and, because of its ruggedness, it is never crowded. As a result, if you wish to get away from it all, it is well worth the extra effort required to reach it.

Mediterraneo Marine Park.

today, St Paul might be tempted to dive back in the water and try his luck elsewhere. However, the settlement of St Paul's Bay is no Bugibba or Qawra. This is a real community where the Maltese live and work and have fished the waters for centuries. Nonetheless, it has suffered major overbuilding.

At the head of the bay is Pwales Beach, though mostly sandless and not fit for swimmers. Continue around the coast road past **Xemxija**. On the hillside there is a Neolithic burial site (not signposted), where the dead were buried in womb-like tombs cut into the rock, suggesting a return to Mother Earth.

The road snakes upwards and just before Mellieha there is a turn-off to the **Selmun Palace**, a 17th-century fortress. Nearby **Ghajn Hadid Bay** offers a little-known small sandy beach.

Mellieha Bay

Superbly positioned on a high ridge, with its parish church of Our Lady of Victory on a spur, **Mellieha** has been named a European Destination of Excellence for its facilities and surroundings. These include excellent restaurants, which attract locals and visitors from across the islands.

Down the long winding hill below the village is the longest sandy beach on Malta. Its proper name is **Ghadira** (pronounced "aa-dee-ra") but to visitors it is better known as **Mellieha Bay ⑩**. Unsurprisingly, the beach is extremely popular and its amenities improve each year. There are cafés, beach establishments and all the facilities for renting windsurfing equipment and canoes, as well as water-skiing and parascending. It is very crowded at weekends, when families arrive early to select the best positions for their parasols.

Marfa Ridge

The best vantage point from which to survey Mellieha and its beach is from **Marfa Ridge ⑪**, the tall ridge of land that on the map looks like a fishtail on the end of Malta. To get there, continue on the main road past the beach and as you ascend

All the fun of the lido at Bugibba.

Bugibba seafront lido.

TIP

An excellent way to get off the beaten track and explore the headlands surrounding Ghajn Tuffieha and Golden Bay is to go horse riding. You can arrange this at the Golden Bay horse-riding stables, tel: 2157 3360.

the steep hill, take a sharp left turn. A short way along this track is the **Red Tower** (occasionally open to the public), built by the Knights in 1649. It takes its name from its distinctive red paint. Immediately below, you can look down to the small lakes of the **Ghadira Nature Reserve** (tel: 2157 2603; Nov–May Sat–Sun 10am–4pm; guided tours only; free), one of the very few places on the islands where birds can rest in safety, as the male population of Malta indulges in the controversial habit of shooting or trapping migrating birds. Marfa Ridge is one of the places that they do this – though the European Union is now stepping in to regulate this practice.

If you drive or walk a little further on past the tower, you will be greeted with marvellous views over to the Gozo Channel. It is very likely that while you are admiring the view from here, you will see the ferry steaming between Mgarr on Gozo and Cirkewwa on Malta.

The Marfa Ridge has a wild beauty, with rocky outcrops, fertile fields, plantations of acacia and the remains of many a *girna* – a small, round stone hut, only slightly taller than a man, dating back to the Bronze Age. Don't confuse these with the recent stone shelters you will see on the ridge, though – these are used by modern-day bird trappers.

Marfa Ridge beaches

At the northern end of the ridge are some pleasant beaches. The small, attractive **Ramla Bay** is dominated by its large hotel, well known for its beach and sports facilities (the hotel is also open to non-residents using the restaurant or café). Alongside is a small, free stretch of sand suitable for family picnics.

Armier and **Little Armier** are small, flat, unsophisticated sandy bays facing towards Comino – not "smart" beaches but nonetheless popular. Generally the facilities in these parts are simple and inexpensive, though for a more luxurious experience, try Baia Lido (www.baiabeachclub.com) next door, for a truly wonderful setting and lovely food.

View from the Red Tower.

Paradise Bay, 2km (1 mile) away on the western edge of the ridge at **Cirkewwa**, near the Gozo ferry terminal, is another attractive option, with a pleasant beach reached by narrow steps. It is usually sandy, but some years there is a lot of shingle. Paradise Bay is very popular with Maltese villagers for their coach outings, and can be particularly crowded at weekends, so it is best to avoid this time if you are looking for some peace and quiet. Kiosks serve simple refreshments.

Scuba diving is a popular sport at Golden Bay.

Popeye Village

Beside Mellieha Beach on the approach road down from Mellieha, there is a roundabout with a sign to Anchor Bay and **Popeye Village** ⓬ (Il-Prajet; www.popeyemalta.com). The former name comes from days long ago when a number of anchors were to be found on the beach in this pretty little sandy bay.

The latter name is much more recent. In 1980, *Popeye*, the movie (with Robin Williams in the starring role) was filmed in Malta, and Anchor Bay was chosen as the location for the rustic Newfoundland-style fishing village of Sweethaven.

Nineteen wooden structures made up the original fictitious village, though two burnt down in 1982, and all the special wood shingles used in the construction of the rooftops were specially imported from Canada. The rest of the wood was shipped from Holland and the village took more than seven months to complete, using a 165-man construction crew, armed with some 8 tons of nails and

Popeye Village.

Relaxing in the sun, Gnejna Bay.

more than 9,000 litres (2,000 gallons) of paint. It is said that the village was only built to last a few months, but it has stood the test of time much better than the film (which was a flop) and is now one of the island's most popular attractions for families with young children. It has really come on in recent years and now boasts a full programme that all ages will love, including fairground rides, activities and boat rides.

Golden Bay and Ghajn Tuffieha Bay

A road cuts through the Pwales valley from St Paul's Bay to two of Malta's most popular sandy beaches, Golden Bay and Ghajn Tuffieha Bay. Both are in a dramatic setting, each surrounded by flat-topped, golden-and-brown-coloured rocky cliffs with excellent stretches of fine sand.

Golden Bay ⓭ is the more accessible of the two, with an attendant-run car park close to the sand and a smart café-restaurant with a viewing platform looking down on to the beach. The Golden Sands Hotel has been totally rebuilt and there are other small beach facilities with plenty of refreshments, as well as the opportunity to rent a windsurfing board, pedalo or canoe. Don't swim if the red flag is flying as there are undercurrents here.

Ghajn Tuffieha ⓮ (pronounced "eye-n-toof-ee-ha"), whose unusual-sounding name has the intriguing translation of "the apple spring", is by far the prettier of the two beaches. There is no building in its backdrop vista, just a hillside planted with struggling tamarisk and acacia plants where, for centuries, goatherds have brought their animals to pasture.

It is a delightful place, accessible only by a long, staggered staircase down the side of the steep hill to the sands. The climb inevitably means that the beach gets less crowded than its neighbour, so head here if you are looking for a more tranquil Maltese beach experience.

Gnejna Bay

At the far end of Ghajn Tuffieha beach is a high and treacherous

Sunset at Gnejna Bay.

narrow clay ridge; below it, on the far side, is a tempting, smooth, cream-coloured rock promontory. On the far side of this ridge is another popular beach, **Gnejna Bay** ⓯ (pronounced "j-nay-na"), reached by road through the village of Mgarr or by clambering over a dangerous hillside. The sand here is mixed with shingle and, to accommodate all tastes, there is even a short stretch of smooth white rock for sunbathing on. On the left of the bay are boathouses cut into the rock. Refreshments are provided by mobile kiosks or vans.

Mgarr

If you don't fancy getting to Gnejna Bay by scrambling over the precipitous rocks from Ghajn Tuffieha, then you will have to go the long way round via the village of **Mgarr** ⓰. As in so many of Malta's villages, the village square is dominated by a handsome, oversized church. Dedicated to the Virgin Mary, it has a dome that is curious not only for its silver patina but also its oval shape (see margin). Mgarr is known for its two village-square restaurants, drawing custom from near and far to join its *fenkata* (rabbit-feast) evenings.

In and around Mgarr are some of Malta's oldest temple remains. Just 200 metres (656ft) off the square, heading back towards Valletta, is **Ta' Hagrat** temple (tel: 2158 6264; Tue, Thu and Sat 9am–noon). It's easy to miss as it is only signposted in one direction, and when you do find it you will wonder whether it was worth the effort. To the untrained eye, this small, tatty clump of stones is practically indecipherable and the site it occupies has been fenced off.

A couple of kilometres east, at Zebbieh, are the **Skorba** temples (tel: 2158 0590; Tue, Thu, Sat 9am–noon), the site of the earliest-known settlement in Malta, perhaps going back as far as 3,800 BC. There are signs of two temples and a number of houses, indicating that a flourishing fishing and farming settlement must have been here at some time. However, as at Ta' Hagrat, the site is unfathomable to the average visitor.

FACT

Mgarr's parish church is often referred to as the Egg church: when the parish needed a larger church, the parishioners went into business selling eggs to fund it.

Ghajn Tuffieha Bay.

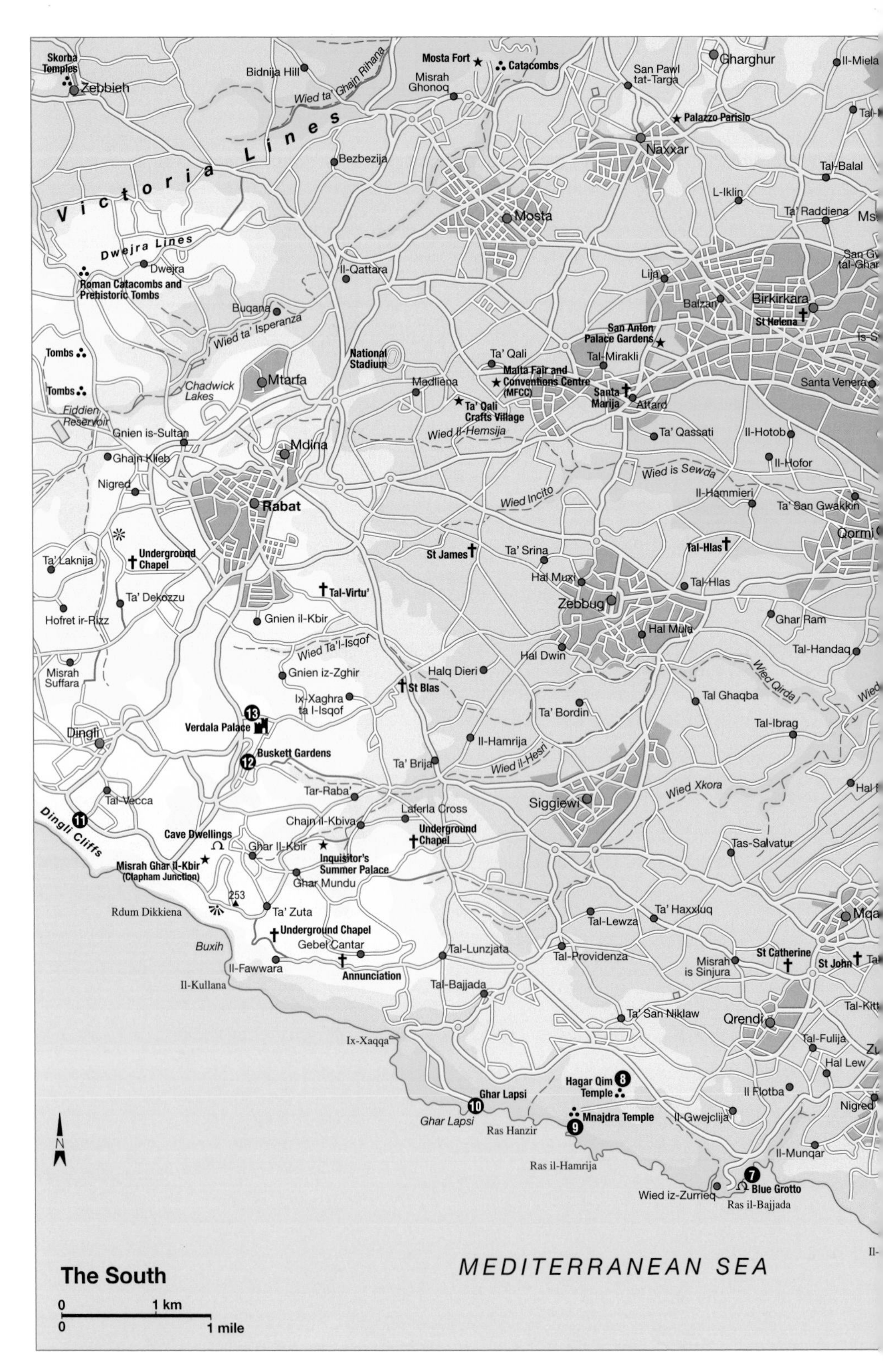
Skorba Temples
Zebbieh
Bidnija Hill
Wied ta' Ghajn Rihana
Mosta Fort
Catacombs
Misrah Ghonoq
San Pawl tat-Targa
Gharghur
Il-Miela
Palazzo Parisio
Naxxar
Victoria Lines
Bezbezija
Tal-Balal
L-Iklin
Ta' Raddiena
Mosta
Dwejra Lines
Dwejra
Roman Catacombs and Prehistoric Tombs
Il-Qattara
Lija
Balzan
Birkirkara
St Helena
Buqana
Wied ta' Isperanza
San Anton Palace Gardens
Tombs
National Stadium
Ta' Qali
Tal-Mirakli
Malta Fair and Conventions Centre (MFCC)
Santa Venera
Mtarfa
Chadwick Lakes
Madliena
Ta' Qali Crafts Village
Santa Marija
Attard
Fiddien Reservoir
Gnien is-Sultan
Wied il-Hemsija
Ta' Qassati
Il-Hotob
Mdina
Ghajn Klieb
Il-Hofor
Wied is Sewda
Nigred
Rabat
Wied Incito
Il-Hammieri
Ta' San Gwakkin
Qormi
Ta' Laknija
Underground Chapel
St James
Ta' Srina
Tal-Hlas
Hal Muxi
Tal-Hlas
Ta' Dekozzu
Tal-Virtu'
Zebbug
Hofret ir-Rizz
Gnien il-Kbir
Ghar Ram
Hal Mula
Wied Ta'l-Isqof
Tal-Handaq
Hal Dwin
Misrah Suffara
Gnien iz-Zghir
Halq Dieri
Wied Qirda
St Blas
Tal Ghaqba
Ix-Xaghra ta l-Isqof
Ta' Bordin
Verdala Palace
Dingli
Tal-Ibrag
Il-Hamrija
Buskett Gardens
Ta' Brija
Wied il-Hesri
Tar-Raba'
Wied Xkora
Tal-Vecca
Siggiewi
Laferla Cross
Dingli Cliffs
Chajn il-Kbiva
Underground Chapel
Cave Dwellings
Ghar Il-Kbir
Tas-Salvatur
Misrah Ghar Il-Kbir (Clapham Junction)
Inquisitor's Summer Palace
Ghar Mundu
253
Rdum Dikkiena
Ta' Zuta
Ta' Haxxluq
Tal-Lewza
Underground Chapel
Buxih
Gebel Cantar
Tal-Lunzjata
Tal-Providenza
St Catherine
St John
Il-Fawwara
Annunciation
Misrah is Sinjura
Il-Kullana
Tal-Bajjada
Ta' San Niklaw
Qrendi
Ix-Xaqqa
Tal-Fulija
Hal Lew
Hagar Qim Temple
Ghar Lapsi
Il Flotba
Nigred
Ghar Lapsi
Mnajdra Temple
Il-Gwejclija
Ras Hanzir
Il-Munqar
N
Ras il-Hamrija
Blue Grotto
Wied iz-Zurrieq
Ras il-Bajjada
MEDITERRANEAN SEA
The South
0
1 km
0
1 mile

Gozo
Pozzallo, Catánia
MEDITERRANEAN SEA
Paceville
Spinola Fort
Il-Ponta Ta'San Giljan
St Julian's Tower
Il-Bajja tal-Balluta
Sliema Point Tower
Sliema
Tigne Fort
Id-Dahla ta' Tas-Sliema
Il-Ponta Ta'Dragut
Gzira
Manoel Island
Fort Manoel
Id-Dahla Ta'L'Azzarett
Ta' Xbiex
Il-Port Ta' Marsamxett
Fort St Elmo
St Elmo Lighthouse
Il-Ponta Ta' Ricasoli
Fort Ricasoli
Valletta
Wied Ghammieq
Rinella Creek
Rinella
Fort St Rocco
Smart City
Floriana
Gwardamanga
Il-Port Il-Kbir
Id-Dahla tal-Kalkara
Kalkara
Dockyard Ck
Senglea
Vittoriosa
Ras il-Gebel
Hamrun
French Creek
Capuchin Monastry
San Pietru
Xghajra
Marsa
Il-Kortin
Cospicua
Kordin
Newport (Marsa Creek)
Cotonera Lines
San Leonardo
Fort Leonardo
Zabbar
Paola
Fgura
Buleben iz-Zghir
Has-Sajd
Zonqor
Hypogeum
Tarxien Temples
Tarxien
Il-Bidni
Ponta taz-Zonqor
Ta' Ciantar
Marsaskala
Marsaskala Bay
Ta' Buleben
Il-Gzira
Luqa
Santa Lucia
St Grigor
Il-Bajjada
Tas-Sienja
St Lucia
Tal-Barrani
Zejtun
Ponta tal-Mignuma
Mamo Tower
St Mary
St Thomas Bay
Bir id-Deheb
Ghaxaq
Ta' Lombardi
Misrah Strejnu
Secca il-Munxar
Gudja
Tal- Munxar
Il-Marnisi
St Paul
Ta' Garda
Neolithic Temples
Xrobb il-Ghagin
Marsaxlokk
Bur Maghtab
Il-Ballut
Fort Tas-Silg
Il-Karwija
Ras il-Fenek
Il-Fiddien
Il-Hofra z-Zghira
Wied Has Sabtan
Tal-Liebru
Ghar Dalam (Cave of Darkness)
Borg in-Nadur
Il-Biez
Safi
Tal-Galuhar Tower
Il-Fossa
St George's Bay
Peter's Pool
St Agatha
Misrah Hlantun
Ponta tat-Tumbrell
Birzebbugia
Il Ponta L-Kbira
Delimara
Fort Delimara
Marsaxlokk Bay
Rambla ta' Birzebugga (Pretty Bay)
Playmobile Fun Park
Slug's Pool
Ponta ta'Delimara
Ta' Ghammer
Ta' Salvun
Il-Mizieb
Hal-Far
Tal-Papa
Kalafrana
Hal-Far Airfield (Disused)
Benghisa
Ponta ta'Benghisa
Il Mara 190
L-Artal
Fort Benghisa
Ghar Hasan Cave
Il-Mara

Clusters of luzzus at the harbour.

THE SOUTH

Some of the world's oldest temples, Malta's most picturesque fishing village, dramatic sea caves, towering cliffs and shady woods are the highlights of the south of the island.

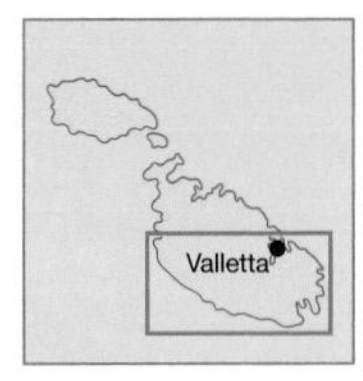

Main Attractions

The Hypogeum
Tarxien Temples
Marsascala
Marsaxlokk
Ghar Dalam
The Blue Grotto
Hagar Qim
Mnajdra
Dingli Cliffs
Buskett Gardens

The most fascinating of Malta's many temples is actually the closest to Valletta – the **Hypogeum** ❶ in Paola. It is also known as the Hal-Saflieni Hypogeum after the name of the immediate locality. Hypogeum means "underground chamber", and its subterranean nature sets it apart from the archipelago's other temples. In fact it was only discovered accidentally in 1902, when workmen were preparing house foundations.

The Hypogeum was dug out of the rock in around 3,000 BC by people using flint and hard rocks. They created a network of corridors and deep chambers on three levels. At the deepest level there appears to be a secret granary, which is reached by seven uneven angled steps that turn sharply to the right and have a sheer drop into a narrow chamber on their left. This deliberate drop is said to be a device to trap would-be thieves as they approach in the enveloping darkness.

Echoes of the past

The Hypogeum was a place for both ritual and burial. When discovered, it was full of fragments of bone and pottery, of which only a little has been retained. An estimated 7,000 bodies were interred here. The chambers are finely finished on a well-proportioned scale. The most impressive, commonly referred to as the "Holy of Holies", has pillars and lintels that are architecturally remarkable. The room was probably used for the sacrifice of animals.

There are patterns and symbols on the walls and there is an oracle chamber where a square niche was cut into a wall so that the priest's voice would echo around the temple. When the deep voice of a man speaks into the niche, the sound reverberates around the chamber; when a woman speaks into it, nothing happens. Two *Sleeping Lady* figurines were found in the middle chambers but, unlike the other

Marsaxlokk Sunday Market.

Taking to the waters of the south coast.

artefacts from the Hypogeum, these are now displayed in the National Museum of Archaeology in Valletta.

The Hypogeum was closed for much of the 1990s for restoration, and there were rumours that it would never reopen as the very breath of visitors damages the soft limestone. It has now reopened, but numbers are limited to a maximum of 80 per day (8 tours daily from 9am to 4pm). It is advisable to book around a week in advance, especially during busier seasons. Book online at www.heritagemalta.org.

Tarxien

A short distance by car, still in the suburb of Paola, are the **Tarxien Temples** ❷ (pronounced *tar-sheen*), which were discovered in 1914 and excavated with great care (tel: 2169 5578; daily 9am–5pm; charge).

This group of four temples is remarkable for the quality of its carvings, which include not only subtle decorative spirals, but also friezes of farm animals, among them a bull, crafted to represent virility, and a suckling sow, crafted to represent fertility.

Of considerable historical importance was the discovery here of the large base of a monumental statue to Mother Earth. It indicates that these early people had created the first-known free-standing statue of a deity. Had it survived, it would have been at least 2.5 metres (8ft) high.

Certain walls and floors of the temples are discoloured with a curious dark patina, which experts believe was caused in the late Bronze Age by the funeral pyres of a new people arriving at the temples. These latter folk cremated their dead, while

Neolithic bowl at Tarxien Temple.

the original dwellers interred bodies. The temples have recently been covered with a new protective tent; a new walkway has also added and an educational mobile application has been released.

The southeast corner

Leave behind the faceless suburbs of Paola and head west to **Zabbar**, which is entered via the Hompesch Arch, dedicated to the very last Grand Master of the Order in Malta, Ferdinand von Hompesch (1797–98). In the centre of Zabbar, the Church of Our Lady of Graces, known locally as Ta Grazzia, is a masterpiece of local church architecture. It was designed by the acclaimed local architect Tomasso Dingli, but took on its present appearance in 1737, when a new facade was added. The church is small but charming.

Marsaskala ❸ was once a quiet fishing village. Today, it has been taken over by apartment buildings and restaurants, and is a popular locals' holiday resort, if not the sort of place where overseas visitors come. Its large bay cuts a pretty picture nonetheless, with its flotilla of fishing boats and pleasure craft and a tall Italianate campanile as a backdrop.

Follow the coast road south to St Thomas Bay, a scruffy sort of place where fishermen's boats and broken huts litter the foreshore in a less-than-picturesque way. There is, however, that rare commodity, a sandy beach and plenty of rocky slabs on which to sunbathe. If it is crowded here, as is often the case, then a better alternative is **Peter's Pool** ❹, just south of here on the main road.

The path down to the pool is well trodden. There is no sand, not even a shore, but if you want to swim in a glorious natural lido, then this is the place to come. Just jump or dive into the deep, clear, blue water from the rocky shelving and watch where the locals get out. But stay away from the currents, which swirl under the rocky outcrops at the pool's end. If swimming is not your thing, there are some good coastal paths to explore and it's easy to find your way.

A word of caution: thieves sometimes operate in this region and will casually break your car windows to gain access. The best defence is to leave nothing in your car. If an "attendant" is there, it is polite to tip.

Marsaxlokk

Marsaxlokk ❺ – which, for the benefit of tongue-tied visitors, is pronounced "Marsa-shlock" – is quite simply the prettiest fishing village on the islands. It also holds Malta's largest fishing fleet, and the harbour, with its multitude of colourful *luzzus* (traditional fishing boats), is a photographer's dream.

A market is held on the quay daily, with fruit and vegetables for the locals and lace for the coach parties. Most visitors enjoy a meal of freshly caught fish, before returning to their coach. Despite its many day-trippers, the basic structure of the village is still largely untouched. Sadly, the

FACT

The south is probably the most traditional part of Malta, but it is home to some very modern developments, including Smart City (www.smartcity.ae/Malta/index.php), just outside Kalkara. This purpose-built, self-sustainable township for knowledge-based industries was built in partnership with the Maltese government and is currently in development. It is set to revolutionise this part of the island.

Young sailor in Marsaxlokk.

FACT

The spectacular Zurrieq *festa*, held to honour St Catherine, is held every year on 4 September.

same cannot be said for Marsaxlokk Bay. It was here that the Turkish fleet anchored prior to the Great Siege of 1565, and the bay was also used by the invading French in 1798. In the late 20th century it was defaced by an obtrusive power station.

The area around Marsaxlokk offers some of the best views of the island and is worth exploring on foot. **Delimara**, with its historic fort, makes for a picturesque stop and is just a few kilometres away from the centre of Marsaxlokk.

Ghar Dalam

Continue on the coast road around St George's Bay and, just before you get into **Birzebbuga**, signs indicate the route a little way inland to **Ghar Dalam** ❻ (tel: 2165 7419; daily 9am–5pm). Its name means "cave of darkness" and it is a natural formation some 200 metres (600ft) long, carved out by a subterranean river and only rediscovered and first scientifically investigated in 1865.

Its upper rock stratum yielded bones of humans and animals dating from the Phoenician period (1st century BC); the second stratum dated to Neolithic times (5,200–4,500 BC) and contained fragments of pottery with animal patterns, imported pieces of obsidian from Lipari and Pantelleria, and the remains of domestic animals. But it was a third layer of rock that yielded the most exciting finds: this dated from the Pleistocene era (1.8 million–11,000 years ago) and contained the fossilised skeletons, antlers and teeth of deer, bears, dwarf elephants and hippopotami (on display in a refurbished exhibition next to the cave).

Several similar fossils have also been discovered on Sicily and have fuelled speculation that the islands once formed part of a land bridge between the African and European continents, between present-day Sicily and Libya or Tunisia. Another theory is that a major earthquake broke up the land and caused severe flooding; this may have created the Maltese archipelago and separated the two continents.

The caves were also put to good use as an air-raid shelter during the intense bombing of World War II.

Ghar Dalam Cave.

From Bronze Age to Industrial Age

Close to Ghar Dalam is another ancient site, the scant remains of the Bronze Age site of **Borg in-Nadur** (visits by prior appointment only). However, there is no interpretation here and only the archaeologically inclined will get anything out of a visit. Of more general interest is the monument on the coast road that commemorates the summit between George Bush Snr and Mikhail Gorbachev that marked the end of the Cold War between the United States of America and the Soviet Union on 23 December 1989 (just a few weeks after the fall of the Berlin Wall). This was held on the SS *Maxim Gorkiy* cruiser moored in Marsaxlokk Bay, and sea conditions were so rough, with some meetings needing to be rescheduled as a result, that the event was nicknamed The Seasick Summit. Although no agreement was signed as such, the summit was largely viewed as marking a turning point in relations between East and West.

Signs along this road point invitingly to **Pretty Bay** and, sure enough, around the Birzebbuga headland is a sandy beach that, indeed, must have been pretty once upon a time. The panorama now, however, is dominated by the giant Kalafrana freeport container terminal, almost within swimming distance of the beach. This is one of Malta's most important sources of income after tourism and here the two clash in a spectacular visual juxtaposition.

The road winds inland past the disused airfield of Hal-Far, while the container port spreads itself thickly over this area, turning it into one giant industrial estate. Just past the airfield, look for the minor road signposted to **Zurrieq**. If you miss it, continue towards Luqa, then pick up the Zurrieq signs.

The Blue Grotto

There is little to detain you in Zurrieq but just south is the tiny picturesque rocky inlet of **Wied iz-Zurrieq**. Here, traditional Maltese fishing boats are moored in the water in great numbers

The design of luzzus may date back to the Phoenicians.

Boat trip to Blue Grotto.

FACT

Between Ghar Lapsi and Dingli Cliffs is the small settlement of Tal-Providenza. This is home to the Madonna Tal-Providenza, one of Malta's best Baroque churches.

or hauled ashore to be repainted in fine colours. It is a spectacular drive into Wied iz-Zurrieq along the cliffs. From its jetty beneath the simple cafés and souvenir shops, small boats taking up to eight passengers at a time ferry visitors to the charming **Blue Grotto** ❼. The best time to go is in the early morning, when the light reflected through the caves brings out the colour. Don't worry about being cheated on the price of a trip. A few years ago this was a concern, but nowadays these are government-regulated and clearly marked with a bona fide ticket booth. Boats start running at around 8am and finish at 4pm every day in summer.

Hagar Qim

Continue on the same road to the famous temples of Hagar Qim and Mnajdra (tel: 2142 4231; daily 9am–5pm, until 7pm in summer).

Hagar Qim ❽, pronounced "hadge-are eem", means standing stones. It is at the top of the hill (by the car park) and is almost completely surrounded by a curtain wall, with three massive standing stones set into it. When the site was discovered in 1839, the *Maltese Venus*, the statue of the *Seated Woman* and several other female figurines were all found here. Many of these figurines, with emphasised body parts, are thought to be ancient tributes to fertility. They now reside at the Archaeological Museum in Valletta. The monumental facade is very impressive and gives a good impression of the huge scale of these megalithic structures. Originally, they had wooden roofs but these have long since rotted away.

A corridor leads to the interior that is made up of a series of round chambers, almost all of which have their own entrance. Both Hagar Qim and Mnajdra were used for sacrifices, with libations of milk and blood presented at the altars. The altars are upturned mushroom-shaped, possibly to stop the sacrificial blood from dripping off the edge. They were shrines to Mother Earth and it was probably believed that the dead returned to her womb only if sacrifices were offered. In the chambers there are decorated stones, libation altars and tie holes where

Hagar Qim temples.

AHEAD OF THE TIMES

According to a recent theory, the temples at Mnajdra, like the circle at Stonehenge in Britain, fulfilled some kind of calendary function. The main entrance faces east, and during the spring and autumn solstice, the first ray of sunlight falls on a stone slab on the rear wall of the second kidney-shaped chamber. Then, during the winter and summer solstice, the first ray touches the corners of two stone pillars in the section connecting the two stone chambers.

Meanwhile, the two kidney-shaped chambers at the main entrance and in the connecting section were created with particular care. Today we talk of the precision of watchmakers; 5,000 years ago, the precision of the "calendar people" of Malta may have been just as famous.

curtains were hung in order to conceal the priestesses.

Mnajdra and Ghar Lapsi

The site of **Mnajdra** ❾ (pronounced "im-na-eed-rah"), a five-minute walk down the steep hillside with the broad blue sea as a backdrop, is much more romantic than that of Hagar Qim. The temples here have been dated to around 3,700 BC, predating Hagar Qim by some 900 years. The badly reconstructed eastern temple consists of just one chamber and is thought to be the oldest; the two-chambered temple attached to it is probably the most recent section. The southern complex is the second oldest.

Just west of the Mnajdra temples is **Ghar Lapsi** ❿, a popular bathing spot with the locals. After a hot day exploring the ancient temples it is an excellent place to take a dip. There is limited foreshore, but the locals have contrived to make this into a natural lido, with iron steps provided to make the cool clear waters easily accessible. Scuba divers also find its underwater world beautiful.

The island of Filfla

The walk to Mnajdra also gives an excellent view of the tiny island of **Filfla**. This island sits right opposite Dingli Cliffs and is a barren and uninhabited islet that has proved fascinating throughout history. Because of the mysterious way the rock stands in the water and the way the setting midsummer sun catches it, Filfla may have been an integral part of temple ritual and the reason why the temples were built in this exposed position.

More recently, the island was used for target practice by British warships. Local lore has it that two-tailed lizards live here among the unexploded shells. Filfla has been declared a nature reserve but law-breakers, instead of landing, now pass by on boats to shoot the resting migratory birds. Access to it is only given for scientific or educational research and prior permission must be given.

The island of Filfla.

Dingli Cliffs

From Ghar Lapsi turn inland towards Siggiewi, head briefly towards Rabat, then south back towards the coast

An aerial view of Ghar Lapsi.

Ghar Lapsi.

and **Dingli Cliffs ⓫**, Malta's highest point. Eventually the road heading north runs out of asphalt. It's a good idea to stretch your legs at this point. There are stunning views down some 250 metres (800ft) to the waves below, and also far out to sea. This is one of the islanders' favourite walking spots.

Close to the Dingli Cliffs is the enigmatic **Clapham Junction** (Misrah Ghar il-Kbir), where the sharp-eyed may see the best examples of Malta's famous cart tracks (see page 31). It was the remaining traces of these mysterious tracks that supposedly prompted a visiting Englishman to remark that the area reminded him of Clapham Junction, one of London's busiest train stations.

The Inquisitor's Summer Palace

Also close by, along a country road down the lush valley to Siggiewi, is the **Inquisitor's Summer Palace**. A remarkable and beautiful house concealed on the side of the hill, it was built in 1625 by the Inquisitor, Horatus Visconti, as his summer residence. The elegant building is only one room deep, with all rooms interconnecting. There is a small chapel at one end and beneath its terrace apron are deep caves where the Inquisitor's staff are said to have lived. For years, the palace lay abandoned. Now it has been renovated and is used by the prime minister as his summer residence (open only occasionally to visitors).

Buskett Gardens

Buskett Gardens ⓬ is Malta's largest wooded area – a delightful spot, cool and shady in summer, ripe with oranges in winter. The name "gardens" is something of a misnomer as this is essentially a wood comprising fir, oak, olive trees and citrus groves, and gets its name from the Italian, *boschetto*, meaning "a place where aromatic firs grow."

Buskett is particularly popular with picnickers, and for more than 300 years, on 29 June, one of the most popular *festas* in Malta, *Mnarja* – the feast day of St Peter and St Paul – has

Dingli Cliffs.

Map on page 180

been celebrated here. Its name comes from the Latin word *illuminaria*, used originally by the clergy to describe the lighting up of the churches of Mdina and Rabat in honour of the two saints.

The day traditionally starts with horse and donkey races on a road that leads up to the Saqqija hill entrance into Rabat. Here, there is a stone balcony on which successive Grand Masters and governors sat to watch the races, and later present banners to the winners. These were then taken by the winners to adorn their parish church.

Today, excitable crowds gather in Buskett Gardens to cook rabbit, drink wine, and sing and dance well into the night.

Verdala Palace

On the northern outskirts of Buskett Gardens, on elevated ground surrounded by woodland, is **Verdala Palace** ⓭, a silent, romantic castle, which is half-villa and half-fort (rarely open to visitors; for information tel: 2122 2966).

Designed by Gerolamo Cassar in 1586 for Grand Master Fra Hugues de Verdale, Verdala may look like a traditional medieval castle, but it was never designed to withstand serious assault. However, its four corner towers are positioned to afford excellent musket fire should it ever be required. The castle has been enlarged and embellished over the centuries – with the British in their later years installing plumbing and sanitation as they converted it into the governor's family's summer residence. Today, palace is the President of Malta's official summer residence.

It has a quiet grandeur, with frescoes in the main room depicting highlights from the life of Grand Master Verdale. There is a fine staircase to one side leading to the roof, from which there is a superb view of the countryside. Within its stone walls is a concealed chamber with rings in the floor and wall where it is said that prisoners were chained and tortured.

The Chapel of St Anthony the Abbot, built in the 16th century, is in the grounds. Viewed from Buskett Gardens below, note the trompe-l'oeil windows painted to create the impression of symmetry.

TIP

December to January is a good time for a stroll in Buskett Gardens as this is when the oranges are picked and their sweet scent permeates the air.

Verdala Palace.

THE SECRETS OF MALTA'S TEMPLES

The island's temples have been jointly declared a Unesco World Heritage Site. A little insight into their history will enhance your enjoyment of them.

Between 3,600 and 2,500 BC there was a building boom in Malta. Prehistoric farmers with no tools but flint, obsidian and bone built well over 50 massive temples, of which 33 survive in various states of preservation. Today they are unique, and considered to be the oldest free-standing stone structures in the world – even predating Stonehenge and the Egyptian Pyramids.

All of them began with the same basic design: a corridor slicing through two kidney-shaped chambers to reach a small altar apse at the far end, with a Herculean outer shell of hard grey limestone. Their entrances are massive uprights of softer, golden stone with equally massive lintels.

The great blocks, many of them over 5 metres (16ft) long and weighing up to 20 tons, were moved around on the stone rollers, shaped like cannon balls, that still lie around most sites. As more temples were added, the outer walls, corbelled in towards the top, were extended to incorporate them. They were probably roofed over with beams, brushwood and clay.

The earliest interiors were plastered and painted with red ochre. All were decorated with intricately carved spirals on steps and altars, friezes of farm animals, snakes and fish, and a simple pattern of pitted dots. Still evident are sockets for wooden barriers or curtains and niches for rituals.

Although measures have been taken to protect the temples, visitors can still walk through them, marvelling at their longevity.

The spiral is by far the most common design in Maltese megalithic art – though its exact meaning is still speculated.

Ta' Hagrat temple, near Mgarr, dates from around 3,600 to 3,300 BC and is one of the earliest temple buildings in Malta.

Porthole doors cut through great slabs of golden stone were a feature of later temples.

Statue on display at Gozo Archaeological Museum.

THE "OBESE FIGURES"

Statues of grossly overweight figures are found in all Maltese temples. Their pleated skirts, generous thighs and small hands and feet led them to being called "Fat Ladies". But they are of indeterminate sex, and, furthermore, it has been noticed that the "ladies" have no breasts. So their name has been revised to the more accurate (and politically correct) term of "Obese Figures".

However, certain figurines, such as the *Sleeping Lady* (above) and the *Malta Venus* (below), show that Neolithic women were well endowed. Meanwhile, pleats are a unisex feature, since statuettes exist of men in skirts with neatly bobbed hair or pigtails.

Fertility, in its widest sense, appears to have been what people worshipped. The male dominance of temple culture is left in no doubt by carved enshrined phalluses.

A wealth of very fine pottery has also been found at all of Malta's temple sites, some of which now rests in the Archaeological Museum in Valletta. This museum is actually a great starting point if you hope to learn more about the temples, with interesting figurines and corpulent statues, as well as photos and maps of the sites.

A statue found at Hagar Qim, dating back to 3,000 BC.

agar Qim is entirely golden, as no grey stone was available.

Celebrating the feast of St Joseph in the village of Kirkop.

Buildings on Triq ir-Repubblika, Victoria, Gozo.

GOZO

Gozo may be tiny but there's plenty to see. It's very popular for day trips, as well as for relaxing weekend breaks.

Taking the Ta Gurdan walk on the island of Gozo.

Tradition has it that Gozo is Homer's Ogygia, the island where the nymph Calypso held the Greek hero Odysseus captive for seven years. There may be other contenders for the honour, but there is certainly a strange enchantment about the place.

The Arabs named the island Ghawdex, meaning "joy", which the Spanish later translated into the Castilian, *gozo*. For some reason, however, the local population still preferred Ghawdex (pronounced "ow-desh"), to which they have remained steadfastly loyal ever since.

No matter what history has thrown at them, the Gozitans appear to have adapted and then proceeded to carry on much as before. As a result, in Malta the Gozitans are known as a strong, resilient people who have the disconcerting habit of walking away with the nation's top jobs. Indeed, there have been more Gozitan presidents, archbishops and chief justices than the Maltese would care to count.

A boat on the Blue Lagoon, Gozo.

Only one-third of the size of Malta, Gozo is still a land of farmers and fishermen. With an area of only 67 sq km (26 sq miles) and a population of about 37,000, it is possible to stroll along Gozo's country lanes and goat tracks for an hour or more and see only a young boy herding his goats and sheep, or a farmer hoeing his fields.

In the countryside, flat-topped hills rise out of valley floors, drystone walls contour every gradient and church domes crest the skyline.

In summer the hot sun bakes any ground that is not devoutly worked, but in spring the landscape is a gaudy patchwork. Carpets of miniature wild flowers sprout from apparently solid rock, thyme and wild fennel scent the air and, as far distant as one can see, there is the cobalt sea and sky.

Sadly (most would agree), larger, modern developments are becoming the norm here, too, and locals are struggling between cosmopolitan ideals and the desire to stay traditional and unique.

The citadel rises above the town.

VICTORIA

The Gozitan capital may be pint-sized, but it's got plenty to offer, including a busy market, top shops and the stunning Citadel.

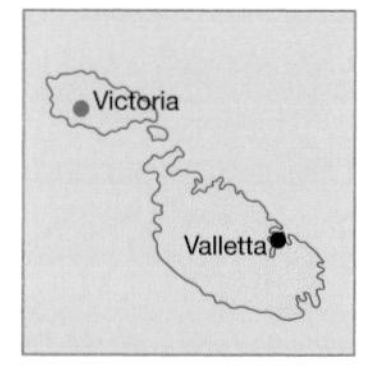

Main Attractions

Triq Ir-Repubblika
Pjazza Independenza
St George's Basilica
The Citadel
The Cathedral

Queen Victoria gave her name to Gozo's capital and elevated it to city status as part of her Golden Jubilee celebrations in 1887. The Gozitans politely installed a fountain and commemorative plaque in Cathedral Square, then went back to using the ancient name of **Rabat** (which means "suburb"). Like Rabat on Malta, which sprawls outside the fortress walls of Mdina, Gozo's suburb nestles beneath the protective bastions of its citadel, a romantic mass of sheer rock faces, curtain walls, ravelins and bell towers that dominates the skyline from almost every approach road.

Origins

The ridge on which **Victoria (Rabat)** ❶ stands has been inhabited at least since the Bronze Age. The Carthaginians left behind a Punic inscription thanking the *prl whds 'm gwl* (the people of Gozo) for helping to restore three temples. A quick tally of Victoria's churches today indicates that, in the religious sphere at least, not a lot has changed. The town was fortified under the Romans and one of the present-day crossroads, Triq Putirjal (Main Gate Street), and three elegant stone crosses mark the limits of the old walls.

The Arabs appear to have spurned the lower town and established themselves on the more easily defended heights of the hill. In the Middle Ages both suburb and citadel were thriving, close-packed communities. Few of the medieval houses have survived, but the narrow twisting lanes and alleyways remain.

Republic Street

Triq Ir-Repubblika Ⓐ (Republic Street) is the town's main thoroughfare, a pleasant mixture of shops and balconied houses that slices through Victoria from east to west. Lined along its stretch are banks, a police

Exploring the back streets.

TIP

Eco-conscious travellers will love Organika (www.organika.com.mt) in St George's Square. This tiny store is packed full of organic food and drink, local delicacies and eco-friendly products.

station, a post office, two opera houses and the Bishop of Gozo's 19th-century palace. It is also home to two shopping malls, Arkadia and The Duke, both of which have become extremely popular with locals and Maltese day-trippers alike.

On the feasts of the Assumption (15 August, known locally as Santa Marija) and of St George (the third weekend in July), it still lives up to its old name of Racecourse Street, when everyone turns out to cheer a medley of thoroughbred trotting ponies and gasping hacks as they pelt uphill towards a lavish carrot – a stupendous array of silver cups and salvers.

The colourful **Villa Rundle Gardens** (Gnien Rundle) have been thoroughly revamped, and now offer recreational facilities as well as an open space for families. They sit at the bottom of the hill, and are also taken over for the celebrations of Santa Marija in August by a jolly agricultural and industrial show, which provides just as much entertainment for people-watchers as for sheep and onion fanciers.

The meeting place

The official title of Victoria's main square is **Pjazza Independenza** **B** (Independence Square) – but it is going to be a long time before this name catches on. Surrounded by tall clipped ficus trees, cafés and busy little shops and market stalls, it has been known locally as **It-Tokk** for as long as the Gozitans can remember. It means "meeting place" and this is exactly what the square has been to locals throughout its many incarnations over the years.

The square is graced, on the right, by the **Banca Giuratale**, a semicircular Baroque confection built in 1733 as the council chambers of Gozo's governing Jurats (the island's jurors). It now houses various government departments, including the tourist information office.

On the left is the small church of **St James the Apostle** (originally constructed in 1740), which has been rebuilt following the collapse of its foundations in the 1980s. The vigorous use of its bells to drown out political meetings in the square is said to

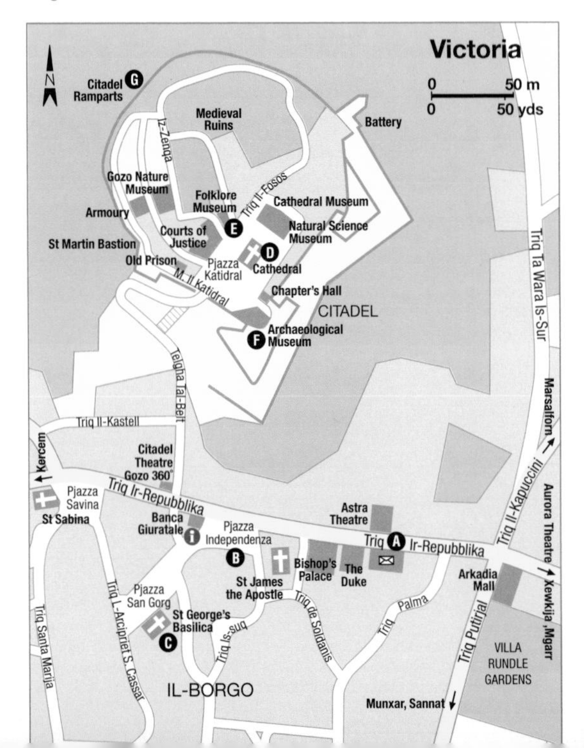

Street signs in Victoria.

have contributed to the delay in the issuing of a restoration permit.

The old town

Pjazza San Gorg (St George's Square), which lies immediately behind the main square, is dominated by the imposing **St George's Basilica** ❸. The present building dates from 1678, though it has been much extended, and the facade was rebuilt in 1818. The paintings on the gilded ceiling and dome were completed between 1949 and 1964, and the striking bronze altar canopy, executed in 1967, is a copy of Bernini's in St Peter's, Rome. The main altarpiece, a glowing triumphant St George, was painted by Mattia Preti (1613–99) of Valletta cathedral fame.

Spreading out behind St George's is the old part of the town, **Il Borgo**, a maze of little streets and alleys designed to baffle invaders and deflect the flight of arrows and shot. Old stone balconies and religious niches are the things to look for here.

Cross back over Republic Street and on the corner, just as you start to walk uphill to the citadel, is the Citadel Theatre showing **Gozo 360°** (www.gozo360.com.mt; shows every half-hour Mon–Sat 10am–3pm). This entertaining audiovisual introduction to the history, geography and culture of Calypso's Isle does for Gozo what the acclaimed Malta Experience does for the bigger sister island.

The citadel

The massive golden-coloured **citadel** bastions, which rise above the town, date from the first years of the 17th century. It is thought that Francesco Laparelli, papal engineer, architect of Valletta and one-time assistant to Michelangelo, drew up the plans for them in 1567, two years after the Great Siege, but it was another 32 years before building commenced. King Philip II of Spain paid a significant sum towards their cost, and the Gozitans provided the rest by way of donations and taxes on wine, oil and agricultural exports.

The effectiveness of these splendid fortifications was never tested. By the time they were finished, the Ottoman Turks had been driven out of

Statue of Pope John Paul II, Victoria.

Victoria citadel.

FACT

The coat of arms on the facade of Gozo Cathedral belongs to Grand Master Perelos, head of the Order at the time of the cathedral's construction.

the western Mediterranean. For a few more years, the upper town retained its importance because, by law, every Gozitan was bound to sleep there. But when this restriction was lifted in 1637, the population began to drift away to more convenient locations in the countryside. In 1693, an earthquake reduced many of the abandoned buildings to rubble.

The citadel reborn

Today, the Knights' impressive bastions are being restored and what remains of the old town is being revived. It takes some imagination to picture it in its medieval heyday, with its small palaces, chapels and warren of crowded alleys, but it is still well worth a visit.

To the left of **Cathedral Square** (Pjazza Katidral), viewed from the great entrance arch, is the early 17th-century Palace of the Governors of Gozo, with the "fat" mouldings (a triple roll form of moulding) that distinguished Maltese architecture in the previous century. It is now part of the adjoining **Law Courts**. On the right are the parish offices and the **Chapter's Hall**, built in 1899. The huddle of domestic dwellings that once filled the square was demolished in the 1860s.

Exhibit on display at the Archaeological Museum.

The cathedral

Built at the turn of the 17th century, on a site previously occupied by at least three churches and two pagan temples, the **cathedral** **D** is the work of the Maltese architect Lorenzo Gafà, who also designed Mdina's cathedral. It has his usual lightness and grace, but because funds ran dry, the dome he intended for it was never completed. This deficiency has cleverly been turned into an asset by a trompe l'oeil substitute, painted by Antonio Manuele of Messina in 1739. From the nave this artful sham soars skywards in perfect symmetry; viewed from near the altar steps, however, it shoots off at an alarming angle.

The cathedral floor is paved with the colourful marble tombstones of bishops and priests. The coat of arms on the facade of Gozo Cathedral belongs to Grand Master Perelos, head of the Order at the time of the cathedral's construction.

Just around the corner, occupying part of the cathedral's vestry, the **Cathedral Museum** (tel: 2155 6087; www.gozocathedral.org; Mon–Sat 10am–4pm) is built entirely from local limestone in a Mediterranean Baroque style. The museum features Ionic columns from the temple of Juno, a bishop's landau from the late 1860s, church silver and much more in its collection. Note the marble coats of arms of Grand Master Ramon Perellos (1697–1720) and Bishop David Cocco-Palmeri (1684–1711), with the coat of arms of the present Bishop of Gozo in the centre.

Citadel museums

All of the capital's small museums are clustered here in the upper town, in buildings that are as important as the collections they hold (http://heritagemalta.org; daily 9am–5pm).

The three houses that form the **Folklore Museum** E date from around 1500. As an architectural group they are unique in the Maltese Islands, admired for the simple delicacy of the stonework and their "Norman" windows. Don't be deterred by the folklore label; the collection is a fascinating look at rural Gozitan life and its bygone times.

The **Archaeological Museum** F is housed in the fortress's last surviving private palace. The design of the sumptuously ornate balcony was reconstructed from the shattered remnants of the original. The exhibits range from Neolithic to Medieval, and among them the 12th-century tombstone of a young Muslim girl, Majmuna, is particularly touching.

High on a wall opposite, a little further up the hill, is an inscription marking the house of the Sicilian soldier, Bernardo DeOpuo *(Audacis Militi)*, a hero of the 1551 attack. Preferring death to slavery, he killed his wife and two daughters, then dispatched several Turks before he himself was felled.

The **Gozo Nature Museum** forms part of a cluster of 16th-century houses and has a good display of fossils, flora and fauna. Across the alleyway a former 17th-century granary is now the **Armoury**, home to helmets, cannonballs, an old carriage and a couple of 19th-century hearses.

Prisons and ramparts

It is also worth checking if the **Old Prisons**, lower down the street, are open. The inmates, incarcerated in the tiny cells here between around 1600 and the 1880s, left poignant carvings of ships on the walls. Attractive little shops selling local crafts line the small street leading to the early 17th-century storehouses and rest rooms of the Knights. From the 1880s right up until 1964, these were the island's "New Prisons". Today, they are used to display a range of handicrafts.

For all the intrinsic interest of the citadel, however, the most enduring memory is the view from the **ramparts** G, a panorama of rolling valleys, strange, decapitated hills and, just in the distance, a glimpse of the big island of Malta.

TIP

In the citadel, alongside the cathedral, Ta' Rikardu is a good place to sample local produce, wines and cheese. Souvenirs are available, too.

OPERA IN VICTORIA

The fact that Victoria has two opera houses is wonderfully Gozitan. The whole thing began modestly enough a hundred years ago, with the founding of two band clubs to provide music for the saint's day processions of the cathedral and St George's Basilica respectively. Then, in the 1960s, the St George's club built the Astra Theatre. The cathedral club, not to be outdone, moved premises to the Aurora Theatre, and since then there has been a tit-for-tat rivalry over everything from facades to discos and opera productions. But thankfully all that angst hasn't gone to waste, as the island has built quite a reputation for its operatic productions. Big international names have been enticed to sing at both theatres, and upcoming seasons promise numerous highlights, too.

A school in Victoria.

Taking a stroll at Qbajjar.

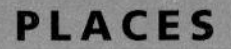
Map on page 206

AROUND GOZO

This tiny island includes the world's oldest free-standing temple, unspoilt villages and near-biblical landscapes. A tour around it will show you why Unesco wants to designate Gozo a World Heritage Site.

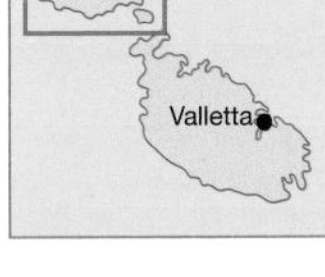

Main Attractions
- Ggantija Prehistoric Temples
- Xaghra
- Calypso's Cave
- Ramla Bay
- Marsalforn
- Ta' Pinu
- The Azure Window
- Xlendi
- Ta' Cenc

Like Odysseus (or Ulysses to the Romans), most visitors still arrive on Calypso's island by boat. It is a 25-minute trip by car ferry from Cirkewwa at the northern tip of Malta. In summer, another ferry service runs between Sliema on Malta and Mgarr on Gozo.

En route, you are sure to have a fine view of Comino. It was once a troublesome pirate's lair and the haunt of invading Turks, which explains its impressive 17th-century fort and gun battery. The flashes of limpid, turquoise sea are its famous Blue Lagoon.

First impressions

Sailing into Gozo's only port, **Mgarr** ❷, gives a concentrated view of all that makes the island special: chapel, church spire and fort line the horizon, small flat-topped houses, tiny fields and greenery rise to meet them, while at the water's edge bob gaily painted fishing boats with Christian shrines amidships and the pagan eye of Osiris on their bows. Only the mock-Gothic church on the skyline is out of character. This cathedral-sized building was started in 1924, delayed for lack of funds, then finished at a gallop in the 1970s after the priest in charge won the National Lottery.

Fort Chambray, adjacent, was also built with prize money, the loot accumulated by the last great admiral of the Order of St John, Knight Grand Cross Jacques de Chambray. Having retired from active service in 1749, and disgusted by the Order's peacetime lack of vigour, the old sea dog became Governor of Gozo and spent his last years fortifying Mgarr harbour at his own expense.

Fifty years on, when Napoleon's troops arrived on the island, the old warrior's ramparts, manned by Knights and Gozitans, gave the French force a good deal more trouble than they had bargained for. Since then, the

First sight of Gozo: landfall at Mgarr harbour.

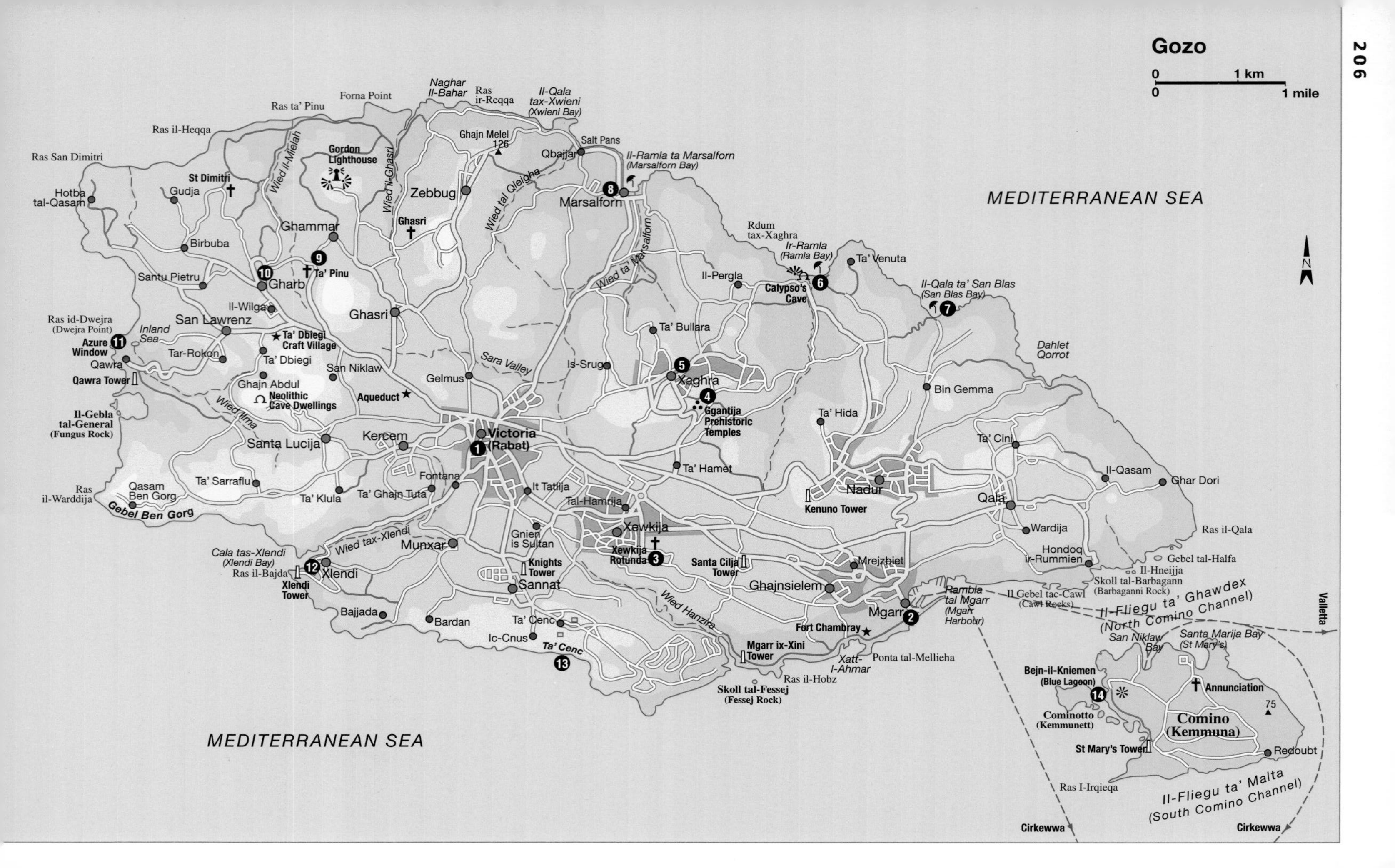

Gozo
0 1 km
0 1 mile
N
MEDITERRANEAN SEA
MEDITERRANEAN SEA
Valletta
Cirkewwa
Cirkewwa
Il-Fliegu ta' Ghawdex (North Comino Channel)
Il-Fliegu ta' Malta (South Comino Channel)
Comino (Kemmuna)
Redoubt
Annunciation
75
Santa Marija Bay (St Mary's)
San Niklaw Bay
Bejn-il-Kniemen (Blue Lagoon)
Cominotto (Kemmunett)
St Mary's Tower
Ras I-Irqieqa
Ras il-Qala
Gebel tal-Halfa
Il-Hneijja
Skoll tal-Barbagann (Barbaganni Rock)
Il Gebel tac-Cawl (Cawl Rocks)
Hondoq ir-Rummien
Ghar Dori
Il-Qasam
Dahlet Qorrot
Wardija
Ta' Cini
Qala
Bin Gemma
Il-Qala ta' San Blas (San Blas Bay)
Rambla tal Mgarr (Mgarr Harbour)
Mgarr
Ponta tal-Mellieha
Fort Chambray
Xatt-l-Ahmar
Ras il-Hobz
Nadur
Kenuno Tower
Ta' Hida
Ta' Venuta
Mrejzbiet
Ghajnsielem
Mgarr ix-Xini Tower
Skoll tal-Fessej (Fessej Rock)
Ir-Ramla (Ramla Bay)
Rdum tax-Xaghra
Calypso's Cave
Il-Pergla
Ggantija Prehistoric Temples
Xaghra
Ta' Bullara
Ta' Hamet
Santa Cilja Tower
Wied Hanzira
Xewkija
Xewkija Rotunda
Il-Ramla ta Marsalforn (Marsalforn Bay)
Wied ta' Marsalforn
Marsalforn
Salt Pans
Qbajjar
Il-Qala tax-Xwieni (Xwieni Bay)
Is-Srug
Tal-Hamrija
Ras ir-Reqqa
Ghajn Melel
126
Wied tal Qleigha
Sara Valley
Victoria (Rabat)
It Tatija
Gnien is Sultan
Knights Tower
Sannat
Ta' Cenc
Ta' Cenc
Ic-Cnus
Naghar Il-Bahar
Zebbug
Ghasri
Wied il-Ghasri
Gelmus
Fontana
Munxar
Bardan
Forna Point
Gordon Lighthouse
Ghasri
Aqueduct
Kercem
Ta' Ghajn Tuta
Wied tax-Xlendi
Bajjada
Ghammar
Ta' Pinu
San Niklaw
Ta' Klula
Xlendi
Xlendi Tower
Ras ta' Pinu
Wied il-Mielah
Gharb
Ta' Dbiegi Craft Village
Ta' Dbiegi
Neolithic Cave Dwellings
Ghajn Abdul
Santa Lucija
Cala tas-Xlendi (Xlendi Bay)
Ras il-Bajda
Il-Wilga
Wied Ilma
St Dimitri
San Lawrenz
Ta' Sarraflu
Ras il-Heqqa
Gudja
Birbuba
Santu Pietru
Tar-Rokon
Inland Sea
Qasam Ben Gorg
Gebel Ben Gorg
Azure Window
Qawra
Qawra Tower
Ras id-Dwejra (Dwejra Point)
Il-Gebla tal-General (Fungus Rock)
Ras il-Warddija
Hotba tal-Qasam
Ras San Dimitri

fort has been both a British garrison and a psychiatric hospital.

Fast-forward to the current day and Fort Chambray has been developed into a unique apartment, villa and hotel complex that combines modern luxury with incredible historic surroundings. The views from this vantage point are simply out of this world, spreading across the sea to Comino and the north of Malta.

The road to Victoria

Most traffic en route to Victoria passes through the busy village of Ghajnsielem. Its name means "the spring of peace" and originates from the water spring found here, around which an arcade containing public washbasins was built in 1700. Around the next bend in the road, the great round church of the **Xewkija Rotunda** ❸ (also known as the Xewkija Dome) rises across the fields to the left.

Gozo's fourth-largest community, Xewkija has disjointed the noses of every other parish by building the biggest church. The dome is said to be the third-largest unsupported church dome in Europe, bigger even than the Mosta Dome on Malta. Based on the design of Santa Maria della Salute in Venice, the church was begun in 1952 and a bell tower was added later.

Remarkably, the whole of this great enterprise was financed by a population of under 3,000 (helped by donations from Xewkijans abroad) and built by willing local labour. Some of the choicest pieces of carved stone from the attractive early 17th-century church that the Rotunda replaced are displayed in a side chapel. The carvings are thought to be the work of two renegade Sicilians who sought sanctuary in the church from the laws of their own country.

A gigantic temple

High on a hill 3km (2 miles) due north, on the edge of the ancient village of Xaghra, is a much earlier and, in its way, an even bigger monument – the Stone Age complex of **Ggantija Prehistoric Temples** ❹ (tel: 2155 3194; daily 9am–5pm, until 6pm in summer).

TIP

The car ferry makes for an easy way to get your vehicle across to Gozo, and it is reasonably priced. While the public-transport system has improved here, a car will always make it easier to really explore the best of what's on offer.

HARVESTING SEA SALT

Saltpans, in use since Roman times, are dotted all along this stretch of coast: glittering little troughs and reservoirs cut into ledges of gold-coloured rock. The most impressive are just past Qbajjar, on the coast road that leads to Ghasri. Not only are they highly photogenic, they also produce tons of prime sea salt a year.

The easy part of the procedure is having them flooded by the sea in stormy weather, and then sizzled dry by the sun. The residual salt crystals are then harvested in rather back-breaking manual labour. If you are an early riser, make the effort to wander down towards the Marsalforn saltpans before sunrise in summer, when you can watch the salt being collected as it glistens under the rising sun's rays.

The saltpans used to harvest sea salt.

The annual Xaghra Feast.

Constructed from 3,600–3,000 BC, this is the oldest free-standing stone building known to man, predating Egypt's pyramids and Britain's Stonehenge by over 1,000 years. And of all Malta's Neolithic remains, this is the largest and the best preserved. The two temples cover 1,000 sq metres (10,800 sq ft), and their astonishing rear wall still rises 6 metres (20ft) and contains megaliths weighing in at 40–50 tons – the most gigantic blocks used in any of the archipelago's herculean structures. The complex is a Unesco World Heritage Site.

Xaghra

At the entrance to the village of **Xaghra** ❺ (pronounced "shur-rah"), just a short walk away from Ggantija, stands the superbly restored **Ta' Kola Windmill** (same opening hours as Ggantija). This is one of the few Maltese windmills still with its sails and original wooden machinery intact. Built in 1725, it contains a forge, ancient tools and living quarters decorated with old country furniture and local fabrics. A Discover Gozo ticket costs €13, with discounts available for children, students and senior citizens, and will save on entrance fees to the most interesting archaeological sites and museums on the island. Alternatively, the Heritage Malta Multisite Pass is available for €50, and offers entry to 22 heritage sites and museums (except Hypogeum). Both are valid for 30 days. Visit www.heritagemalta.org for more details.

Xaghra's main square is one of the most attractive squares on Gozo, with old-fashioned shops, a good restaurant and a café-bar. Just off here (signposted) are three more small visitor attractions, two caves and a wonderful toy museum. Caves seem to be a speciality of Xaghra, with two choices: **Xerri's Grotto** (Mon–Sat 9am–6pm) and **Ninu's Cave** (daily 8.30am–6pm). It is certainly a novel experience to walk through the front door of an ordinary family home and be shown into a basement which displays an array of weird and wonderful stalactites and stalagmites.

There is one more pleasant surprise in store in Xaghra: the fantastically

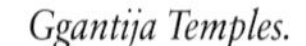

Ggantija Temples.

named **Pomskizillious Toy Museum** (Jun–Sept Mon–Sat 10.30am–1pm and 4–6pm, Oct–May 10.30am–1pm) . Full of old-fashioned toys and automata, this is a delight for children who have never grown up. The strange name derives from the English nonsense poet Edward Lear, who visited Gozo and described it as "pomskizillious and gromphiberous, being as no words can describe its magnificence". A wax model of Lear himself is a prize exhibit.

The legend of Calypso

Take the road heading north out of Xaghra to Ramla Bay, and within a few minutes you will come to the island's most mythical spot, **Calypso's Cave**.

Set high in the cliff face at the northeast corner of the Xaghra plateau, it is reputed to be a labyrinth, reaching down to sea level in some places. It is here, if we are to believe local legend, and the works of Homer and Callimachus, that the Greek hero Odysseus (Ulysses to the Romans) was washed ashore and into the arms of the golden-haired temptress, Calypso, on his epic return from Troy. It is said that Calypso wished to detain Odysseus on the island and make him her immortal husband, but after a number of years, Odysseus returned home to his wife Penelope.

Following a rock fall, the cave can no longer be explored. However, it is not the cave but the view from the adjacent platform that makes a visit worthwhile.

Best beaches

Looking down from Calypso's Cave there is a splendid vista of the former domain of the sea nymph: tumbling rocks, a wide, fertile valley and the red-gold sweep of **Ramla Bay** ❻, Gozo's finest beach.

A lucky Roman once had a villa in the dunes behind the bay. Since then it has been a no-go area for the building trade. Except for a few bamboo huts serving drinks and snacks in summer, it is as uncommercialised as it was when Calypso ruled the land.

The island's second-best beach, **San Blas** ❼, is also close by – a mere 1.5km (1 mile) due east as the crow

The beach at Ramla Bay.

TIP

Ta' Frenc (http://tafrenc restaurant.com), along the main road towards Marsalforn, is considered to be one of the best – if not the best – restaurants on the island. This is the ideal spot if you're planning a special evening.

flies, some 6km (4 miles) via Nadur, as the roads go. If you want to walk it, take a good local map. San Blas is a delightful little cove with just enough sand for a few families to share, so try to get there early.

Marsalforn

By contrast to San Blas, **Marsalforn ❽**, a few kilometres west along the north coast from Ramla Bay, is a proper seaside resort; indeed, it is the largest on the island, though on Gozo, large is always a relative term. It's a cheerful if somewhat bland place, pulsing with life in the summer and just as much a playground for the Gozitans and Maltese as for foreign tourists.

On summer evenings, family groups stroll like a tide, back and forth, around the bay. There is one main hotel, several smaller hostelries, wall-to-wall restaurants and snack bars, along with souvenir shops piled high with hand-knitted sweaters, which have ousted lace as the favoured local craft. The bay has a tiny fishing harbour tucked under one of its arms and a choice of rock, shingle and sand for swimmers.

The Basilica of the National Shrine of the Blessed Virgin of Ta' Pinu.

Going west

Malta's national shrine, **Ta' Pinu ❾** stands on a plateau off the road between Victoria and Gharb. It was near here, in 1883, that a local peasant woman, returning from working in the fields, heard a voice calling to her. A friend confided that he too had heard the voice and together they prayed for the woman's critically sick mother, who then miracously recovered. From then on, miracle cures multiplied and the little chapel became a place of pilgrimage.

To accommodate the thousands of devotees, a huge neo-Romanesque church was built in the 1920s, though the original chapel is tucked into it, behind the main altar. In a corridor to the rear is a display of naïve votive paintings, baby clothes and crutches that poignantly attest to cures and escapes from peril.

If you have time, take a walk into the Gozitan countryside towards **Gordan Lighthouse**. This building, constructed by the British, dates back to 1851. Climb to the top and take in the stunning views of the hills, valleys and sea below.

A short distance west, the village of **Gharb ❿** features a flamboyant 17th-century Baroque church. The Church of the Visitation was built between 1679 and 1729 and its yellow butterfly facade is one of the finest and most original church fronts in the entire archipelago. The bell towers flanking it to the west are typically Maltese. Gharb also has some fine old houses alongside the church and a delightful **Folklore Museum** (tel: 2156 2034; daily 9am–5pm) in a rambling house on the square. An old printing press, carriages, costumes and a mass of intriguing rural items are on show.

Backtracking to the main road and heading for San Lawrenz, you will soon reach the **Ta' Dbiegi Craft Village**, where knitwear, lace, leatherwork and pottery are on sale.

Dwejra

Beside the church of San Lawrenz, the road dips down to the geological curiosities of **Dwejra Point** ⓫. The tarmac finishes here and to the right is a stunning natural rock arch – the **Azure Window,** which has eroded significantly in recent years and there are increasing fears that will collapse soon. Beside it, over a small hill, the **Inland Sea** is a crater into which the sea flows through a cavernous fissure in the cliffs. Little boats sail through the gap on sightseeing trips.

To the left is **Fungus Rock**, once highly prized by the Knights for the odd red plant that grows on top of it. Partly because of its colour, they used it to treat blood diseases, to staunch wounds and for other medicinal purposes. Its phallic shape encouraged them to apply it to other parts of the body, too. To protect the crop they made this a knightly preserve, shaved down its sides to deter poachers, and placed a sentry on the rope-and-pulley bridge that was erected to reach it. Entry was forbidden to the locals and punishable by death.

The Knights even sent samples of the fungus as princely gifts to the monarchs of Europe. Recently, however, it was sadly discovered that the plant has no medicinal properties whatsoever and isn't even a fungus. It's a rare kind of parasite that attaches itself to other plants' roots and only comes up for air during its short flowering season.

South of Victoria

The road south from Victoria passes downhill through **Fontana**, where there is a cavernous 17th-century public washhouse, still used by the locals. On the last stretch down to the sea is *the* meeting-place of the summer, La Grotta (www.lagrottaleisure.com), an open-air disco set in a lovely terraced garden.

At the seafront, the tiny resort of **Xlendi** ⓬ looks on to what is said to be the smallest bay on the island. It resembles a grey-cliffed mini fjord, with a protective tower at its entrance and colourful fishing boats anchored off the small sandy strip of beach. Although it has been much built up in recent years, with banks of holiday apartments being added, it still has charm. Tamarisks and pastel-painted buildings line the small promenade and there are restaurants, bars and souvenir sellers. Try to stay a night here, for when the day-trippers have gone, the tiny village regains its small-time, atmosphere.

Due east of Xlendi, on bumpy minor roads, is the village of Sannat and, nearby, the wonderfully wild cliffs of **Ta' Cenc** ⓭ – from which there is a 150-metre (500ft) sheer drop to the sea. This area is the home of nesting birds and rare plants, as well as Stone Age remains and the most unostentatious luxury hotel on the islands, called Ta' Cenc (www.tacenc.com). Behind the hotel is a Neolithic necropolis, an intact dolmen (a megalithic tomb with a large flat stone laid on upright stones) and some of Malta's mysterious cart tracks, though they are not easy to spot.

TIP

Ta' Pinu has a dress code that is strictly enforced. Men must wear trousers or long shorts and women must wear a skirt and cover their shoulders. Shawls are provided and can be used as skirts.

Fungus Rock, highly prized by the Knights.

Blue Lagoon, Comino Island.

The Blue Lagoon.

COMINO

Once a pirates' haven, this tiny uninhabited rock attracts throngs of day-trippers to its famous Blue Lagoon.

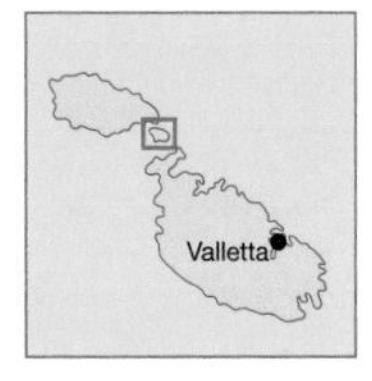

Main Attractions

The Blue Lagoon
St Mary's Tower
Liberty Square

If Malta is the busy island, and Gozo the quiet island, then Comino is surely the great escape island, where relaxation and sports are the only staple items on the day's menu. Lying midway between Malta and Gozo, Comino is all of 2.5 sq km (1 sq mile) in size. The island is too minute for it to attract any serious large-scale development, and so is likely to remain what it has always been: a barren, rocky wilderness with a variegated coastline of jagged cliffs interspersed by two small sandy beaches, lots of pretty coves and creeks, arches, stacks, rock tunnels and, of course, the stunningly beautiful **Blue Lagoon** ⓮ – a true gem of the Mediterranean.

Natural beauty

The colours of the waters surrounding the island are breathtaking: deep-water indigo and navy, sky and turquoise blue in the sandy bays, peaking to the sparkling azure and emerald of the Blue Lagoon, which lies between Comino and Cominotto, an island 100 metres (328ft) northwest of Comino and only one-quarter sq km (0.1 sq miles) in area.

This is the Mediterranean at its best, and there are even playful dolphins that bob up and down in the deep-sea channels between the islands. Clearly they like it here, too.

The nearest point to Comino is Mgarr in Gozo, 3km (2 miles) away. The Gozitans have always affectionately regarded Comino as their own. And the Maltese, who think they own Gozo anyway, have never raised any serious objections to this happy state of affairs.

Game reserve of the Knights

It is said that when the Knights of St John arrived in the 16th century, the island was teeming with wild boar and

On a boat to Comino.

Windsurfing off Comino.

hares. The vegetation also attracted pelicans and quail. For this reason, successive Grand Masters of the Order kept Comino as a private game reserve.

They were very serious about it, too. In 1695 an edict issued to the people of the islands stated in no uncertain terms: "Admission is strictly forbidden to subjects of any class or condition, armed with gun, dog, ferret, net or any device intended for game; under penalty of the galley for three years without pay, if the trespasser is an ordinary person; or a fine of forty ounces of gold, if a cleric or a member of the learned professions; and if a minor, of banishment from the dominions of the Prince during His Highness's pleasure."

Pirate threat

But the island was certainly not a paradise, and was far from peaceful. Throughout the Middle Ages, both Malta and Gozo were constantly attacked by Saracen pirates, who used Comino as a base from which to assault the islands. In 1416, the Maltese petitioned the Viceroy of Sicily to improve their defences. Two years later, a tax on wine was introduced to raise the money with which to finance the building of a fortified tower on Comino; but the Maltese were swindled by King Alfonso V of Spain, who used the money for his many adventures elsewhere. Comino remained unprotected and towerless for the next 200 years.

A fortified island

So it was not until 1618 that Grand Master Alof de Wignacourt, keenly aware of the need to protect the Malta Channel more efficiently and deter further assailants, arranged the erection of **St Mary's Tower** on Comino. Of the many such towers that were built around the islands during this period, St Mary's was the most expensive and was equipped and manned by 30 soldiers.

A century later, more forts were constructed, including a battery on the southeast corner of Comino to guard the Channel, as well as a redoubt at **St Mary's Bay**. In 1722, in preparation for an expected attack, **St**

An aerial view of Gozo fields looking out to Comino.

Mary's Battery, also known as Perellos Battery, was complete and ready for action. But the perceived threat from Turkish forces did not materialise and so the fortifications were never seriously tested.

Once the tower was in place, however, a small community blossomed, but it was an impoverished existence, with little hope of economic improvement, and the population inexorably declined. Today, you can count the number of people who live here all year round on the fingers of one hand.

In World War I, the British built an isolation hospital on the island for serious cases of infection. This military-style compound of stone buildings around a central square can still be seen. **Liberty Square**, as it was called, acted as a kind of village centre, complete with a grocery shop, postbox and even a bar. Two well-trodden paths, named Battery Street and Congreve Street, lead to it.

Not far away, at St Mary's Bay, is the only chapel on Comino. It is said to be of great antiquity, predating the fort.

Modern times

Comino entered the 20th century with the tourist boom that followed Malta's independence in 1964. And when its only hotel was up and running properly, this little island was at last ready to carve out a name for itself on the upper echelons of Europe's willing and eager tourist market.

Water sports are a big draw on Comino and the expanded water-sports centre now includes a surf centre, a first-rate diving base and a diving school, all staffed by qualified instructors. The tennis centre has several sand courts, one of which is floodlit, and a resident tennis coach.

Progress, if unchecked, does have its price, however, and day boats piled high with tourists regularly dart in and out of Comino's pretty coves and inlets, making it very busy during the summer months.

Fortunately for its residents, the hotel is out of earshot of most of the hubbub and the crowds go home early anyway. The result is very much the idyll hailed by the advertisements as the last jewel of the Mediterranean.

TIP

Day visitors to Comino may be able to use the sports facilities of the Comino Hotel, subject to resident demand; tel: 2152 9821.

CUMIN AND THYME

In ancient times, Ptolemy referred to the island as Cosyra, but the name that stuck is Comino, from the spice cumin, which used to be grown in vast quantities here. In fact, cumin still grows wild in clumps all over the island, but it is the pink and mauve wild thyme that hits the eye and scents the air as you walk around the island, especially in the spring months when the bees start buzzing to produce what is arguably the region's best honey.

Today, Comino is practically uninhabited – with just one summerhouse and large hotel built on the island. At its peak, through, a small agricultural community of around 200 made Comino their home and eked a living out of growing cumin and cotton, and producing honey.

Wild thyme growing on Comino.

A TRIP TO SICILY

With daily flights and catamaran trips, Sicily is just a hop, skip and jump away from Malta. It makes for an alluring day excursion, with plenty of new sights and sounds.

Main Attractions
Mount Etna
Sylvester Craters
Teatro Greco, Taormina
Corso Umberto, Taormina
Giardino Pubblico, Taormina

Just 90km (60 miles) north of Malta, the Mediterranean's largest island is a simple day trip away. Sign up with Virtu Ferries, jump aboard its catamaran (tel: 2123 2522; www.virtuferries.com), and within 90 minutes you can set foot on Sicilian soil at Pozzallo. Admittedly, the journey can prove a little rough, and travellers are advised to take anti-seasickness medication before boarding. Thankfully, the journey is over before you know it and luxurious air-conditioned buses will then whisk you north to Etna and Taormina. If you don't mind whistle-stop packages, and if you are short of time and/or money, then this is the way to go. However, be warned that you have to get up very early in the morning to catch the catamaran.

Independent travellers can also take the same catamaran route to Pozzallo, hire a car and then embark on the long drive north (approximately 4 hours to Etna). A quicker alternative is to take the catamaran to Catania (a crossing time of 3 hours), which is only some 25km (16 miles) south of Taormina and Etna.

The view from Taormina towards Mount Etna.

North from Pozzallo

Don't expect an immediate change in topography. After all, long ago these two countries were one landmass and this part of southern Sicily, like Malta, is also mostly barren and flat. After an hour or so, however, the landscape begins to rise and fall. It becomes lush and promising, even in summer, and you will pass over two of Europe's highest road bridges while looking down to the ancient town of **Modica** – a Unesco World Heritage Site. The historic town of **Ragusa**, a stunning example of a Baroque town, divided in two by a deep gorge, lies just a few kilometres further north.

Mount Etna

Rising above the plain of Catania to a height of over 3,300 metres (11,000ft), **Mount Etna** is the highest and the most active volcano in Europe. In 1669, lava reached as far afield as Catania, and in 1928, the city of Mascali was devastated. The volcano also erupted in 1971, 1983, 1998, 2001, 2007, 2014 and 2015.

As you ascend the slopes you will see the legacy of this destruction, including houses wrecked and buried up to their rooftops in lava following the 1983 and 2001 eruptions.

Yet, tempting fate, the locals continue to inhabit its slopes and, as a reward, harvest its rich benefits. Etna's fertile soil produces wonderful fruit and vegetables, including the island's best wines and some of the finest olive oil in the world.

The Sylvester Craters

Most itineraries stop at the **Sylvester Craters**, created in the 1892 eruption. The craters form a spectacular lunar landscape with massive panoramic views down the slopes. Dotted here and there, far below, are smaller, earlier volcanic cones, many now cloaked in mature greenery.

The higher the mountain climbs, the darker the colours become; greenery disappears, reds and purples dominate, then in turn give way to greys and blacks. Then, in the cooler months, pure white snow caps the volcano, which is transformed into a popular ski resort.

Taormina

Taormina is Sicily's most dramatic resort, a stirring place celebrated by poets and literary figures from classical times onwards; D.H. Lawrence stayed here for three years, from 1920 to 1923. Today, it would still figure highly in any Mediterranean beauty contest, not least for its magnificent hilltop setting. Critics point out that this is a safe, sophisicated un-Sicilian pocket, that it is a Sicilian St-Tropez, but in a place this beautiful, few visitors seem to mind.

The Taormina Arte Festival is held in June every year. If you are lucky enough to catch it, you'll enjoy a series of events dedicated to cinema, theatre, music, dance and art held at the Ancient Theatre, the Congress Palace and the Palace of the Dukes of St Stefano.

The jewel in Taormina's crown is its **Teatro Greco**, originally built by the Greeks and then rebuilt by the Romans when Taormina enjoyed a period of considerable status and prosperity. Constructed on the very crest of the old town and hewn out of the hillside, this is one of the most spectacularly sited ancient amphitheatres in the world.

Views plunge down to the coast in three directions, overlooking the aptly named Isola Bella and the mouthwatering beach resort of **Giardini Naxos**, which was the site of the very first Sicilian colony, founded by Greek settlers. On a clear spring or winter's day, with snow-capped Etna in the background, the scene is truly breathtaking and prompted the German writer Goethe to comment that, "Never did any audience, in any theatre, have before it such a spectacle".

One of the ships transporting passengers to Sicily.

The magnificently sited Greco-Roman Theatre at Taormina.

Giardino Pubblico.

A walk along Corso Umberto

Most of Taormina's sights lie on or just off its pedestrianised main street, **Corso Umberto**. Here, former palazzi and other venerable buildings, dating from late Medieval times onwards, have been turned into chic shops, romantic restaurants and delightful cafés. Luxury food emporia display bottled peppers, candied fruits and fresh kumquats. Majolica tiles, leather goods and traditional puppets vie for window space with chandeliers and reproductions of classical statuary. The prices here, of course, reflect the outstanding setting.

Start your visit at the corner of Piazza Emanuele and Corso Umberto, where you will find the **Palazzo Corvaja**, a handsome 15th-century structure, formerly home to the Sicilian parliament. The upper part houses an excellent small historical museum (free admission), while below is the tourist office. While here, look out for the ornamentation of black and white lava. Head straight for the Teatro Greco (well signposted) then return to the Corso Umberto and walk its whole length.

There's lots more to admire along this thoroughfare, including the **Torre dell' Orologio** (Clock Tower), halfway along the street, and near the very end, the **Duomo** (Cathedral), which dates from the 13th century.

Giardino Pubblico

Try to make time to visit the lush tiered park, the **Giardino Pubblico** (a 5–10-minute walk, signposted from the Teatro Greco; free). The park was bequeathed to the town by an eccentric Englishwoman in the 1920s and features a number of follies. The largest of these – the Villa Communale – has become synonymous with the park itself. From this point you can wonder at the rows of cypress and cedar trees that frame spectacular views of the sea.

The return journey to Malta is, thankfully, usually calmer than the outgoing journey. Also, prepare yourself for an extremely long day on the move as you won't return to Valletta until late evening.

A ceramic picture of San Pancrazio, patron of Taormina.

SICILIAN CUISINE

It may be just across the water, but Sicilian cuisine has plenty of new tastes to offer foodies. Here, food is an important part of the locals' way of life, and nothing but love and passion goes into every dish. Of course, most of the dominant flavours are Italian, but you will notice Greek, Arab and Spanish influences, too.

If you want something local, be on the lookout for dishes that include *aranchini* (deep-fried cheese- or meat-stuffed rice balls), *pasta alla Norma* (which is served with aubergines and salty cheese) and sardines cooked with fennel.

Of course, the Sicilians are also renowned for their sweet tooth, so be sure to leave plenty of room for dessert. These include the rich *cassatta* cake and the crispy *cannoli*, both stuffed with sweet ricotta. Ice cream is also ingrained in Sicilian culture, and it is believed that, during Roman times, runners would bring snow down from Mount Etna, which they would then flavour and serve to the upper classes. Today you will find a range of refreshing and delicious flavours available, including rum, jasmine and hazelnut.

Meanwhile, if you are on a day trip, be sure to research the many places to stop for lunch, as all the restaurants will be vying for your business as you walk by.

Piazza IX Aprile, Taormina.

An old Street, Mdina.

TRAVEL TIPS

Transport

A – Z

Language

Further Reading

TRANSPORT

GETTING THERE AND GETTING AROUND

GETTING THERE

By Air

All schedule and charter flights arrive at Malta International Airport at Gudja. There is also a small landing field on Gozo to service private planes.

Malta's national airline, Air Malta (in the UK, for enquiries, tel: 0207 660 0543 or check www.airmalta.com) operates from Heathrow, Gatwick, Birmingham, Bristol, Cardiff, Edinburgh, Exeter, Manchester airports in Britain. In Europe, it flies from Athens, Frankfurt, Paris, Rome, Milan, Naples, Catania, Munich, Geneva, Copenhagen.

Many other airlines also operate scheduled services to Malta, as do low-cost airlines such as Ryanair (www.ryanair.com), Meridiana (www.meridiana.it), easyJet (www.easyjet.com) and Wizzair (www.wizzair.com).

Flying time from the UK is about 3hrs 15mins.

Travel to and from the airport

As part of the transport reform, four express buses now take visitors from the airport to all parts of Malta. The X1 goes to Cirkewwa, the X2 to St Julian's, the X3 to Bugibba and the X4 to Birzebbugia (for details see www.publictransport.com.mt). There is also a shuttle service provided by Malta Transfer (www.maltatransfer.com) that connects the airport with hotels in Malta and Gozo. Taxi services are available around the clock and prices have now been fixed. Consult www.maltairport.com for details.

Transit/Transfer to Gozo

If your final destination is not Malta, but the nearby islands of Gozo or Comino, the tourist information office within the airport concourse will be able to advise on ferry services from Cirkewwa. Check the Gozo Channel Company website (www.gozochannel.com) for details.

Taxis, as well as the X1 bus to Cirkewwa, will get you to the ferry. For transfers to Comino, contact Capitain Morgan Cruises (www.captainmorgan.com.mt), United Comino Ferries (www.cominoferries.com) or Ebsons Comino Ferries (www.cominoferryservice.com).

A cruise ship in Grand Harbour.

A Maltese bus.

By Sea

Many cruise ships call in at Malta's Grand Harbour with tourists on day visits. But, for independent travellers, the only means of getting to the islands by sea is by car catamaran (www.virtuferries.com) from Sicily. Services leave Pozzallo, the southernmost point of Sicily. The timetables change constantly and the catamaran runs only when there is good weather. There is also a three-hour catamaran service from Catania, Sicily, on certain days.

By Car

Arriving with a car does not require a permit, but the car must have "Green Card" insurance specific to Malta. Cars may be imported to the islands for a period of up to three months (the maximum permitted stay for a tourist); any longer will require special police permission.

On arrival, the car's engine and chassis numbers may be logged by customs officers. This is to ensure that the same items reappear for departure and are not sold as spare parts or exchanged on the local market. The same officials may examine the car for goods on which duty is payable.

Wardens

Wardens' major roles are the management of parking restrictions and the control of traffic, roles they enforce with enthusiasm. Visitors are regarded as harshly as locals. Other roles include checking dogs are on leashes and the apprehending of drivers throwing rubbish out of car windows. Wardens wear brown uniforms with a distinctive yellow sash.

GETTING AROUND

Orientation

Malta is a small island and nowhere is more than half an hour or so by bus from Valletta. The same rule applies to Gozo, which is even smaller. The new bus system is no longer centralised around Valletta and Gozo, so it is best to check routes at www.arriva.com.mt.

Car hire is recommended for its cheapness and the flexibility it offers over the bus service, but be warned that the quality of driving is erratic, to say the least.

By Bus

Return visitors to the island will notice that the bright orange buses – and their unpredictable ways – are things of the past. Today, international operator Arriva runs the local system, which has pushed prices up slightly. But a more comprehensive service is now available, with buses running around the clock and to more locations than ever before. As the system is so new, changes are still taking place, so it's best to consult www.arriva.com.mt for details.

Between Islands

By Boat

The Gozo Channel Company operates a car ferry (which also takes foot passengers) between Cirkewwa on Malta and Mgarr on Gozo, offering up to 21 return crossings daily from 5.30am. Journey time is about 25 minutes. During the summer, services continue into the night and there is a nonstop shuttle service during peak holiday periods.

For more detailed information on timetables, contact the Gozo Channel Company on 2210 9000, or visit www.gozochannel.com.

If your destination is Comino, the Comino Hotel runs a ferry service from April to October (open to all, including non-guests). For details, contact the Comino Hotel, tel: 2152 9821.

By Taxi

Taxis are generally white and, more often than not, are Mercedes. You can pick one up at the various ranks around town, at the airport, harbours and outside hotels. Street hailing is not normal, though on a Saturday night, passing cabbies may hoot to let you know they're available for hire.

It is wise to insist that either the meter be switched on, or make sure you agree a price before you start your journey. All garages run chauffeur-driven cars as taxis, too. A taxi from the airport to Valletta costs about €15.

Carriages

Karrozzin are today more of a tourist attraction than a practical means of getting from A to B. But a jaunt in a Maltese "surrey with a fringe" *gharry* is a labour-saving and picturesque way to take in the sights of Valletta, St Julian's, Sliema or Mdina. Your driver will halt every now and then to tell you a little about each view or monument. Cost depends on the length of the journey and the time of day (bargain first) and usually includes a chance to be photographed at the reins. There has been some controversy over the treatment of the horses in recent years, and shelters for them are now popping up all over the place.

Driving

Driving Conditions

Ask any Maltese about driving on their islands and they'll laugh and warn you to go carefully. The most important thing to remember is that though they may drive on the left (like the British), the mentality on the roads is pure Mediterranean. Do not expect direction signals. Overtaking on the inside, reversing into main roads and cutting up is the norm. There are many traffic lights, and a long series of roundabouts that seem to enlarge as the traffic grows heavier.

Saturday night in the Paceville, St Julian's and Spinola Bay areas is one long rush hour, and at the weekend, good weather brings out all the island's cars, with families heading for the seaside and countryside beauty spots. Coast roads are heavily congested. Whatever the provocation, drive defensively. The speed limits are 80kmh (50mph) on highways and 50kmh (30mph) in built-up areas.

Licences

All current national and international driving licences are recognised. Visitors from non-EU countries arriving by car should ensure that they are covered by a Green Card with insurance extension to cover Malta.

Fuel

Petrol stations are open daily 7am–6pm. None open on Sundays and public holidays. Most have an automatic pump in operation out of hours. In Gozo, stations are in Victoria or on the road to Mgarr's harbour. Fuel is comparatively inexpensive; €1.37 per litre as of June 2016.

Parking

Parking is always difficult and fines are imposed if you leave your car blocking an exit or in a restricted zone; tow zones and traffic wardens are in operation (see box).

Car Hire

All the familiar European firms, such as Hertz and Avis, have car-rental services, and there are also innumerable small garages that will rent you a car at even more attractive rates. Make sure that the car is an equally attractive proposition, and check insurance cover and liability.

Karrozzin can be hired on the islands.

Rates range from about €16–28 per day. Prices are subject to increases during the holiday season, so book well in advance if visiting in the summer. Payment by credit card is fine for large companies; smaller hire firms may prefer cash. The minimum age for hiring a vehicle is 25 and you will need to produce a valid driving licence or international driver's permit. Chauffeur-driven cars are quite popular with tourists and most car-hire companies also offer this service.

The following are car-hire companies on Malta and Gozo:

Malta

First/Johns
Elija Zammit Street, Paceville, St. Julians;
tel: 2298 2298; http://johns.com.mt.

Avis
50 Msida Seafront;
tel: 2567 7550; www.avis.com.mt.

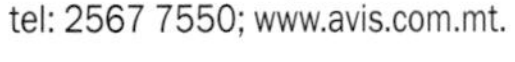

Hertz
66 United House, Triq il-Gzira, Gzira;
tel: 2131 4636/7.

Percius
85 Triq Annibale Preca, Lija;
tel: 2144 2530; www.percius.com.

Wembley's Rent-a-Car
115 St George's Road, St Julian's;
tel: 2137 4141; http://wembleys.com.

Gozo

Gozo Garage
5 Triq Luigi Camilleri, Victoria;
tel: 2155 1866; www.gozogarage.com.

Mayjo Rent-a-Car
Triq Fortunatu Mizzzi, Victoria;
tel: 2155 6678; www.mayjocarhire.com.

Cycles and Motorbikes

Cycling has become more popular in Malta despite heavy volume of traffic and poor standard of driving. The situation is somewhat better on Gozo, but you should still take great care. Cyclists should still beware of badly potholed roads and poor drivers.

Bicycles and motorbikes are available for hire throughout the islands:

The Cyclist
Triq Ir-Rihan, San Gwann,
tel: 2766 1166; www.thecyclistmalta.com.

Eco Bikes
Triq L-Imsel 8, Bugibba,
tel: 2750 0022; www.bikerentalmalta.com

Gozo Adventures
7 Triq Sant Indrija, Victoria, Gozo,
tel: 9999 4592; www.gozoadventures.com.

Hertz Bike Hire
66 Gzira Road, Gzira (also has a branch at the airport open 24 hrs),
tel: 2131 4636; www.hertz.com.mt

Malta Scooters
MedSun LTD 100A, Dr Gorg Olivier Street, Spinola Bay, ST.Julians, tel: 2137 8711; www.maltascooters.com. (Scooters only)..

Gozo "safari" cars.

A – Z

A HANDY SUMMARY OF PRACTICAL INFORMATION

A

Admission Charges

Most museums do have admission charges. These average at around €7, but may be higher.

B

Budgeting for Your Trip

Malta is on a par with most other European countries when it comes to costs – and may even be more expensive than Italy and Spain. Most meals will set you back an average of €18, although you can eat for less. Hotels average at around €70 per night, while a day ticket on the bus costs €1.50.

C

Children

Despite its popularity as a family-holiday destination, Malta has relatively few attractions or even natural features (such as soft sandy beaches or grassy parks) that appeal specifically to children.

Perhaps the most important thing to consider is whether you require a sandy beach. If this is a major consideration, then head for Ghadira at Mellieha, Gnejna or Golden Bay.

The most child-friendly spot is White Rocks, home to **Splash & Fun Waterpark** (www.splashandfun.com.mt), **Mediterraneo Marine World** (www.mediterraneopark.com) and a dinosaur-themed playground. However, you can visit all of these quite easily in a day.

The other well-advertised family attraction is **Popeye Village** (www.popeyemalta.com). By mainland European standards, however, it is very low-key and will occupy only a few hours at most.

Older children may enjoy taking a few traditional archery lessons, organised by Falcon Archery Malta (www.archerymalta.com), as well as learning about the history of this ancient activity.

The good news is that the locals, in true Mediterranean style, love children and there is little in the way of food and drink or sanitary conditions that is likely to cause problems. Do beware of the sun, however. Use sunblock creams and keep children well covered up.

Leading hotels provide entertainers to organise activities for children – and grown-ups.

Climate

The climate of Malta has been the nation's fortune. Even in winter, the temperature rarely drops below 12°C (54°F). Snows and frosts are unknown and rain is likely to fall only between November and February. During the summer months it can top 43°C (109°F), although 29°C (84°F) is more usual. Between April and September, there is virtually nonstop sunshine and soaring temperatures.

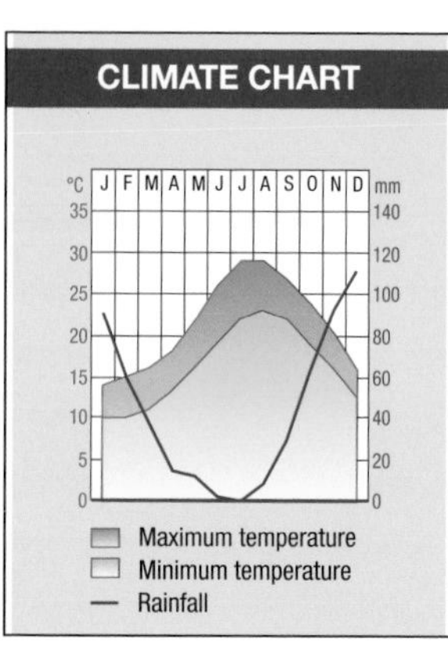

Crime and Safety

The islands are a comparatively safe place for a holiday. Even so, common sense should always prevail. Take the usual precautions against bag-snatchers or pickpockets in crowded places.

Should you be the victim of a crime, you must notify the police immediately and, if necessary, seek assistance from your embassy or consulate. Contact the relevant diplomatic mission, too, for advice should you happen to be detained by the police.

The police are quite approachable, although rarely in evidence on the streets. There is a police station in each town.

Police General Headquarters

Malta: Calcedonius Street, Floriana, tel: 2122 4001–7.
Gozo: 113 Triq ir-Repubblika, Victoria, tel: 2156 2040.

Emergency Numbers

Malta: tel: 112.
Gozo: tel: 112.

Customs and Entry

When travelling between EU countries, personal effects intended for one's own use are not subject to any duty. Travellers from outside the EU may bring into Malta, duty free, either 200 cigarettes, 50 cigars, or 250g in loose tobacco. In addition, 1 litre of spirits (or fortified/sparkling wine) and 2 litres of still wine are permitted. Perfume is limited to 50 grams and eau de toilette to 250ml.

Unless pets are arriving from an EU country with a valid pet passport, most animals entering Malta require official documentation and undergo a period of quarantine. For detailed information and conditions, consult the Veterinary and Phytosanitary Regulation Department website: www.vafd.gov.mt or call: 2292 5216 (EU countries) or tel: 2165 3013 (non EU countries).

D

Disabled Travellers

Malta is not an easy country for travellers with disabilities. The hilly streets, particularly of Valletta and Victoria, and the poor condition of the pavements mean that getting around can be difficult. Many pavements are truly hazardous. However, the hotels on Malta have done a great deal to accommodate people with disabilities, and exhibitions such as The Malta Experience in Valletta (www.themaltaexperience.com), for example, cater well. The natural willingness of Maltese people can be counted upon to help if needed, but always telephone ahead to check facilities.

For further information regarding facilities for disabled travellers, contact the National Commission for Persons with a Disability (tel: 2278 8555; www.knpd.org). Tourist-information centres can also advise on the accessibility of sites and museums. Malta International Airport offers help to disabled travellers, both on arrival and on departure.

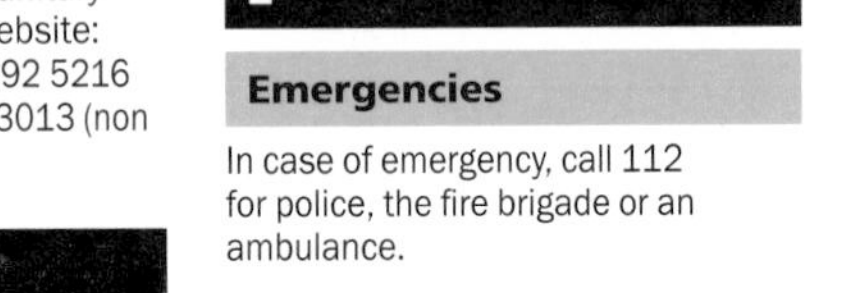

E

Emergencies

In case of emergency, call 112 for police, the fire brigade or an ambulance.

Etiquette

Churches

Women, on entering church, must cover shoulders and avoid plunging necklines. If they are deemed to be unsuitably attired they may be handed a scarf to cover up, or refused entrance. A similar principle applies to men with shorts – though the only church that strictly applies this rule is Ta' Pinu on Gozo.

Sunbathing

Topless and nude bathing is (officially) against the law in Malta and is punishable by fines. In fact, in spite of deep-rooted Catholic disapproval and indignant letters to the newspapers, both are customary on certain secluded (and some non-secluded) beaches, but may attract peeping Toms with binoculars.

Enjoying the sea near Mellieha.

Electricity

220/240 volt, 110 volt for shavers. Electricity is expensive. Visitors from the UK may use their normal three-pin plug items. Visitors from elsewhere may need an adaptor.

G

Gay and Lesbian Travellers

The gay scene is not obvious, but it exists. There are a few gay clubs but their popularity and locations, in Paceville, change frequently. The Gay Malta website, www.gaymalta.org, carries all of the latest information. The age of consent is 16.

H

Health and Medical Care

Inoculations

For visitors arriving from the US, Canada, Australia and Europe, no inoculations are required, though it is a good idea to check when you last had a tetanus booster.

Sun

The Maltese islands are bathed in sunshine virtually year-round. In the summer, don't underestimate the intensity of the sun's rays. Take precautions: the wearing of a hat in the middle of the day is recommended for everyone, especially the elderly and the very young. Begin with a high SPF-factor sun cream or total sunblock until your skin has acclimatised to the sun's rays. Popular brands of sun tanning creams are available everywhere.

Pests

As with any Mediterranean country, the usual troupe of gnats, mosquitoes and cockroaches may be resident. Insect-repellent creams and sprays are readily available. Malta has a few snakes but happily they are not poisonous. Sometimes the odd jellyfish lurks in the island's clear waters.

Drinking Water

Tap water is quite safe to drink (although it doesn't taste that great) but fountain water must be avoided as it may not come directly from the mains supply.

General Medical Care

Malta follows the World Health Organisation's recommendations for health safety. Pharmacists and chemists have quite wide prescribing powers and most well-known prescribed drugs are generally available here. Visitors with specific requirements must ensure they have an adequate supply of medication, or bring a prescription to present to the pharmacist or doctor.

To receive free treatment in cases of illness, accident or even childbirth, EU citizens (and citizens of certain other countries such as Monaco and the former Yugoslavia) must obtain (in their country of residence before arriving in Malta) the European Health Insurance Card (EHIC). In the UK, the EHIC can be applied for at post offices or online at www.ehic.org.uk. The card entitles bearers to the same medical assistance offered to Maltese citizens. (Note: it won't provide repatriation in case of serious illness or accident.) Citizens of non-EU countries must pay for medical assistance and medicine.

All doctors in Malta and Gozo speak English and, probably, Italian.

Pharmacies

There are numerous pharmacies and chemists throughout the islands, all with a green cross symbol by which to identify them. Most keep normal shop opening times, from 8.30 or 9am until 12.30pm and then 4–7pm. A roster of pharmacies open over the weekend is listed in the weekend newspapers. The airport pharmacy (in the Arrivals Lounge) is open daily from 7.30am-10pm. The qualified staff can dispense many products without a doctor's prescription.

Ambulance/Emergency Service

Malta: tel: 112.
Gozo: tel: 112.

Principal Hospitals

Mater Dei Hospital:
Tal-Qroqq, Msida; tel: 2545 0000.
Gozo General Hospital:
Triq l'Arcisqof Pietru Pace, Victoria; tel: 2156 1600.
There are also a number of government-run health centres and district health centres (polyclinics) in towns and villages that are able to offer first aid.

L

Lost Property

Contact the police in the case of lost property, but do not expect too much by way of recovery. Items are rarely deposited in police stations. If the item lost is valuable, a small box advertisement offering a reward in *The Times* often brings the item back. If it is a passport that is lost, contact the relevant embassy or high commission as well as the police. Alternatively, call 2122 4781.

M

Media

Newspapers

Most European daily newspapers arrive in Malta on the day of publication – some are even published here, with newsagents stocking everything from *Le Monde*, *Die Welt*, *La Repubblica*, London's *Times* and *Sun* to the *International Herald Tribune*. An up-to-date supply of international magazines and journals is also widely available.

There are several English-language newspapers: *The Times* (www.timesofmalta.com), which takes a pro-establishment stance, the *The Malta Independent* (www.independent.com.mt), which purports to take an independent line but is equally establishment-biased, and *MaltaToday* (www.maltatoday.com.mt), which tries to be a bit more controversial. The main source of news in English on Gozo is *Gozo News* (http://gozonews.com). There are also a number of dailies and Sundays in Maltese.

Radio and Television

TVM is the national public television station, with local programmes shown in Maltese and some imported ones in English.

Radio Malta, on 93.7 FM (999MW), broadcasts popular music and general news, mainly in Maltese. There are also numerous commercial radio stations, some of them broadcasting in English.

There are also six independent television stations that broadcast in Maltese but show some English programmes. Most hotels and homes will have satellite TV.

Money

The Maltese lira was replaced by the euro on 1 January 2008.

Changing Money

Sterling traveller's cheques are recommended, though it is just as easy to change US dollar cheques. When changing traveller's cheques, remember to take your passport for identification. Hotels accept traveller's cheques, but restaurants and shops will take only cash or credit cards. However, you will probably find a better rate of exchange at banks than at hotels.

Credit Cards

Visa and MasterCard are widely accepted, even by the women who sell their lace tablecloths on the village waterfront; American Express is also widely accepted.

ATMs are available at most localities and accept major credit and debit cards.

Banking Hours

Opening hours vary but are usually Mon–Fri 8.30am–2pm, Sat 8.30am–noon. Certain foreign-exchange bureaux are open after normal banking hours, while others are closed in winter. Both the Bank of Valletta (www.bov.com) and HSBC publish maps of Malta with complete lists of their branches and opening times. They are available from the banks and from tourist information centres.

Tipping

If you wish to show your appreciation, here's a rough guide:
airport baggage 50c (total)
10 percent for a waiter or hairdresser.
tipping taxi drivers is not necessary.

O

Opening Hours

Malta opens early for business, with the working day usually running from 8am–5pm. In the summer months, work starts and finishes even earlier.

Shops are generally open Mon–Fri 9am–7pm, with a long siesta-like lunch break between 1pm and 4pm, and mornings only on Saturdays. However, increasingly, especially in tourist resorts, some shops may open throughout the day and at weekends.

Most businesses close on public holidays, though museums may operate Sunday opening hours.

P

Postal Services

Post offices are found in most towns and villages. Hours of business are Mon–Sat 7.30am–12.45pm. Stamps are obtainable from post offices, hotels, newsagents and some souvenir shops in tourist areas. Post boxes are painted red.

The main post offices are:
Malta: The General Post Office, 305 Triq Qormi, Marsa.
Gozo: Main Post Office, 129 Triq ir-Repubblika, Victoria. Mon–Sat 7.30am–5.15pm.

A poste restante service is available. Write in advance to The Postmaster General at the General Post Office address in Marsa listed above. A passport or identity card may be necessary as identification when collecting post.

Public Holidays

There are several public holidays commemorating patron saints' feast days. Every parish celebrates its own as well as those that are national. On these days, shops, businesses and schools are closed, though restaurants and bars will most likely remain open.

Below is a guide to the national public holidays. On New Year's Day and Christmas Day, buses stop between noon–3pm to allow everyone time with their families.

1 January New Year's Day.
10 February St Paul's Shipwreck.
19 March Feast of St Joseph.
31 March Freedom Day.
March or April Good Friday.
1 May St Joseph the Worker.
7 June Commemoration of 7 June 1919.
29 June Feast of St Peter and St Paul. *Mnarja* harvest festival.
15 August Feast of the Assumption.
8 September Feast of Our Lady of the Victories.
21 September Independence Day.
8 December Feast of the Immaculate Conception.
13 December Republic Day.
25 December Christmas Day.
See also Fireworks, Bands and Saints, page 82.

R

Religious Services

Malta is a Roman Catholic country but all religions are tolerated and services are held in various languages for foreign visitors (on Sunday). For Catholics, there are as many churches for Mass as there are days of the year.

In English

Rabat: St Dominic's, St Dominic's Square, 11.15am.
St Paul's Bay: Parish Church, St Paul's Street, 11am.
Sliema: St Patrick's, St John Bosco Street, 7.30, 9 and 10am, 6.30 and 7.30pm.
Valletta: St Barbara's, Republic Street, noon.

In Italian

Valletta: St Catherine of Italy, Victory Square, 11am.

In French

Valletta: St Barbara's, Republic Street, 10am.

In German

Valletta: St Barbara's, Republic Street, 11am.

Other Denominations

Anglican: St Paul's Anglican Cathedral, Valletta, tel: 2122 5714. Holy Trinity, Rudolph Street, Sliema, tel: 2133 0575.
Union Church of Scotland and **Methodist**: St Andrew's, South Street, Valletta, tel: 2122 2643.
Greek Orthodox: 83 Merchants Street, Valletta, tel: 2122 1600.
Jewish: The Synagogue, Spur Street, Valletta. Secretary of Jewish Community, tel: 2162 5717.
Ecumenical: The Seminary, Triq Enrico Mizzi, Victoria, Gozo. Services in English on first and third Wednesday of every month, 11.15am.
Islamic Centre: Corradino Hill, Corradino, tel: 2169 7203.

Malta knows how to celebrate in style.

Remnants of British rule are to be found all over Malta.

S

Student Travellers

NSTS (http://nsts.org), the Student and Youth Travel organisation in Malta, is located at 220 St Paul's Street, Valletta, tel: 2558 8000. The Gozo office is at 45 Pjazza San Frangisk, Victoria. Both offices can provide you with an invaluable little booklet, the Student Saver Discount Scheme, which lists shops, exhibitions, restaurants and transport, offering reductions of 15–40 percent on prices to those with an ISIC (International Student/ Scholar Identity Card). Entrance to museums is free to students anyway.

T

Telephones

The telephone system is very much in line with European standards, including for internet services. It is now possible to dial any country on the international direct-dialling system if you know the prefix.

For internal directory enquiries, dial: 1182. International calls should prove no problem, but for overseas operators' help, or prefix number enquiries, dial Freecall: 1152. For faults on the line, tel: 133.

Time Zone

GMT + 1 hour. From the last Sunday in March until the last Sunday in October, clocks are a further hour ahead of GMT.

Call boxes throughout the Maltese islands almost exclusively take phonecards, which are on sale at stationery shops. It is possible to rent mobile telephones; call Vodaphone, tel: 1189; or Go Mobile, tel: 1187.

Toilets

There are public toilets in most towns and villages – and near public beaches – but their cleanliness varies. It varies, too, in cafés, bars and restaurants. The best public toilets in Valletta are on Strait Street – where you're in for quite a treat. Historical sites are striving to add facilities.

Tourist Information

Local Tourist Offices

The address of the main tourist office is **Malta Tourism Authority**, Auberge d'Italie, Merchants Street 229, Valletta; tel: 2291 5440/2; www.visitmalta.com. Other tourist information offices are located at:
Valletta Waterfront, tel: 2122 0633
Mellieha, tel: 2152 4666
Mdina, tel: 2145 4480
Malta International Airport, Gudja, tel: 2369 6073/4.
Gozo, Independence Square, Victoria, tel: 2291 5452.

Embassies in Malta

US Embassy
Ta' Qali National Park, Attard, ATD 4000
Tel: 2561 4000
Australian High Commission
Villa Fiorentino, Rampa Ta' Xbiex
Tel: 2133 8201
British High Commission
Whitehall Mansions, Ta' Xbiex
Tel: 2323 0000

Tourist Offices Abroad

United Kingdom
Malta Tourist Office, Unit C, Park House, 14 Northfields, London SW18 1DD
Tel: (44) 020 8877 6991
United States and Canada
Malta Tourist Office, 249 East 35th Street, New York NY 10006
Tel: (1) 212 213 0944

V

Visas and Passports

EU visitors require a valid passport or identity card. Members of the Commonwealth require a valid passport or a visitor's passport. This entitles them to a maximum stay of three months as a tourist. This also applies to visitors from British dependencies, Japan and the US. Should you wish to extend your stay beyond three months, or perhaps to take up temporary residence, apply to the Immigration Police at Police Headquarters, Calcedonius Street, Floriana, tel: 2122 4001.

Most other nationals require visas. No visitors may take up employment without a work permit.

Malta is represented by an ambassador, high commissioner or consulate in most major cities throughout the world, with offices where information or advice on passport and visa queries can be obtained. Where Air Malta is represented, its offices can offer assistance, too.

In Britain, the Malta High Commission is at 36–38 Piccadilly, London W1J OLE; tel: 020 7292 4800.

W

Websites

The Malta Tourism Authority runs its own website: www.visitmalta.com. You can also find essential information at www.malta.com.
The *Times of Malta* is a good place to catch up on daily news at www.timesofmalta.com. For insiders tips and advice see www.maltainsideout.com. For details of current exchange rates, visit www.centralbankmalta.org.

Weights and Measures

Metric is used almost exclusively in Malta, with road signs showing metres and kilometres. Kilos are more commonly used than pounds.

LANGUAGE

UNDERSTANDING THE LANGUAGE

LANGUAGE TIPS

Malti, or Maltese, is spoken daily in Malta and Gozo, but nowhere else in the world. It is a Semitic language with roots that go back to Phoenician and Carthaginian times. Given that it is both complicated and of no use outside the islands, the Maltese people *never* expect visitors to speak to them in it.

English is the second language and is spoken, or at least understood, by the vast majority of the population. However, it is useful to know a little Malti if only to pronounce place names properly. And, of course, it is good manners, and pleasing to both parties, to be able to return the most basic greetings and phrases in Malti.

PRONUNCIATION TIPS

There are 29 letters in the Maltese alphabet: five familiar vowels (pronounced long or short, depending on the position in the word) and 24 consonants. There is no "y".

The additions to the Roman alphabet are c˙, g˙, x˙, which are dotted like an i, and h and h-. Dotting the consonant changes the way it is pronounced:

dotted c˙ becomes the English ch – as in church;
dotted g˙ as the soft j in the French word *je* (or the second syllable in pleasure);
dotted x˙ as in zebra (without a dot, z is *ts*, as in nuts).
gh, although common, is not pronounced.
h is silent unless it is crossed *h-* like a t; then it is pronounced, as in hand.
q is a glottal stop, faintly like a k, impossible to most visitors.
m, when it is at the beginning of a word, is pronounced *im*.

PLACE NAMES

The following is a list of Maltese towns and villages and how to pronounce them.

Birgu *bir-goo*
Birzebbuga *bir-tsay-boo-jah*
Bugibba *boo-jee-bah*
Dwejra *dway-ruh*
Ggantija *j-gan-tee-yah*
Gharb *ahrb*
Hagar Qim *h-ajar eem*
Luqa *loo-a*
Marsaxlokk *marsa-schlock*
Mdina *Im-deena*
Mellieha *mel-lear-ha*
Mgarr im-jar
Msida *im-seeda*
Naxxar *na-shar*
Paceville *par-tchay-ville*
Qawra *ow-rah*
Tarxien *tar-shin*
Xaghra *shah-ra*
Xewkija *she-key-yah*
Xlendi *sch-len-dee*

USEFUL WORDS/ PHRASES

Good morning *bongu (bon-jew)*
Good evening *bonswa (bon-swah)*
Goodbye *sahha (sa-ha)* (also "Cheers", when drinking)
How are you? *kif int?*
I'm very well, thank you female response: *tajba grazzi (tay-ba grat-see)*, male response: *tajjeb grazzi (tay-szeb gratsee)*
Do you speak English? *Inti tit-kellem bl'Ingliz? (int-tit-kellem blin-gleez)*
Please *Jekk-joghbok (yeck yogbock)*
Thank You *Grazzi (grat-see)*
Yes *Iva (eeva)*
No *Le* (*le*, with e as in "get")

The Maltese language can appear mind-boggling to unfamiliar eyes.

FURTHER READING

HISTORY

The Cross and the Ensign: a Naval History of Malta, 1798–1979 by Peter Elliot. The first detailed account of the British Navy's connection with Malta.
The Great Siege: Malta 1565 by Ernle Bradford. Compelling account of the struggle between the Knights of Malta and the Ottoman Empire for the control of the Mediterranean.
Malta Convoy by Peter Shankland and Anthony Hunter. A classic account of Operation Pedestal, the convoy that braved all the enemy could throw at it in 1942 as it sailed to save Malta from starvation and surrender in the islands' second great siege.
Siege: Malta 1940–1943 by Ernle Bradford. Penguin (1987). Malta's second great test of wartime fortitude, written with the immediacy of a novel.
The Story of Malta by Brian Blouet. A rich, comprehensive history, engagingly recounted.
Malta: A Thorn in Rommel's Side by Laddie Lucas. Gripping account of the 18 months when Malta was the most bombed spot on earth and Lucas was commanding the islands' top-scoring squadron.
Fortress Malta: An Island Under Siege, 1940 - 43 by James Holland. A poignant story of the island's siege followed through the eyes of pilots, submariners, soldiers and civilians.

ARCHAEOLOGY

Before Civilization by Colin Renfrew. One of Britain's foremost archaeologists shows how the carbon dating of Malta's prehistoric monuments changed the whole theory of human development and proved that Maltese temples are the oldest free-standing buildings known to man.
Malta: An Archaeological Guide by David Trump. The essential guide to Malta's astonishing prehistoric remains.
World Heritage Sites in Malta by Reuben Grima. With photographs by Enrico Formica.

ARCHITECTURE

British Military Architecture in Malta by Stephen C. Spiteri. A detailed study with many plans and photographs.
Malta: A Guide to the Fortifications by Quentin Hughes. Reprint of a classic guide to Malta's forts and bastions.
5,000 years of Architecture in Malta by Leonard Mahoney. A Maltese architect takes a learned look at the architecture that makes the islands so distinctive. Finely illustrated.

ART

Iconography of the Maltese Islands 1400–1900 by Mario Buhagiar. A critical survey of 500 years of painting in Malta by a leading art historian.
International Dictionary of Artists who Painted Malta by Nicholas de Piro. Illustrated biographies of 600 artists from many nations spanning several centuries.

MISCELLANEOUS

At Home in Malta by Geoffrey Aquilina Ross. With photographs by Jonathan Beacon. The way of life plus some of the islands' finest houses, gardens and nation heritage.
Saints and Fireworks by Jeremy Boissevain. An instructive and entertaining survey of religion and politics in rural Malta.
The Way We Ate by Matty Cremona. A vibrant cookbook dedicated to Maltese cooking through history, and brought to life once again by this talented local foodie.

FICTION

For Rozina... a husband, and other Maltese Stories by Francis Ebejer. A charming insight into the minds and manners of the rural Maltese by one of the country's finest writers.
The Kappilan of Malta by Nicholas Monsarrat. A wartime love story interwoven with a whole sweep of Maltese history.
Like Bees to Honey by Caroline Smailes. A women returns to Malta after many years to face the skeletons in her closet. Very readable, and many references to the islands.

OTHER INSIGHT GUIDES

Insight Guide: Explore Malta features several walking and driving routes, designed to help readers get the most out of Malta during a short stay.
Insight: Fleximap Malta is the perfect navigational companion, featuring the top 30 sights on an easy-to-use, weatherproof, compact map of the islands.
Insight Guide: Italy gives a fascinating insight into Italy's history and culture.

Send Us Your Thoughts

We do our best to ensure the information in our books is as accurate and up-to-date as possible. The books are updated on a regular basis using local contacts, who painstakingly add, amend and correct as required. However, some details (such as telephone numbers and opening times) are liable to change, and we are ultimately reliant on our readers to put us in the picture.

We welcome your feedback, especially your experience of using the book "on the road". Maybe we recommended a hotel that you liked (or another that you didn't), or you came across a great bar or new attraction we missed.

We will acknowledge all contributions, and we'll offer an Insight Guide to the best letters received.

Please write to us at:
Insight Guides
PO Box 7910
London SE1 1WE
Or email us at:
hello@insightguides.com

CREDITS

Photo Credits

Alamy 139TR
AWL Images 7ML
Corbis 45BR
Getty Images 10/11, 12/13, 14/15, 28, 29, 37, 38, 39, 59, 60, 61, 62, 64, 65, 66, 68, 85, 106/107, 108/109, 110/111, 112, 119, 125B, 127B, 140, 145, 148, 198, 201B, 212/213, 222
Glyn Genin/Apa Publications 129T, 131T, 135, 157T, 165T, 193ML
Illustrated London News 54, 55, 57
iStock 31, 44/45T, 44BR, 44BL, 45ML, 48, 69, 89, 102, 139ML, 146B, 149, 165B, 220B, 233
Lysy 30
Malta Culture 9TL, 76
Malta Tourism Authority 7MR, 9TR, 9BR, 67, 72, 73, 74, 75, 77, 79, 80, 83BL, 88, 91, 92R, 97, 99, 100, 101, 120, 124, 154B, 156, 166, 172, 177T, 182, 184B, 187T, 197T, 205, 209, 211, 216T, 216B, 224B
Neil Buchan-Grant/Apa Publications 219B, 220T, 221
Public domain 35, 42, 43, 45TR, 49, 50, 51L
Scala Archives 36, 52/53, 56, 58
Shutterstock 4/5, 146T, 176, 218
Sovereign Order of St John 40, 41, 47
SuperStock 46
Sylvaine Poitau/Apa Publications 1, 6MR, 6ML, 6BR, 6BL, 7ML, 7TR, 7TL, 8BL, 8BR, 8MR, 16, 17T, 17B, 18, 19, 20, 21L, 21R, 22, 23, 24/25, 26, 27, 45BR, 51R, 70/71, 81, 82/83T, 82BR, 82BL, 83ML, 83BR, 83TR, 84, 86, 87, 90, 92L, 93, 94, 95, 96, 103, 104, 105, 113T, 113B, 116, 117, 121T, 121B, 122, 123T, 123B, 125T, 126T, 127T, 130, 132, 133T, 133B, 134/135, 136/137, 138/139T, 138BR, 138BL, 139B, 141, 143, 147, 150, 151T, 152B, 153, 154T, 155, 157B, 159, 160, 161T, 162, 163, 167T, 168, 169T, 169B, 174, 175B, 175T, 177B, 178T, 178B, 183, 184T, 185, 189B, 190T, 192BR, 192/193T, 192BL, 193BR, 193TR, 193BL, 194/195, 196, 197B, 199, 200, 201T, 202, 203, 204, 207, 214, 215, 217, 219T, 224, 225, 226B, 226T, 227, 228, 232T, 232B
TopFoto 63
Viewing Malta 7B, 32, 33, 34, 78, 98, 126B, 128, 129B, 131B, 142, 144, 151B, 152T, 158, 161B, 167B, 173, 179, 186, 187B, 188, 189T, 190B, 191, 208B, 208T, 210, 230, 231

Cover Credits

Front cover: Azure Window *Shutterstock*
Back cover: St Leonard's church, Kirkop *Sylvaine Poitau/Apa Publications*
Front flap: (from top) Boat detail *Sylvaine Poitau/Apa Publications*; St John's Cathedral *Sylvaine Poitau/Apa Publications*; Gozo glass *Sylvaine Poitau/Apa Publications*; The Blue Lagoon *iStock*
Back flap: Valletta *Sylvaine Poitau/Apa Publications*

Insight Guide Credits

Distribution
UK, Ireland and Europe
Apa Publications (UK) Ltd;
sales@insightguides.com
United States and Canada
Ingram Publisher Services;
ips@ingramcontent.com
Australia and New Zealand
Woodslane; info@woodslane.com.au
Southeast Asia
Apa Publications (SN) Pte;
singaporeoffice@insightguides.com
Hong Kong, Taiwan and China
Apa Publications (HK) Ltd;
hongkongoffice@insightguides.com
Worldwide
Apa Publications (UK) Ltd;
sales@insightguides.com
Special Sales, Content Licensing and CoPublishing
Insight Guides can be purchased in bulk quantities at discounted prices. We can create special editions, personalised jackets and corporate imprints tailored to your needs.
sales@insightguides.com
www.insightguides.biz

Printed in China by CTPS

First Edition 1992
Sixth Edition 2017

Every effort has been made to provide accurate information in this publication, but changes are inevitable. The publisher cannot be responsible for any resulting loss, inconvenience or injury. We would appreciate it if readers would call our attention to any errors or outdated information. We also welcome your suggestions; please contact us at: hello@insightguides.com

www.insightguides.com

Editor: Tom Fleming
Author: Jo Caruana
Head of Production: Rebeka Davies
Update Production: AM Services
Picture Editor: Tom Smyth
Cartography: original cartography Berndtson and Berndtson, updated by Carte

Contributors

This new edition was updated throughout by Maciej Zglinicki. The update was supervised and edited by Tom Fleming at Insight Guides.

This edition builds on the earlier editions, written and updated by Malta-based journalist and writer Jo Caruana, and Geoffrey Aquilina Ross, a journalist and author who has edited magazines in both London and Malta.

Ross's text built on that produced by experienced Maltese Islands guidebook author Paul Murphy for the previous edition.

Literally at home in Gozo is Ann Monsarrat, who contributed to the Gozo section in a previous edition. An experienced journalist, she is also the author of several books.

Other writers whose text has been adapted from earlier editions and used in this edtion are Rowlinson Carter, Maud Ruston, Daphne Caruana Galizia, Anthony Montanaro, Michael Ellul, Louis Mahoney and Eric Gerada-Azzopardi.

About Insight Guides

Insight Guides have more than 45 years' experience of publishing high-quality, visual travel guides. We produce 400 full-colour titles, in both print and digital form, covering more than 200 destinations across the globe, in a variety of formats to meet your different needs.

Insight Guides are written by local authors, whose expertise is evident in the extensive historical and cultural background features. Each destination is carefully researched by regional experts to ensure our guides provide the very latest information. All the reviews in **Insight Guides** are independent; we strive to maintain an impartial view. Our reviews are carefully selected to guide you to the best places to eat, go out and shop, so you can be confident that when we say a place is special, we really mean it.

Legend

City maps

Freeway/Highway/Motorway
Divided Highway
Main Roads
Minor Roads
Pedestrian Roads
Steps
Footpath
Railway
Funicular Railway
Cable Car
Tunnel
City Wall
Important Building
Built Up Area
Other Land
Transport Hub
Park
Pedestrian Area
Bus Station
Tourist Information
Main Post Office
Cathedral/Church
Mosque
Synagogue
Statue/Monument
Beach
Airport

Regional maps

Freeway/Highway/Motorway (with junction)
Freeway/Highway/Motorway (under construction)
Divided Highway
Main Road
Secondary Road
Minor Road
Track
Footpath
International Boundary
State/Province Boundary
National Park/Reserve
Marine Park
Ferry Route
Marshland/Swamp
Glacier
Salt Lake
Airport/Airfield
Ancient Site
Border Control
Cable Car
Castle/Castle Ruins
Cave
Chateau/Stately Home
Church/Church Ruins
Crater
Lighthouse
Mountain Peak
Place of Interest
Viewpoint

INDEX

Main references are in bold type

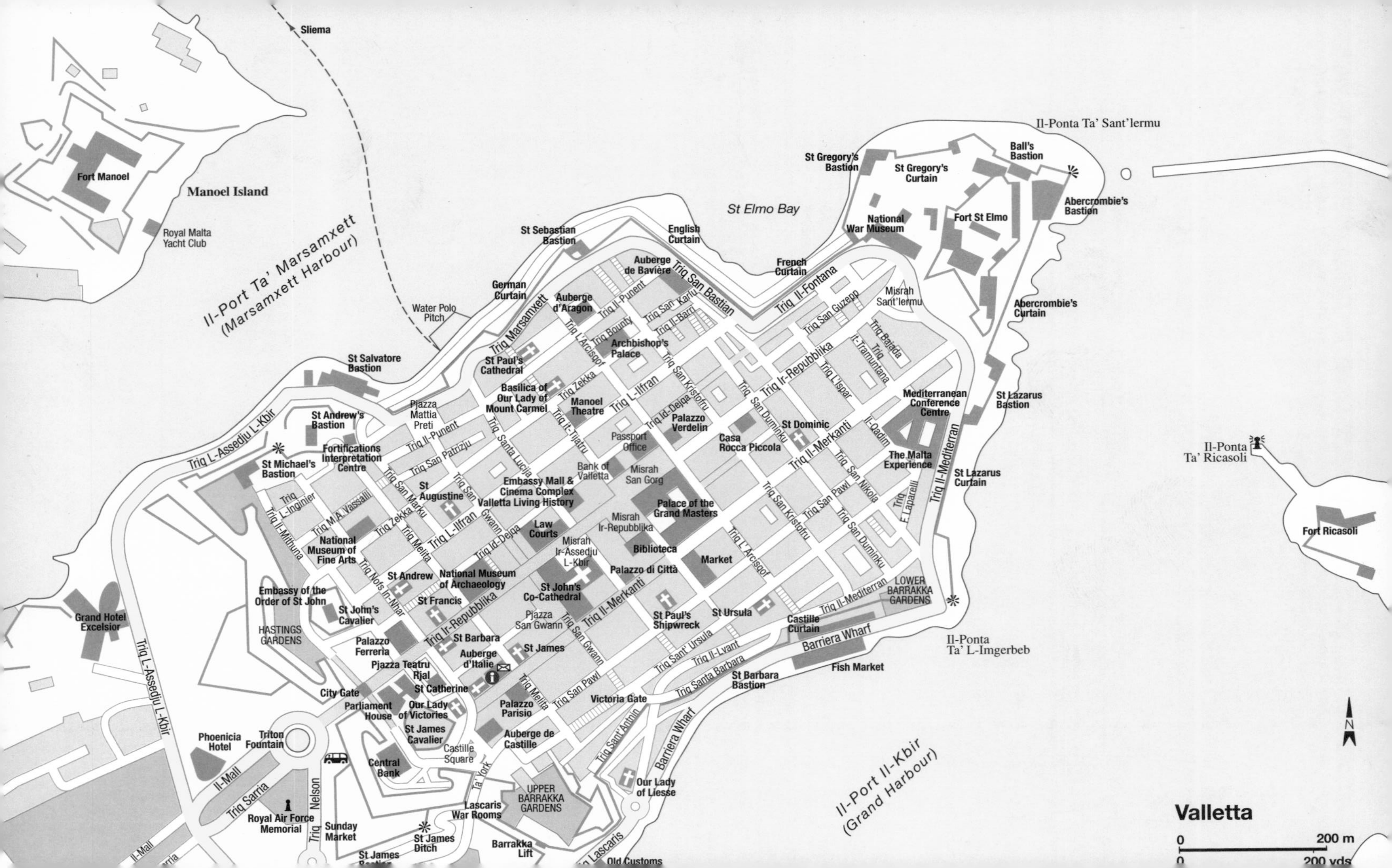
Valletta
0
200 m
0
200 yds
N
Sliema
Fort Manoel
Manoel Island
Royal Malta Yacht Club
Il-Port Ta' Marsamxett
(Marsamxett Harbour)
Il-Ponta Ta' Sant'Iermu
St Gregory's Bastion
St Gregory's Curtain
Ball's Bastion
Abercrombie's Bastion
Fort St Elmo
National War Museum
St Elmo Bay
St Sebastian Bastion
English Curtain
French Curtain
Abercrombie's Curtain
Misrah Sant'Iermu
Auberge de Bavière
Triq San Bastian
Triq Il-Fontana
German Curtain
Auberge d'Aragon
Triq Il-Punent
Triq San Karlu
Triq Il-Barri
Triq San Guzepp
Water Polo Pitch
Triq Marsamxett
Triq L'Arcisqof
Triq Bounty
Archbishop's Palace
Triq Ir-Repubblika
Triq Bajada
Triq It-Tramuntana
Triq L'Ispar
St Salvatore Bastion
St Paul's Cathedral
Basilica of Our Lady of Mount Carmel
Triq Zekka
Manoel Theatre
Triq L-Ilfran
Triq San Kristofru
Triq San Duminku
St Dominic
Mediterranean Conference Centre
St Lazarus Bastion
Pjazza Mattia Preti
Triq It-Tijatru
Triq Id-Dejqa
Palazzo Verdelin
Casa Rocca Piccola
Triq Il-Merkanti
Il-Qadim
The Malta Experience
Il-Ponta Ta' Ricasoli
St Andrew's Bastion
Triq Il-Punent
Passport Office
Triq Il-Mediterran
St Lazarus Curtain
Triq L-Assedju L-Kbir
Fortifications Interpretation Centre
Triq San Patrizju
Triq Santa Lucija
Bank of Valletta
Misrah San Gorg
Triq San Nikola
Triq E Laparelli
St Michael's Bastion
Triq San Marku
St Augustine
Triq San Gwann
Embassy Mall & Cinema Complex
Valletta Living History
Palace of the Grand Masters
Triq San Pawl
Fort Ricasoli
Triq L-Inginier
Triq M.A. Vassalli
Triq Il-Mithuna
Triq Zekka
Triq Melita
Triq L-Ilfran
Law Courts
Misrah Ir-Repubblika
Triq Id-Dejqa
National Museum of Fine Arts
Misrah Ir-Assedju L-Kbir
Biblioteca
Market
Triq L'Arcisqof
Triq San Duminku
Triq Nofs In-Nhar
St Andrew
National Museum of Archaeology
Palazzo di Città
LOWER BARRAKKA GARDENS
Embassy of the Order of St John
St John's Cavalier
St Francis
St John's Co-Cathedral
Triq Il-Merkanti
Grand Hotel Excelsior
HASTINGS GARDENS
Triq Ir-Repubblika
Pjazza San Gwann
St Paul's Shipwreck
St Ursula
Triq Il-Mediterran
Castille Curtain
Palazzo Ferreria
St Barbara
Auberge d'Italie
St James
Triq San Gwann
Triq Sant' Ursula
Barriera Wharf
Il-Ponta Ta' L-Imgerbeb
Pjazza Teatru Rjal
Triq Il-Lvant
Fish Market
City Gate
St Catherine
Triq Melita
Triq San Pawl
Triq Santa Barbara
St Barbara Bastion
Parliament House
Our Lady of Victories
Palazzo Parisio
Victoria Gate
Triq L-Assedju L-Kbir
St James Cavalier
Auberge de Castille
Phoenicia Hotel
Triton Fountain
Castille Square
Triq Sant'Antnin
Barriera Wharf
Il-Port Il-Kbir
(Grand Harbour)
Central Bank
Ta' York
Il-Mall
UPPER BARRAKKA GARDENS
Our Lady of Liesse
Triq Sarria
Triq Nelson
Royal Air Force Memorial
Lascaris War Rooms
Sunday Market
St James Ditch
Barrakka Lift
Il-Mall
Lascaris
Old Customs
St James Bastion